Informatik aktuell

Herausgeber: W. Brauer
im Auftrag der Gesellschaft für Informatik (GI)

Springer-Verlag Berlin Heidelberg GmbH

Markus Schumacher   Ralf Steinmetz (Hrsg.)

Sicherheit in Netzen und Medienströmen

Tagungsband des GI-Workshops
"Sicherheit in Mediendaten"
Berlin, 19. September 2000

Springer

Herausgeber

Markus Schumacher
Informationstechnologie Transfer Office
Fachbereich 20, Informatik, Technische Universität Darmstadt
Wilhelminenstr. 7, 64283 Darmstadt

Ralf Steinmetz
Industrielle Prozess- und Systemkommunikation KOM
Fachbereich 18, Elektrotechnik und Informationstechnik
Technische Universität Darmstadt
Merckstr. 25, 64283 Darmstadt

Die Deutsche Bibliothek - CIP-Einheitsaufnahme

Sicherheit in Netzen und Medienströmen : Tagungsband des GI-Workshops
"Sicherheit in Mediendaten", Berlin, 19. September 2000 / Hrsg.:
Markus Schumacher ; Ralf Steinmetz. - Berlin ; Heidelberg ; New York ;
Barcelona ; Hongkong ; London ; Mailand ; Paris ; Singapur ; Tokio :
Springer, 2000
 (Informatik aktuell)
 ISBN 978-3-540-67926-4   ISBN 978-3-642-58346-9 (eBook)
 DOI 10.1007/978-3-642-58346-9
CR Subject Classification (2000): C.2, E.3, H.5, K.5

ISSN 1431-472-X
ISBN 978-3-540-67926-4

Dieses Werk ist urheberrechtlich geschützt. Die dadurch begründeten Rechte, insbesondere die der Übersetzung, des Nachdrucks, des Vortrags, der Entnahme von Abbildungen und Tabellen, der Funksendung, der Mikroverfilmung oder der Vervielfältigung auf anderen Wegen und der Speicherung in Datenverarbeitungsanlagen, bleiben, auch bei nur auszugsweiser Verwertung, vorbehalten. Eine Vervielfältigung dieses Werkes oder von Teilen dieses Werkes ist auch im Einzelfall nur in den Grenzen der gesetzlichen Bestimmungen des Urheberrechtsgesetzes der Bundesrepublik Deutschland vom 9. September 1965 in der jeweils geltenden Fassung zulässig. Sie ist grundsätzlich vergütungspflichtig. Zuwiderhandlungen unterliegen den Strafbestimmungen des Urheberrechtsgesetzes.

© Springer-Verlag Berlin Heidelberg 2000
Ursprünglich erschienin bei Springer-Verlag Berlin Heidelberg New York 2000

Satz: Reproduktionsfertige Vorlage vom Autor/Herausgeber

SPIN: 10749680   33/3142-543210

Vorwort

In immer mehr Bereichen des öffentlichen und privaten Lebens werden die neuen Möglichkeiten, die sich durch die weltweite Vernetzung eröffnen, genutzt. Immer mehr Menschen nehmen aktiv an der neuen, digitalen Welt teil, das Sammeln, Verarbeiten und Verteilen von Informationen rückt immer stärker in den Mittelpunkt.

Allerdings haben jüngste Vorfälle, wie etwa die *Distributed Denial-of-Service* Angriffe im Februar oder der *I Love You* E-Mail Virus im Mai 2000 verdeutlicht, wie verletzbar die Infrastruktur Internet ist; die Konzeption und Durchsetzung eines adäquaten Sicherheitsniveaus steckt leider noch in den Anfängen. Es hat sich außerdem gezeigt, daß eine einzelne Sicherheitslösung nicht unabhängig von der Sicherheit aller anderen Systeme betrachtet werden kann.

Die rasche Evolution auf dem Gebiet des Internet erfordert es, daß traditionelle Sicherheitskonzepte überdacht werden müssen. Neue Technologien führen zu anderen Sicherheitsanforderungen und stellen höhere Ansprüche an entsprechende Sicherheitslösungen: in vielen Bereichen muß die Sicherheit "neu erfunden" werden.

Kommunikationsprotokolle und Ende-zu-Ende Sicherheit

Die Authentizität von Daten und der Nachweis der Unverfälschtheit können nur dann gewährleistet werden, wenn dem Aspekt der Ende-zu-Ende Sicherheit durch geeignete infrastrukturelle Komponenten und die Integration in bestehende Systeme Rechnung getragen wird. Die Verarbeitung von multimedialen Informationen erfordert die Anpassung und Weiterentwicklung von traditionellen Sicherheitslösungen und Kommunikationsprotokollen.

Die klassischen Grenzen von Telekommunikationsnetzen und dem Internet verschwimmen zunehmend. Große Teile des Internet verwenden Telefonleitungen als physikalisches Transportmedium, umgekehrt gibt es vermehrt Ansätze, das Internet für Dienste wie die Telefonie einzusetzen. Das daraus resultierende Netzwerk ist sicherlich flexibler und vielseitiger, aber auch deutlich komplexer, insbesondere hinsichtlich des Aspektes Sicherheit. [1]

In diesem Zusammenhang werden hier aktuelle Arbeiten u.a. auf den Gebieten *Multimedia Firewalls, IPSec und IP Multicast* sowie *IP Telefonie* vorgestellt. Die Schleusentechnologie *Lock-Keeper* stellt einen Ansatz für den hochsicheren Datenaustausch dar. Am Beispiel des *CORBA Security Service* wird gezeigt, daß ein mächtiges Werkzeug für die Entwicklung verteilter, objekt-orientierter Systeme weitgehend transparent abgesichert werden kann und welche Probleme dabei noch zu lösen sind. In einem kritischen Beitrag am Ende des ersten Teils wird erläutert, wie Sicherheit aus der Sicht von Unternehmen gesehen wird.

---

[1] Siehe u.a. hierzu die Übersichten in: S. Fischer, A. Steinacker, R. Bertram, und R. Steinmetz. Open Security. Springer Verlag, 1998. ISBN 354064654X
und: S. Fischer, C. Rensing, und U. Roedig. Open Internet Security - Von den Grundlagen zu den Anwendungen, Springer Verlag, 2000. ISBN 3540668144

Digitale Wasserzeichen

Digitale Medien haben in den letzten Jahren ein gewaltiges Wachstum erfahren und sind dabei, die analogen Medien abzulösen. Allerdings gelten im digitalen Zeitalter Urheberrechte nicht viel: Musik, Videos, Bücher - alles, was in digitalisierter Form im Internet zu finden ist, wird raubkopiert. Auch Fotografen und Bildjournalisten sind davon betroffen. Und oft können sie nicht einmal nachweisen, daß es sich um ihr Eigentum handelt, wenn sie eins ihrer Bilder auf einer Website entdecken: Das Foto in seiner digitalen Form ist beliebig manipulierbar, der Fotograf hat keinen Beweis. Daß er das Foto in seiner Digitalkamera gespeichert hat, zählt an dieser Stelle nicht, da es auch aus dem Internet heruntergeladen sein könnte.

Seit Anfang der 90-er Jahre beschäftigt sich Wirtschaft und Wissenschaft intensiver mit digitalen Wasserzeichen zur Prüfung von Authentizität und Integrität für Mediendaten, viele Arbeiten zu geeigneten Protokollen wurden durchgeführt. Eine Vielzahl von Publikationen und Lösungen sind bereits entstanden, allerdings sind die existierenden Verfahren oft anwendungsspezifisch, haben sehr uneinheitliche Verfahrensparameter und teilweise sehr geringe Sicherheitsniveaus. [2]

Ausgehend von einer Klassifizierung von Wasserzeichen, werden in dem Workshop u.a. einige neue Verfahren diskutiert, wie z.B. *Wasserzeichen für polygon basierte 3D-Modelle* oder *Asymmetrische Schemata für Wasserzeichen*. Interessant sind auch Kombinationen traditioneller Konzepte mit dem Ansatz des Watermarking, wie z.B. in einem Beitrag über biometrische Merkmale und Wasserzeichen gezeigt wird. Die Audio-Industrie ist bereits heute sehr daran interessiert, ihre Produkte entsprechend zu schützen, insbesondere auf dem Vertriebsweg über das Internet. Interessant dürften daher die Konzepte des Audio-Watermarking, aber auch des Watermarking von MIDI Daten sein.

Zielsetzung des Workshops

Im Rahmen des Workshops *Sicherheit in Mediendaten* werden aktuelle Ansätze auf dem Gebiet vorgestellt und Fragen der Anwendbarkeit, Sicherheit und Qualitätsgüte diskutiert. Unsere Zielsetzung ist es, erfahrene Wissenschaftler, Entwickler und Anwender aus Industrie und Forschung zu einer State-of-the-Art Bestandsaufnahme der Situation Multimedia und Security zusammenzubringen und die Ergebnisse in diesem Tagungsband zu präsentieren. Unser besonderer Dank gilt Jana Dittmann, die viel zu der Bewertung und Auswahl der Beiträge zu dem Vertiefungsthema *Digitale Wasserzeichen* beigetragen hat.

Juni 2000 Markus Schumacher, Ralf Steinmetz

---

[2] Siehe hierzu die Übersicht: J. Dittmann, Digitale Wasserzeichen, Springer-Verlag, 2000, ISBN: 3540666613

Organisation

Workshop-Leitung

R. Steinmetz	TU Darmstadt & GMD-IPSI
P. Horster	Universität Klagenfurt Österreich
R. Oppliger	eSECURITY Technologies Schweiz

Programm- und Organisationskomitee

J. Dittmann	GMD-IPSI (Programmvorsitz)
M. Schumacher	TU Darmstadt (Organisationsvorsitz)
G. Müller	Universität Freiburg
R. Oppliger	eSECURITY Technologies Schweiz
C. Rensing	HTTC
O. Spaniol	RWTH Aachen
R. Steinmetz	GMD-IPSI
J. Swoboda	TU München
H. Thielmann	GMD-SIT
P. Wohlmacher	Universität Klagenfurt

Inhaltsverzeichnis

Teil I

Sicherheit in Netzen

A Distributed Firewall for Multimedia Applications

Utz Roedig[1], Ralf Ackermann[1], Christoph Rensing[1], Ralf Steinmetz[1,2]

[1] Darmstadt University of Technology, Merckstr. 25, D-64283 Darmstadt, Germany
[2] GMD IPSI, Dolivostr. 15, 64293 Darmstadt, Germany
{Utz.Roedig, Ralf.Ackermann, Christoph.Rensing, Ralf.Steinmetz}
@KOM.tu-darmstadt.de

Abstract. Firewalls are a widely used security mechanism to provide access control and auditing at the border between "open" and private networks or administrative domains. As part of the network infrastructure they are strongly affected by the development and deployment of new communication paradigms and applications.Currently we experience a very fast rise in the use of multimedia applications. These differ in many aspects from "traditional applications", for example concerning bandwidth usage, dynamic protocol elements or multiple data flows for one application session. Corresponding firewall mechanisms and techniques did not change with the same dynamics though. Currently existing firewalls have problems supporting these new type of applications because to some extent they try to map the new characteristics to the manner of conventional applications which they are able to handle. We strongly believe that new application types require new firewall techniques and mechanisms. In this paper, we identify typical characteristics of multimedia applications that cause problems using traditional firewalls. Based on this analysis we deduce enhancements to existing firewalls that can be used to better adapt to a communication environment in which multimedia applications are used. We describe these enhancements in general, show a adequate systems architecture and present a implementation based on this design. The feasibility of that approach has been shown in the example scenario that we finally present.

1 Introduction

Today, security aspects have become more and more important and access control at the network border is considered essential. Therefore, most organizations replaced their basic internet routers by devices that perform additional packet-filtering. This option is cost effective, because most routers are able to perform packet-filtering tasks anyway and the functionality has just to be activated. For some institutions, however, this level of security may be insufficient. Packet filters usually just do a pattern matching on predefined fields within the packet (header) but do not pay attention on the semantics of the packets payload which represents application specific data. A more sophisticated method that can be used to control the communication over a network border are so called "stateful filters". They act like a filter, but they are also able to extract information from the application layer and most significant - may change their behavior according to what passed through them in advance.

For higher security users must consider additional options and have to augment packet filter security with proxying. A proxy server offers additional security because the session flow is retained, inspected and forwarded at the application layer. Many firewall vendors prefer stateful filters instead of proxies because that way it is easier to implement support for new protocols. Furthermore filters generally allow for better performance. However, there are strong claims that stateful filters are less secure than proxies [1]. To combine the advantages of all these firewall techniques [2] a mix of packet filters, stateful filters and proxies is often utilized. We call the combination of these elements as shown in Figure 1 *firewall system.*

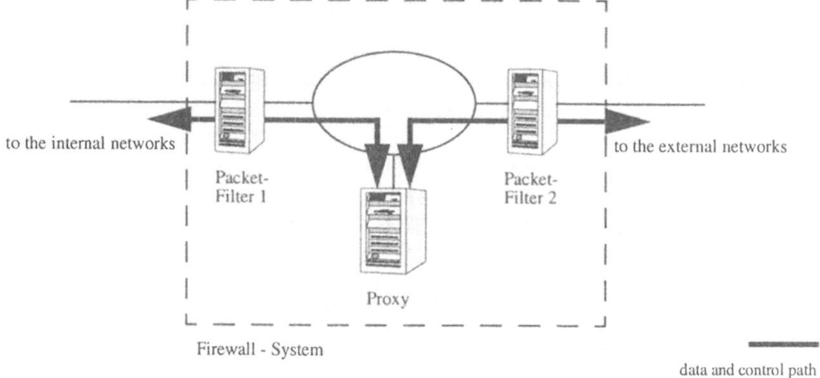

Figure 1: Firewall System

In this scenario, communication between the internal and the external network is only possible by passing data through both filters and the proxy. To enforce the hosts to not communicate directly but only via the proxy, the filters are configured in a way that only packets sent from or to the proxy server are forwarded. Applications that access a server in the other network have to be configured to use the proxy server either explicitly or by means of an element doing address or port translation. The area between the two filters is usually called *demilitarized zone* (DMZ) [3]. The described structure is often used for firewalls and is in general considered to provide a secure configuration to protect the internal network. Therefore, we use it as a reference scenario.

Under certain circumstances, however, the protection is consciously weakened - hazarding obvious security risks. This is usually done if such a practice seems to be the only applicable short-term way to use a certain service at all. Some non-representative examples are given below:

- Some applications complicate the use of a proxy since they were designed and implemented with end systems communicating directly in mind. So they do for instance transmit lower layer addresses as part of their application specific payload data again. In this case, the firewall filters may be configured to selectively pass data streams directly to the external net and vice versa. The same is necessary if no proxy is implemented (yet) for an application.
- Most firewall components that are used today are not designed to support multicast communication. To use applications which demand multicast the security policy of

the firewall must usually be weakened on a "all-or-nothing" basis. This conflicts with the intended policy to handle data streams at a firewall individually and with a fine-grained granularity. Approaches are currently made to remedy that drawback [4].

In this paper we deal with the ever increasing class of multimedia applications which lead to serious problems. For many of these applications, the firewall system has to be configured in a way that it does not provide the maximum possible protection for the internal network. In section 2 we describe characteristics of multimedia applications as well as the resulting problems. Based on these considerations, we present a new approach, the *Distributed Dynamic Firewall Architecture*, which may solve the specified problems, in section 3. Further, we describe our firewall system implementation based on the architectural ideas. To demonstrate the usability of it we show an example of an appropriate multimedia application in section 4. In section 5 we discuss related work and then conclude the paper.

2 Multimedia Applications and Firewalls

We concentrate on a special type of applications - multimedia applications. These use continuous media and discrete media data [5], with the continuous media being audio and/or video streams that demand a high throughput and compliance to real-time specifics like a bounded delay or jitter. The discrete media usually consists of control data streams for the audio and video data streams and additional information (e.g. meta data).

2.1 Communication Principles

In order to describe communication scenarios, we define the following terms to distinguish the granularity at which an application's data stream is considered. A *flow* is a single data stream, identified by a tuple of characteristic values (source address, source port, destination address, destination port, protocol number). The term *channel* is often used to describe a single data stream and will be treated synonymously throughout this paper. A *session* describes the association of multiple flows that together form an application's data stream.

The protocol behavior of most multimedia applications may be generalized in the following manner. A client typically connects to a server using an initial direct TCP or UDP "connection", often called control channel. After control channel setup, the multimedia application opens one or more data channels to transmit audio or video data. The port numbers used for these data channels are dynamically negotiated on the control channel. Detailed examples for that behavior will be given in section 4.

Some multimedia applications do not only use a unicast data channel to send the requested data but make use of multicast mechanisms to reach several clients in a very effective manner. Additionally, if the intermediate network supports these option, the server and client could negotiate QoS parameters to ensure that time critical content can be transmitted through intermediate nodes as desired.

2.2 Characteristics

Multimedia applications differ from traditional applications in many characteristics. Especially the following issues cause problems in a network which is protected by a firewall:

- **Multiple flows for one logical session:** The audio and video content is in most cases sent using additional TCP or UDP flows separate from the control data. Sender and receiver are "connected" by several flows though there is only one logical session between them.
- **Dynamic behavior:** Many of the connection parameters are not fixed and therefore possibly unknown when the communication starts. As an example, the number of audio or video streams, the bandwidth needed to transmit the streams or the TCP and UDP ports used for the streams could be initially unknown. Intermediate systems like firewalls have to consider that fact and do probably have to adapt to this dynamic behavior.
- **Complex protocols:** The Protocols used to control multiple flows and the dynamic communication are usually more complex than those used for a static flow. Firewalls and especially proxies do observe the communication and may benefit from interpreting the semantics of the communication protocols.
- **Data rate and required throughput:** The increased data rate and data volume which characterizes multimedia applications demands higher network but also transfer node performance. Firewalls have to explicitly cope with this fact to prevent transmission bottlenecks.
- **QoS:** The transmission of continuous media typically requires a guaranteed quality (e.g. described in terms of bandwidth or delay). When using the current IETF IntServ approach these are insured by means of explicitly requesting and keeping resource reservations. A firewall as a network element should not hinder the corresponding protocols and could even actively take part in resource reservations. The same applies to the use of the DiffServ approach where QoS specific operations are especially performed at edge nodes which could coincident with firewall systems.
- **Multicast:** Many multimedia applications use multicast communication to transmit audio and video content. To ensure a handling of data streams at a fine granularity, the components of a firewall system have to individually relay multicast streams. Firewall systems therefore need additional mechanisms to determine which multicast groups should be relayed [4].

In this paper we describe problems caused by the first four aspects in more detail and derive a framework to cope with them.

2.3 Security Specifics

As described above, multimedia applications negotiate the number and the specifics (e.g. port numbers) of the data channels dynamically. Therefore, these applications require intermediate systems which are capable to adapt to the current communication situation. In our basic reference scenario, only the central component in the system, the proxy, has these capabilities. It is able to recognize the flow allocation commands of the applications based on the information transmitted via their control channels. According to an appropriate interpretation of these commands it relays the communication paths towards the communication endpoints. The filters at the border of the DMZ are not involved in this dynamic adaptation to the situation. So in a standard scenario they have to be configured to let all possible connections to and from the proxy pass through. That way they are used in an operation mode not providing their maximum protection functionality. From these considerations we deduce the first design criterion for our enhanced framework:

- **Criterion 1:** All components of a firewall system should be able to autonomously adapt or should allow other components to influence and change their individual configuration. In that case there must be mechanisms to coherently control the state of the whole firewall system according to the requirements of the current communication situation. To reach that target, firewall components should be able to dynamically pass information to others.

Another typical problem caused by firewall systems in a multimedia scenario is that of a certain performance penalty. In our reference scenario every packet is sent through two filters and one proxy. This reduces the performance and limits the amount of connections that can be sent through the system.

To increase performance, many firewall vendors use a stateful inspection machine instead of a proxy, which usually allows for a higher throughput. The proxy or stateful inspection machine just forwards the data channel packets without any processing. However, the general problem remains, all traffic is sent through three components. Performance-sensitive streams could be sent directly via both filters.

Additionally it is useful to achieve more flexibility by using dedicated components with special characteristics. These arguments lead to our second criterion.

- **Criterion 2:** Generally speaking there should be means of "routing" packet streams individually through the firewall system. As an example, control channels should be separated from the data channels and can then be treated differently and by different well-suited, dynamically loadable and extensible components.

3 DDFA Systems Architecture

We develop a Distributed Dynamic Firewall Architecture (DDFA), which follows the communication paradigma explained by our two criteria. The following sections describe its components, their internal functionality and interaction.

3.1 Functional Specifications

The first of our criteria requires that all components within the firewall system have to adapt to the current communication state to increase firewall security. This requirement can be met by two general approaches. First, all components can be enhanced with additional functionality so that they are able to analyze the semantics of the communication at all protocol layers. So both filters and the proxy have to be replaced by "stateful filters". In this case all components can adapt their configuration to the current communication state. Therefore, they use information that they have retrieved themselves from the observed communication paths.

Second, the communication between the components can be enabled. By communicating, a component can distribute information (about a stream, or commands to adapt to a stream) to other components. In this case the configuration of all components can be adapted by themselves or by other components. Therefore, the components can use information that they retreive themselves from the observed communication paths (if this information is sufficent) or information that is retrieved from another component and is distributed to them.

To choose between both approaches, the possible impact has to be considered. Our main goal is that the provided security of the overall system should be enhanced. Changes should not strength the system at a single point by weaking it at an other point. The first approach therefore has serious disadvantages. The number of complex and independent policy engines is increasing. It is difficult to set up and maintain all three policy engines in a consistent and secure way. By using the second approach, the complexity of the system also increases, but a central and consistent view of the policy engine is maintained.

When comparing both approaches with respect to performance, the following facts have to be considered. The first method reduces system performance because the desired information must be extracted at least three times from the communication channels. The second method needs to extract the necessary information only once, but the extracted information has to be distributed to the other components which also reduces system performance. As shown, both approaches have an inferior performance than the initial system shown in figure 1, but therefore an increased security. We believe that the realization of our second criteria will outweight this performance drawback.

For security reasons, we decided to use the second approach. As described later, this decision also allows the realization of our second criteria. To fulfil the first criterion we specify requirements for the internal firewall communication subsystem as follows:

- The firewall components, e.g. filters or proxies have to be enhanced so that they are able to communicate with each other. That way they become enabled to receive missing information about the communication state from another component and may also act as an information source.
- All firewall components have to provide an interface, so that other components are able to manipulate their behaviour if this is necessary. This changes the overall system behaviour and must therefore be done in a secure manner.

The second of our criteria could be met in two ways. First, the "routing" could be performed by the components at the edges of the firewall system. This requires that these components are able to split and reassemble the flows of the multimedia sessions. Therefore these components have to support a redirect function e.g. by means of rewriting IP addresses. This redirect functions may act transparently and do not influence the behavior of the involved end systems. To perform the splitting and reassembling of the session flows, edge components have to communicate with components which observe the control channels. The edge components have to split and reassemble the session, the observing component (e.g. a proxy for the control channels) knows about the dependencies of the single flows and has to distribute this information to the filters.

Second, the routing could be performed by the proxy. The proxy handles the control flows of the multimedia session. Therefore this component is able to modify the data transmitted on the control channels. By modifying the negotiated ports on these channels, the proxy could inform the participating endsystems to send specific flows on different ways.

Both methods can be used to split the flows of a multimedia session. The first method does this transparent for the endsystems, while the second method does not. The first method is therefore practicable in all use cases, but more difficult to implement than the second method. To support all communication scenarios, and to be able to keep it simple where possible, we use both methods. These thoughts lead to the following firewall design requirements:

- The same design requirements as derived from the first criterion are also necessary to fulfil the second criterion. Flow information has to be exchanged between the components to split and reassemble the flows of the multimedia session.
- The components at the firewall systems edges must be able to split and reassemble packet streams individually according to specific logical sessions.

3.2 Systems Structure and Components

The internal communication requirements can be met by interconnecting each component with each other. Each of the boxes represents a firewall component with the necessary software enhancements for inter-component communication. A resulting system structure is shown in Figure 2a.

Such a design has some serious drawbacks though. There is a problem for the components to learn about the overall system state. Components have to find each other and keep track about the state of each component. Additionally we need to support the maximum number of possible communication relations. Those can not be assumed to be unique and homogenous. A component can easily become over-featured and therefore over-sized and difficult to implement on different systems. That directly leads to portability problems. The whole complex software enhancement has to be rewritten every time it is ported to another system type. To avoid these problems we use system structure as shown in Figure 2b.

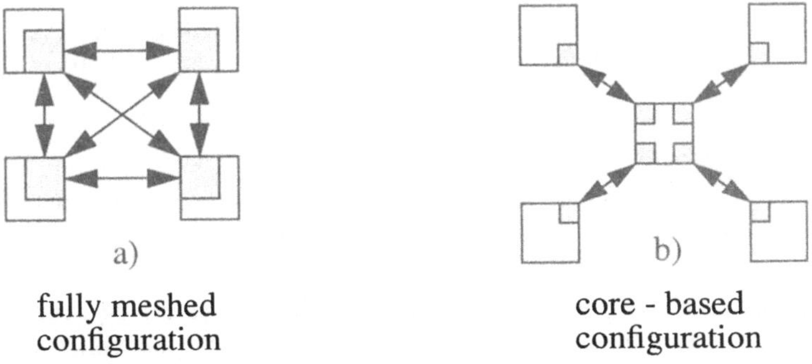

Figure 2: System Structure Alternatives

A central component (we further on call it DDFA-core) forms the central part of our firewall system. This component provides registration mechanisms which allows components to announce theire presence within the system. The core is then able to provide a location mechanism which enables the components to find each other.

The system enhancement for each firewall component are split in two parts.
- The system-dependent part is located on the component itself.
- The system-independent part is located within the core component.

That way a special additional adaption layer is inserted, which makes it easier to tailor the software. It allows to use different types of components providing the same functionality. The core can also be used to maintain tasks which control and organize the interaction of all interconnected components.

4 DDFA Prototype

The functional specifications and the derived system structure has been used to improve the standard firewall scenario shown in figure 1. The enhanced version of the standard scenario is shown in figure 3.

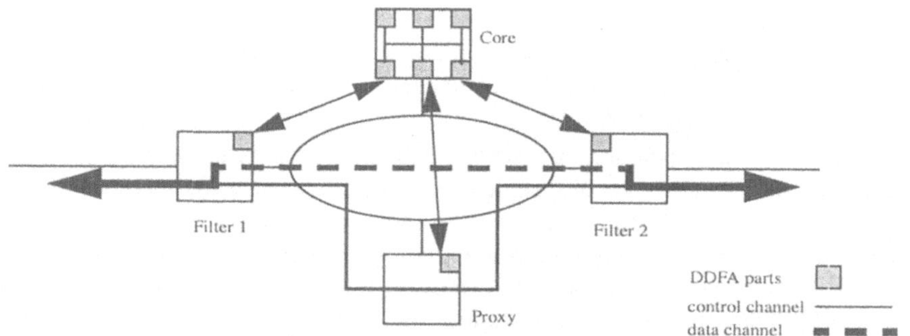

Figure 3: Standard Scenario with DDFA

This DDFA prototype system consists of two filters (FreeBSD 3.2 with IP-Filter 3.2.10) and a proxy host (FreeBSD 3.2 with a self implemented H.323 Proxy) and a core host. Therefore the prototype only supports IP-Telephony apllications based on the H.323 protocol.

4.1 Core Component

The DDFA core forms the main component of our system. The system independent parts of the software enhancements for the firewall components are also located there. The following tasks are fulfilled by the core component:
- **Location mechanism:** The components which participate in the firewall system use the core as a central contact point. The core registers the components and publishes their presence so that they can be addressed by other components.
- **Communication:** The core provides a general communication mechanism, so that the components can interact with each other. This communication is coordinated by

the core, so that requests are submitted and computed in a strict sequential order and an atomic way.

- **Authentication:** The interaction between the components can be controled and restricted. The core provides access control mechanisms and thus decides which components are allowed to participate in the system.
- **Protocol specific features:** Tasks that are usually located at separate firewall components can dynamically be loaded into the core. This is an implementation detail and allows for a higher systems throughput through the efficient use of a single address space.
- **Control tasks:** System startup and individual control functions such as clean-up of component specific data structures are also located at the DDFA core.
- **System independent parts:** The core provides mechanisms to load the system independent parts of the connected components.

The design of our system is modular to simplify enhancement of system functionality. The design is flexible to adapt to different firewall policies. The internal mechanisms and programming details are described in [14].

4.2 Component Adapters

We now show two different adapters to integrate firewall components into the DDFA. One adapter is used to integrate a filter, the other to integrate an IP-Telephony (based on the H.323 protocol family) proxy. Every adapter consists of a system dependent part, installed on the firewall component itself, and a system independent part which is loaded as described into the core.

IP-Filter Adapter:

An IP-Filter adapter is used to integrate "IP-Filter" packet filters hosted on a FreeBSD operating system into the DDFA system. The system independent part provides a generic interface within the DDFA-core to access filters in a standardized manor. Other components can reconfigure the filter, redirect streams or request flow information from the filter by using this interface. The system dependent part is hosted on the filter machines. This part is system dependent because it has to communicate with the filter software, the operating system and the network interfaces on the filter host. It translates the standardized commands from the core into the specific language used for the particular filter. Therefore, parts of this system dependent component must be rewritten in most cases when the target operating system or filter software is changed. System dependent and system independent part are connected via a secured TCP link [14].

IP-Telephony Proxy Adapter:

An IP-Telephony-Proxy adapter can be used to make H.323 proxy functionality available within the DDFA system. The system independent part provides an interface, which allows other components to modify the proxy behavior or to receive informations about the flows processed by the proxy. In addition, the proxy uses this interface to communicate with other components. This proxy is described in [15].

4.3 Communication example in Detail

A representative example of a Multimedia Application supported by our system is Microsoft NetMeeting . It is used for multimedia conferencing and is based on the H.323 protocol suite [9]. Figure 4 shows the communication mechanism between two H.323 based IP-telephony clients. In this figure the caller (later assumed to be on the internal network behind the firewall) initiates an IP-phone call to the called (later assumed to be on the external network) client. Only audio streams will be considered between both clients. If video streams between the clients are used too, two additional streams (RTCP and RTP) in each direction are added.

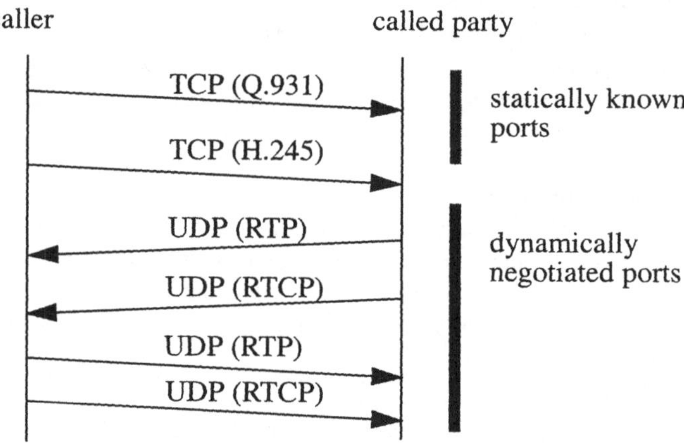

Figure 4: H.323 communication

In a H.323 session two TCP control channels are utilized. The first control channel is employed for call setup and uses the Q.931 protocol. The ports used for the second control channel are dynamicaly negotiated on the Q.931 channel. After the second (H.245) control channel is established, this channel is used between the clients to establish the audio and video streams between both clients. The ports used for these flows are negotiated dynamically on the H.245 control channel.

To show the difference between a standard firewall system (shown in Figure 1) and our extended DDFA system (shown in Figure3), we will explain how both systems handle a H.323 application. The H.323 Application is handled by a system shown in Figure 1 in the following manner:

1. Boundary conditions:

- The calling H.323 client has to support a proxy. The application has to know that it must route the call over the proxy.
- Filter 1 must pass the initial Q.931 (TCP, destination port 1720) connection from the caller to the proxy, Filter 2 to must pass the initial Q.931 (TCP, destination port 1720) connection from the proxy to the called client.

- Filter 1 must pass the H.245 (TCP, destination port greater than 1023) connection from the caller to the proxy, Filter 2 to must pass the H.245 (TCP, destination port greater than 1023) connection from the proxy to the called client.
- Filter1 and Filter 2 must be configured to allow all UDP flows with a destination port greater 1023 to and from the proxy.

2. Communication:

- The calling host connects to the proxy via TCP at port 1720. The proxy then relays this connection to the destination host. This Q.931 connection is now survied by the proxy.
- The proxy recognizes that the H.245 port is negotiated on the Q.931 control channel. The proxy also relays and observes this control channel between both endpoints.
- The proxy recognizes the negotiation of the audio channels. By modifying the submitted ports and IP-addresses the proxy gets these audio streams and relays them between both endpoints. The bulk data transfered between the clients are relayed by the proxy.

If the application is handled by our modified firewall system, the boundary conditions and the communication mechanisms change. The system configuration and the session flows are shown in Figure 3.

1. Boundary conditions:

- Filter 1 must pass the initial Q.931 (TCP, destination port 1720) connection from the caller to the proxy. In addition, all TCP connection attempts, made from the internal client to the external client on port 1720 should be redirected to the proxy. In this case, the application does not need to support a proxy, the proxy is transparently inserted in the communication path.

2. Communication:

- The calling client tries to connect to the called client via TCP on port 1720 to set up the Q.931 connection. Filter 1 redirects this request to the H.323 proxy. The proxy then asks via itscore connection the Filter 1 component about the state of this flow. As result the proxy gets the information that this connection was primary made to the destination client. The proxy now uses the core connection to inform filter 2 that he will connect the destination client on port 1720 via TCP. Filter 2 adjusts his configuration to allow this connection. The proxy now connects to the destination client and relays and observes the Q.931 connection between both clients.
- By observing the Q.931 connection, the proxy recognizes the negotiation of the H.245 connection. To negotiate the H.245 connection, the destination client passes information about the target IP-address and port for the H.245 connection to the calling client. This information is modified by the proxy, so that it will receive the connection request for the H.245 connection. Before the proxy passes the modified message to the calling client, it uses the core connection to inform Filter 1 about the connection that will be made to the proxy. Filter 1 adjusts his filter rules.
- The proxy now receives the H.245 connection request. It informs the Filter 2 via the core about the outgoing connection to the destination client. Filter 2 adjusts its filtering rules. The proxy now connects to the destination client and relays and observes the H.245 connection.

- Next the audio data streams are negotiated on the H.245 channel. The proxy observes this communication and informs both filters about the negotiated streams. The filters then change the filter rules according toinformation passed by the proxy. The bulk data are now sent directly between the clients. These data do not have to be relayed by the proxy.
- When the communication is going to be finished, special messages are sent on the control channels. This is recognized by the proxy, and it distributes this information to the filters, so that all previous opened paths within the filter rules could be closed. When the communication is finished, the system configuration is again in the state described in the section "Boundary conditions".

4.4 Security Concerns

As we described, the main difference between the standard firewall and our DDFA system is the initial configuration. In the standard system several predefined "holes" within the filter configurations are necessary because an adaption of the system during the communication is not possible. The DDFA System does not need these predefined holes, because the system can open and close the actual necessary paths on all components during the communication. The DDFA System, therefore, allows a more secure operation, regarding the filter configuration, than the standard system.

Finally we have to consider if the overall DDFA System is also more secure then the standard system. The overall system is more complex then the standard one, but a central and consitent view of the policy engine is maintained. An administrator of the firewall system will not recognize the difference between configuring the central component in the standard scenario or configuring the DDFA system. Therefore configuration errors could be possible with equal probability in both systems. Because the internal design and implementation of the DDFA system is secure, this system provides a higher security level then the standard one.

4.5 Performance Concerns

As shown, in the DDFA system, the bulk data (audio and video flows) are sent directly via both filters between the endpoints. In the standard scenario, the audio and video streams are additionally processed by the proxy located between both edge filters. Therefore our DDFA system has the following performance advantages:
- The bulk data are only processed by filters. By avoiding the usage of proxies for the data flows, performance is increased [13].
- The bulk data are only processed by two components. By reducing the amount of hops, the performance is increased.

As mentioned, the distribution of flow information within the DDFA system leads to an inferior performance. This performance reduction only affects the control channels of the multimedia session. Therefore, theoretically, the usage of the DDFA system leads to a slower session setup (and session tear down), because of the delay on the control channels. Subjective we could not recognize this delay during our first tests. The theoretically proof proposition according the DDFA performance has to be verified. Therefore measurements have to be done.

5 Related work

As the increased use of multimedia applications not only in the research community but also in commercial environments generates an increasing demand for adequate secure and yet performant solutions - there is a lot of further research activity on that topic. An approach to support the requirements of high data rates is described in [10]. The authors propose parallel firewalls to support high performance networks. In their approach, the connections are dynamically distributed to different proxies because the proxies represent the bottlenecks of firewall systems. The distribution is done by one or several packet filters at the edge of the system via network address translation. This approach allows for scalability, yet at significant costs since the data streams are still routed through a proxy, which is not necessary in our implementation.

Using the SOCKS protocol, specified by the Authenticated Firewall Traversal Working Group [11] of the IETF, a client that wishes to establish a connection to an object that is reachable only via a firewall must open a TCP connection to the SOCKS server system and has to authenticate at the server. The SOCKS server evaluates the request and if that proceeded successfully - establishes the appropriate connection directly. This approach has some major disadvantages. The implementation of the SOCKS protocol typically involves the re-compilation or re-linkage of TCP-based client applications to use the appropriate encapsulation routines in the SOCKS library. Often this is not possible. Also it can be used only for communication between known partners, which restrict its usability.

The PIX firewall system developed by Cisco [12] is based on a combination of stateful filters and proxies. Their approach is to authenticate a user at a proxy and to build up the initial connection. If this is successful all session flows are directly passed-through between the two parties while maintaining control of the session state. This architecture reaches a high throughput but there is a limited possibility to configure additional components (e.g. packet filters) dynamically to adapt the whole firewall system. We consider our approach at least as comparable and even more flexible for emerging new multimedia protocols.

6 Summary and Outlook

We presented a distributed firewall architecture and implementation, which is targeted to solve the problem of efficiently supporting multimedia applications in a secure manner. The main idea of our approach is, to treat a firewall system as a distributed architecture of specialized components and to dynamically adapt all these as well as their interactions to the current communication situation.

By implementing a prototype we showed the general usability of our approach. In a representative example scenario we described how the data channels are directly passed through the system, whereas the control flow is handled by a proxy. The prototype system determines which connections are allowed by using IP-, TCP- and UDP-filter lists. Communication paths through the firewall system are opened on demand and only when they are really needed. The proxy approach allows us to also implement support for a user specific authentication which will definitely be needed in a production environment.

Based on our implementation we actually measure the performance of the system, using the utilities and methods presented in [13] in order to compare with other approaches. Finally we plan to add features to both the systems architecture and the user interface to improve the usability of the system. In a future implementation step CORBA usage in the core system will be evaluated. Thereby we intend to transparently distribute the functionality of the core component over several hosts in order to increase the resilience of the system and its overall performance.

7 References

[1] Network Associates: Application Gateways and Stateful Inspection, http://www.avolio.com/apgw+spf.html

[2] Chapman, D.B.: Building Internet Firewalls, O'Reilly, Cambridge, 1995

[3] Cheswick, W.R., Bellovin S.M.: Firewalls and Internet Security, Addison Wesley, 1994

[4] Finlayson, R.: IP Multicast and Firewalls, Internet Draf draft-ietf-mboned-mcast-firewall-02.txt, 1998

[5] Steinmetz, R., Nahrstedt, C.: Multimedia: Computing, Communications & Applications, Prentice-Hall, 1995

[6] Comer, D.E.: Internetworking with TCP/IP, Volume I, 2nd Edition, Prentice Hall, 1991

[7] Reed, D.: IP-Filter, http://coombs.anu.edu.au/~avalon/

[8] Progressive Networks: Real Audio, http://www.real.com/

[9] ITU: ITU-T Recommendation H.323, Packet-Based Multimedia Communications Systems, 1998

[10]Ellermann, U., Benecke, C.: Parallel Firewalls: Scalable solutions for High-speed Networks [German], DFN-CERT Workshop Sicherheit in vernetzten Systemen, Hamburg 1998

[11]Leech, M., Ganis, M., Lee, Y., Kuris, R., Koblas, D., Jones, L.: SOCKS Protocol Version 5, RFC 1928, 1996

[12]Cisco: Cisco's PIX Firewall Series and Stateful Firewall Security, White Paper, 1997

[13]Ellermann, U., Benecke, C.: Tools for measuring the Performance of Proxies [German], published in MMB-Arbeitsgespräche: "Leistungs-, Zuverlässigkeits- und Verläßlichkeitsbewertung von Kommunikationsnetzen und verteilten Systemen", Hamburg 1998

[14]Utz Roedig, Ralf Ackermann, Christoph Rensing, and Ralf Steinmetz. DDFA Concept. Technical Report KOM-TR-1999-04, KOM, December 1999

[15]Utz Roedig, Ralf Ackermann and Ralf Steinmetz. Evaluating and Improving Firewalls for IP-Telephony Environments. The 1st IP Telephony Workshop, Berlin 2000

Integration der Schleusentechnologie "Lock-Keeper" in moderne Sicherheitsarchitekturen

E.-G. Haffner[1], Thomas Engel[1], Christoph Meinel[1]

[1] Institut für Telematik, Bahnhofsstr. 30-32,
D-54292 Trier, Germany
`{Haffner, Engel, Meinel}@ti.fhg.de`

Zusammenfassung. Moderne Sicherheitsarchitekturen sind darauf ausgerichtet, die diversen Kommunikationsanforderungen von Abteilungen und Unternehmensstrukturen nach außen und untereinander durch geeignete, adäquate Maßnahmen gegen unbefugten Missbrauch zu schützen. Hierzu werden unterschiedliche *Security Level* mit den jeweilig erlaubten Anwendungen definiert und zum Einsatz gebracht. Auf den niedrigsten Leveln sind alle Protokolle erlaubt, während eine Erhöhung der Sicherheitsanforderungen zugleich eine Restriktion an möglichen Anwendungen nach sich zieht, die gewöhnlich durch *Firewalls* kontrolliert werden. Am oberen Ende der Sicherheitsskala sind die kommunizierenden Netze physikalisch getrennt und die zugelassenen Protokolle entsprechend eingeschränkt. Die *Lock-Keeper Architektur* als eine Möglichkeit für hochsicheren Datenaustausch wird hier vorgestellt und seine Integration in komplexe Sicherheitsstrukturen aufgezeichnet.

1 Einleitung

Mit der weltweit wachsenden Vernetzungsdichte von Computern über das Internet und den sich daraus ergebenden Möglichkeiten zum Datentransfer zu den unterschiedlichsten Zwecken steigen auch die betrieblichen Anforderungen an die Rechnerkommunikation. Kaum ein Unternehmen kann es sich heutzutage leisten, ohne Zugriff auf den gigantischen Datenspeicher des Internets auszukommen und selbst der Datenaustausch zwischen Filialen eines Konzerns erfolgt nicht selten - zumeist verschlüsselt - über das Netz der Netze.

Dabei steigt ebenfalls der Anspruch an die Qualität der Datenformate. Moderne Medien verbessern jedoch nicht allein die Brauchbarkeit der dargestellten Informationen, sondern erfordern überdies Transferkanäle hoher Bandbreite.

Allerdings wachsen mit den vielen Chancen des heutigen Informationsaustausches ebenso die Risiken. Anbindungen von Institutionen, Behörden und Unternehmen an das Internet über Standleitungen generieren gefährliche Angriffsmöglichkeiten für Attacken. Die Integrität der unternehmenseigenen Daten zu schützen, die Authentizität der Kommunikationspartner zu gewährleisten und die Abhör- und Manipulationssicherheit während eines Datenaustausches zu garantieren wird in den sogenannten

Security Policies geregelt. Je nach Sicherheitsbedürfnis der betroffenen Stellen sind unterschiedliche Maßregeln für den elektronischen Datenverkehr sowie Verhaltensvorschriften für die Mitarbeiter Bestandteil dieser Dokumente. Allerdings sind für große Konzerne keineswegs gleiche Anforderungen aller Abteilungen vorauszusetzen. Vielmehr sehen die Sicherheitsvorschriften komplexer Sicherheitsarchitekturen unterschiedliche *Security Levels* vor, wobei im Einzelnen zu klären ist, welche Kommunikationsziele - unter welchen Sicherheitsbedingungen - zu erreichen sind. Nicht selten müssen hier schwerwiegende Entscheidungen gefällt und Kompromisse eingegangen werden.

Als Werkzeuge zur Realisierung der angestrebten Ziele dienen im Bereich der Sicherheitsinfrastrukturen für den elektronischen Informationsaustausch zumeist *Firewalls*. Der Zweck dieser Systeme besteht in einer Art Filterfunktion: nur berechtigte Zugriffe für authentifizierte Benutzer[1] mittels der erlaubten Protokolle dürfen zugelassen werden. In diesem Artikel werden wir darüber hinaus Einsatzmöglichkeiten der Schleusentechnik des *Lock-Keepers* vorstellen, der vermittels physikalischer Trennung der kommunizierenden Netzwerke in der Lage ist, höhere Sicherheitsanforderungen zu gewährleisten und bestimmte Attacken von Angreifern auszuschließen. Wir werden weiterhin aufzeigen, an welchen Stellen der Sicherheitsarchitekturen eine geeignete Analyse eingehender und ausgehender Daten erfolgen kann.

In den folgenden Abschnitten wollen wir zunächst die Gefährdungspotentiale von Angriffen gegen firmeneigene Netze aufzeigen und hier ebenfalls grundlegende Fragestellungen der Security Policies berücksichtigen (Abschnitt 2). In einem weiteren Abschnitt folgen dann diverse Ansätze zur Abwehr derartiger Angriffe, die zu komplexen Sicherheitsarchitekturen führen (Abschnitt 3). Im Vordergrund wird dabei die Funktionsweise des Lock-Keepers stehen. Eine Zusammenfassung mit Ausblick auf künftige Aktivitäten beschließt die Ausführungen (Abschnitt 4).

2 Angriffe gegen Datennetze

2.1 Die Bedeutung der Security Policy

Um Technologien gegen Angreifer auf Datennetze geeignet beurteilen und bewerten zu können, werden wir zunächst die wesentlichen Aspekte moderner Sicherheitskonzepte aufzeigen.

Wir unterscheiden hierbei zwischen einem inneren Computer-Netzwerk (IN) und einem äußeren (ON). Das IN beinhaltet jedwede Art vertraulicher und zu schützender Information eines Unternehmens, einer Behörde oder sonstigen Institution. Das ON ist ein Netzwerk oder ein Verbund von Netzen, über das Datenaustausch mit Kommunikationspartnern erfolgen soll. Ein prominentes Beispiel eines ON ist das *Internet*.

---

[1] Zumeist wird anstatt der Überprüfung der Authentizität des Benutzers auch eine solche des Quellrechner-Systems als statthaft empfunden.

Firmeneigene Intranets stellen INs dar. Allerdings können die Netzwerkstrukturen auch komplexer sein. Innerhalb größerer Unternehmen und Konzerne kann auch der Datenaustausch untereinander mittels INs und ONs modelliert werden.

Ein wesentlicher, allerdings nicht der einzige Sicherheitsaspekt konzentriert sich hierbei auf die Frage, wie der Datenaustausch zwischen IN und ON gegen mögliche Angriffe von außen (aus dem ON) geschützt werden kann. Allerdings darf hierbei nicht vergessen werden, dass de facto die meisten Attacken gegen Netze aus den INs selbst erfolgen [1].

Mögliche Risiken im Datenaustausch sind nicht-gewährleistete Authentizität von Sender und Empfänger, Abhör- und Manipulationsmöglichkeiten von Seiten Dritter und das unbefugte Eindringen in das IN, während gerade ein Datentransfer zwischen den Netzen erfolgt. Auch die Daten selbst können das Computernetzwerk gefährden. „Viren", „Würmer" und andere sogenannte „Beastware" stellen eine Bedrohung des INs dar.

Aufgrund dieser komplexen und umfangreichen Gefährdungspotentiale sollte ein Unternehmen zunächst eine *Security-Policy* [2] aufstellen, die im Detail die wichtigsten Sicherheitsfragen beantworten muss. Wie bereits in der Einleitung erwähnt, geht das größte Sicherheitsrisiko im Umgang mit elektronischem Datentransfer mit dem höchsten *Quality of Service* (QoS) einher. Wenn alle Arten von Programmen und Protokollen zu Verfügung stehen, wächst die Begeisterung des Anwenders mit dem Missfallen der Sicherheitsexperten. Typische moderne Internet-Protokolle und - Anwendungen wie *http, ftp, telnet, rlogin* [3], *smtp* und *sendmail* [4] stellen ebenfalls enorme Risiken dar[2].

2.2 Klassifikation von Attacken

Zum Erstellen einer spezifischen Security-Policy, die als Grundlage zur Absicherung gegen Angriffe von innen oder außen dient, ist es erforderlich, die möglichen Arten von Attacken zu klassifizieren und dabei festzuhalten, welche Abwehrmaßnahmen geeignet sind, den Bedürfnissen des jeweiligen Unternehmens bzw. der entsprechenden Abteilungen zu genügen.

Die nachfolgende Tabelle 1 gibt einen kurzen Überblick über die möglichen Klassen von Attacken und zeigt, ob es sich hierbei um einen „Online-Angriff" handelt, bei dem der Angreifer interaktiv über das Netz auf die Systeme im IN gelangt (vgl. [2]).

Diese Klassifikation zeigt auf, dass zahlreiche Möglichkeiten für den Angriff gegen ein IN existieren. Rein zahlenmäßig gehören die Offline-Angriffe mittels Beastware inzwischen zu den meistverbreiteten Angriffstypen, jedoch gelten die Online-Angriffe als die gefährlichsten, da die gesamte Integrität des inneren Netzwerks potentiell in Frage gestellt wird.

---

[2] Zu generellen Sicherheitsrisiken von UNIX siehe [5].

Klasse	Beschreibung der Quelle	On-line
Passwort-Diebstahl	Passwörter befinden sich in Klartext-Dateien oder werden abgehört auf IP-Ebene. Dictionary-Attacks raten Passwörter systematisch.	✓
„Social engineering"	Passwörter werden durch menschliche Interaktion bewusst oder unbewusst übermittelt (z.B. telefonisch).	✓
Bugs und Hintertüren	Fehlverhalten von Software; bewusste Abweichung von der Programmspezifikation durch den Programmierer; oder Viren und Würmer schaffen neue „Hintertüren".	✓
Authentifikationsfehler	Programme zeigen Einwahlmasken im IN und senden die Passwörter ins ON.	✓
Fehler auf Protokollebene	Sicherheitslücken im TCP-Protokoll, etwa „TCP sequence number attack"; Tunneling; „message encapsulating"; „tiny fragment attack"; „overlapping fragment attack" [6].	✓
Offline-Angriff (meist „Denial-of-service")	Würmer, Trojanische Pferde und Viren („Beastware") können das IN in seiner Funktion beeinträchtigen oder gar zerstören. Daten des IN können ins ON gelangen.	--

Tabelle 1: Klassifizierung von Angriffsmöglichkeiten gegen Computernetze

2.3 Psychologische Faktoren

Interessanterweise spielen für den Einsatz von Sicherheitswerkzeugen neben der technischen Relevanz zunehmend psychologische Faktoren eine zentrale Rolle. Das „Gefühl der Sicherheit" ist kein bloßer Zusatz oder gar ein Nebeneffekt in der informations- und kommunikationsbetonten Arbeitswelt. Ein aus sicherheitstechnischer Sicht objektiv überzeugendes System kann – wenn die Security-Policy in dieser Frage noch Lücken aufweist – durchaus verunsichernd auf die betroffenen Personen wirken. Eine zentrale Rolle spielt hierbei die Klarheit und Überschaubarkeit des Sicherheitskonzepts, die sich in der Security Policy offenbart.

2.4 Beastware

Wie Tabelle 1 aufweist, stellen Attacken über Inhalte der Daten selbst, die Viren, Würmer, Trojanische Pferde und andere „Beastware" ([7],[8]) enthalten können, grundsätzlich hohe Risiken dar [9].

Hierzu ist jedoch die Frage zu klären, worin sich das hohe Gefährdungspotential dieser Daten äußert. Inzwischen existieren zwar eine Reihe von Werkzeugen und Analysetools, die einen gewissen Anteil wohlbekannter Beastware erkennen und eliminieren können (Virenscanner, Mail-Analyser etc.), allerdings sollte dies nicht darüber hinwegtäuschen, dass ein Großteil des Sicherheitsrisikos grundsätzlich für ausführbaren Code bestehen bleibt.

Es handelt sich jedoch informationstheoretisch de facto um ein unentscheidbares Problem, dass ein Programm prinzipiell nicht herausfinden kann, welche Handlungen eine bestimmte Software auszuführen in der Lage ist. Und dies gilt nicht nur für eine automatische Analyse der Beastware: wie sollte ein menschlicher Administrator alle Wirkungen eines Programms mit den verschiedensten Eingabewerten ermitteln (z.B. wenn eine unendliche Testmenge erforderlich ist)?

Deshalb sind es durchaus berechtigte Sorgen, die Sicherheitsexperten von Unternehmen dazu veranlassen, keine unbekannte Software von außen in das firmeneigene Netz aufzunehmen und sehr restriktive Maßnahmen anstrengen, damit nicht durch diverse Kompilations-, Umwandlungs- oder Dekodierprozesse aus einfachem ASCII-Text ein Stück Software wird. Im Rahmen einer klar definierten Security-Policy lassen sich derartige Maßnahmen für gewöhnlich, insbesondere in Hochsicherheitsbereichen, als völlig legitim vertreten.

3 Abwehrmaßnahmen gegen Angriffe

3.1 Firewalls

Als ein sehr wichtiges Werkzeug zur Gewährleistung von Netzwerksicherheit hat sich in den vergangenen Jahren die bereits erwähnte *Firewall* etabliert. Eine Firewall ist eine Sammlung von Komponenten zwischen zwei Netzwerken, die zusammen folgende Eigenschaften erfüllen:

- Der Datenverkehr zwischen den beiden Netzen muss in beiden Richtungen die Firewall passieren
- Nur autorisierter Datenverkehr - gemäß der jeweiligen Security-Policy - darf die Firewall passieren
- Die Firewall selbst kann nicht angegriffen werden.
  (vgl. [2])

Die meisten modernen Firewalls sind Paketfilter. Sie analysieren TCP/IP[3]-Pakete, indem sie Sender und Empfänger gemäß der IP-Adresse verifizieren; sie kontrollieren den TCP-Port um sicherzustellen, dass der gewählte Dienst auch in Anspruch genommen werden darf. Allerdings gibt es zahlreiche Methoden, mit denen die Analysemechanismen einer Firewall hintergangen werden können. Mängel und Sicherheitslücken in der Konstruktion einer Firewall versuchen die Hersteller schnellstmöglich zu schließen. Es gibt jedoch keine absolute Sicherheit, dass sich Unbefugte nicht trotz Absicherung durch eine Firewall aus dem ON in das IN Zugang verschaffen.

Die Ursache hierfür liegt in der prinzipiellen Aufgabenstellung dieser Sicherheitsmaßnahme: eine Firewall muss erlaubte Anfragen von nicht-autorisierten unterscheiden und hierbei erstere ermöglichen, während letztere abzuwehren sind. Angriffe mit hoher krimineller Energie basieren in der Regel darauf, dass die Kriterien für den berechtigten Zugriff durch den unberechtigten Angreifer gefälscht werden, und somit

---

[3] Transmission Control Protocol/Internet Protocol

die Firewall ungehindert passiert werden kann. Es besteht hier demnach durch die prinzipielle Funktionsweise dieses Systems ein inhärentes Sicherheitsrisiko.

3.2 Die Lock-Keeper Architektur

Grundlagen. Bei sehr hohen Sicherheitsanforderungen von Unternehmen und wenn nicht alle Dienste zwischen den Netzen bereitgestellt werden müssen, stellt das Datenaustauschverfahren des *Lock-Keepers* (LK) eine echte Alternative oder Ergänzung zu klassischen Firewalls dar.

Der LK operiert dabei wie eine Schleuse. Zu keinem Zeitpunkt besteht eine direkte Verbindung zwischen den Netzen IN und ON, statt dessen werden die Daten zunächst in ein Vermittlungsnetz, das LKN transferiert, um nach Abtrennung vom jeweiligen Quellnetz eine Verbindung zum Zielnetz aufzubauen (vgl. Abb. 1).

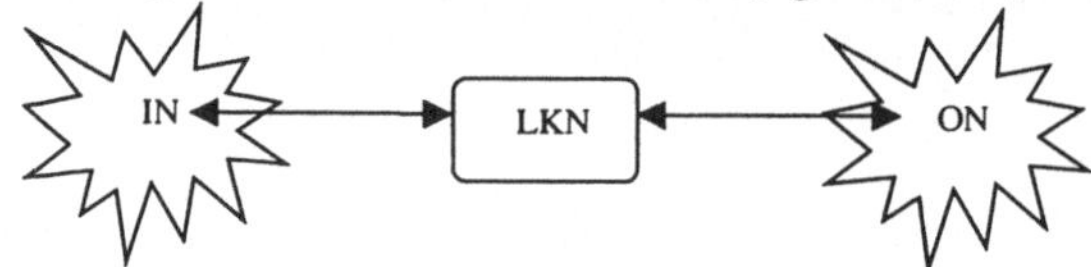

Abbildung 1: Topologie der Schleusentechnologie des Lock-Keepers

Die Abbildung 1 stellt eine abstrakte Darstellung der Netzwerktopologie des LK dar. Zentral für die Funktionsweise des LK ist dabei, dass die Trennung der beiden Netze auf einer *physikalischen Ebene* stattfindet. Damit wird es auch für den Systemadministrator kaum möglich, die Funktionsweise des Lock-Keepers auch nur vorübergehend zu umgehen. Somit kann zwar eine fehlerhafte Software-Komponente oder eine falsche oder unzureichende Konfiguration dazu führen, dass der Datenaustausch beeinträchtigt wird (*denial-of-service*), allerdings wird die Integrität der Daten des IN dabei nicht beeinträchtigt. Die dynamische Verbindung der jeweiligen Netze basiert dabei auf *PPP*[4], so dass hierüber Datentransfers und Mailübergabe stattfinden kann. Eine symbolische Darstellung der Funktionsweise des LK findet sich in Abbildung 2.

Eine Schleusentechnologie, wie die des Lock-Keepers, bleibt für die möglichen Online-Angriffe immun (vgl. 2.2), da das zugehörige Sicherheitskonzept nicht etwa berechtigte von nicht-erlaubten Anfragen trennt (wie bei einer Firewall, 3.1), sondern grundsätzlich – unabhängig von einer optionalen Analyse – jedweden Datenverkehr zwischen IN und ON zwischenspeichert und hierdurch alle direkten Angriffsmöglichkeiten unterbindet. In der Umkehrung bedeutet dies natürlich ebenfalls, dass bestimmte Dienste, die eine direkte und unmittelbare Verbindung zwischen den Computer-Netzwerken erfordern, durch den Lock-Keeper nicht bereitgestellt werden können. Im Ausblick wird auf künftige Entwicklungen in diesem Bereich hingewiesen.

---

[4] Point to Point Protocol

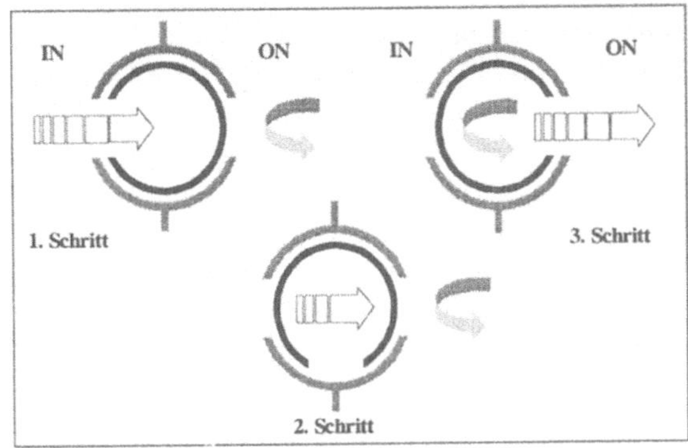

Abbildung 2: Funktionsweise des Lock-Keepers

Die in 2.3 angesprochenen psychologischen Aspekte einer Sicherheitsarchitektur sprechen aufgrund der Klarheit des Schleusenverfahrens für den Einsatz eines Lock-Keepers. Ohne genaue Kenntnis der (TCP-)Protokoll-Spezifikationen lassen sich die prinzipiellen Sicherheitscharakteristika vermitteln. Sowohl Software-Fehler als auch versehentliche oder absichtliche Misskonfigurationen des Systems gestatten aufgrund des hardwarenahen Aufbaus keine direkte Verbindung der Netze durch die Schleuse.

Der Preis für eine sichere Abwehr von Online-Attacken muss jedoch durch Einbußen im *Quality of Service* gezahlt werden. So ist beispielsweise ein klassisches Browsen im Internet nicht möglich, wenn die Netze mittels Lock-Keeper verbunden sind. Einen Ausweg aus diesem Dilemma bieten hier mehrschichtige Sicherheitsarchitekturen. So kann ein Unternehmen das eigene Netz in mehrere Subnetze aufteilen, wobei – je nach Sicherheitslevel – diese Netze untereinander mittels einer Firewall oder eines Lock-Keepers gesichert sind. Selbstverständlich können Firewall und Lock-Keeper auch kombiniert eingesetzt werden (vgl. 3.3).

Praktische Implementierung. Die theoretische Funktionsweise des Lock-Keepers als Schleuse für sicheren Datenaustausch kann auf mehrere unterschiedliche Arten implementiert und realisiert werden. Entscheidend für die Einhaltung der Sicherheitscharakteristika ist dabei die Trennung zwischen der Schleusen-steuernden Software und der Trennung der beiden Netze. Jedwedes – absichtliches oder unbeabsichtigt-fahrlässiges – Fehlverhalten der Software darf keinesfalls dazu führen, dass die beiden zu trennenden Netze verbunden werden.

Im einfachsten Falle, wo der LK nur aus einem einzigen Rechnersystem besteht, kann dies zum Beispiel dadurch realisiert werden, dass die Verbindungen zwischen den Netzen über den Lock-Keeper mit ISDN-Leitungen realisiert werden. Schließt man den LK und die beiden zu verbindenden Systeme an *denselben* NTBA[5] an, so ist stets gewährleistet, dass jeweilig maximal 2 Leitungen belegt werden können. Da jede Verbindung zwischen dem Lock-Keeper und einem der beiden Netze (IN oder ON)

---

[5] Network Termination Basic Access

jedoch bereits 2 Leitungen beansprucht, kann keinesfalls per Software eine direkte Verbindung zwischen IN und ON hergestellt werden; selbst dann nicht, wenn der LK durch eine erfolgreiche Attacke von außen kompromittiert worden wäre. Wie leicht zu sehen ist, verlagert sich die Sicherheitsanforderung an den Lock-Keeper selbst somit auf die bereitgestellte Infrastruktur. Eine Sicherheitsbeurteilung eines solchen Verfahrens ist deswegen günstig zu beurteilen, weil auch durch Eingriffe des Systemadministrators (ohne die Infrastruktur zu verändern) die Systemcharakteristik nicht gefährdet wird. Die Möglichkeit für Denial-of-Service Attacken bleibt jedoch bestehen; allerdings sind die Daten im IN stets geschützt vor direkten (online-)Angriffen aus dem ON.

Eine alternative Implementierung besteht in einer hardwareseitigen Lösung, die per se den LK stets nur *entweder* mit dem IN *oder* dem ON verbindet. Wiederum ist eine solche Lösung gegen mögliche Software-Attacken gefeit. Allerdings muss gewährleistet bleiben, dass die Umschaltzeit zwischen den Netzen nicht so niedrig gewählt wird, dass sie für das robuste IP-Protokoll transparent wird.

3.3 Kombinierte Sicherheitsarchitekturen

Typischerweise beinhalten die IT-Architekturen von Unternehmen mit Internet-Standleitungszugängen neben der Absicherung durch eine Firewall (FW) ebenfalls Virenscanner (VS) und Mail-Analysetools (MA).

Router (R) und Bridge-Router (BR) sind ebenfalls in der Lage, durch sogenannte Access-Listen verschiedene Segmente interner Netze voneinander zu trennen. Dazwischen entsteht eine „demilitarisierte Zone" (DMZ).

In diese komplexe Architektur lassen sich ebenfalls Schleusenkomponenten des Lock-Keepers (LK) für Hochsicherheitsanwendungen einflechten. Eine mögliche Ausbaustufe skizziert die Abbildung 3.

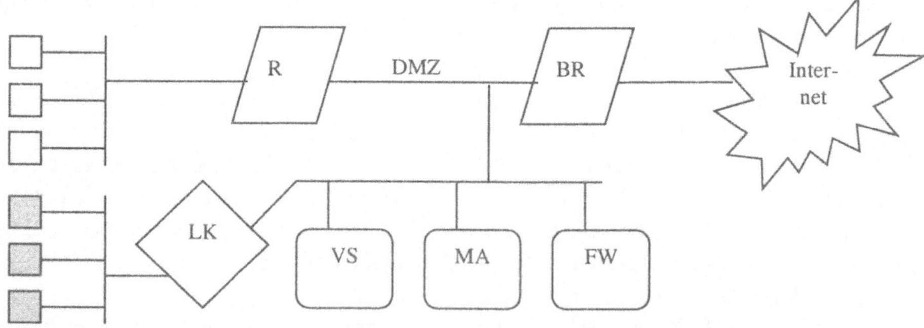

Abbildung 3: Moderne Sicherheitsarchitekturen mit Schleusenkomponenten

Die Schleusentechnologie lässt sich jedoch ebenso mit dem Internet direkt verbinden. Dann werden für derartig abgesicherte Netzsegmente allerdings typische Internet-Dienste (wie z.B. das Browsen) grundsätzlich unterbunden, oder zumindest nur mit starken Einbußen in den Antwortzeiten ermöglicht (über Cache-Proxies).

Die physikalische Trennung von Netzwerken hat eine längere Historie. Woodward erwähnt den Begriff des „Security-Guard" als ein Verbindungsstück zwischen einem unsicheren und einem vertrauenswürdigen Rechnersystem bereits 1979 [10]. Hier spielt jedoch die menschliche Kontrollkomponente eine entscheidende Rolle. Außerdem wird der Datentransfer zunächst nur in einer Richtung betrachtet. Dieser Gedanke wurde schließlich erneut aufgegriffen und erweitert von Denning, lange bevor das *World Wide Web* das Internet populär gemacht hat [11].

3.4 Zeitversatz der Schleusentechnik reduzieren

Ein prinzipielles Problem beim Einsatz der Schleusentechnologie ergibt sich durch den zwingenden Zeitversatz, den wir auch *Zyklus* nennen. Selbst wenn Daten mit optimaler Geschwindigkeit bis zum zentralen Schleusenserver gelangen, müssen sie spätestens hier auf das nächste Öffnen des Schleusentores warten. Im schlechtesten Falle jedoch gelangen die Daten nicht einmal ohne Zeitversatz bis zur Schleusenzentrale. Dann ist ein zusätzlicher Zyklus bis zur Auslieferung der Daten ins Zielnetz erforderlich.

Eine Erweiterungslösung des Lock-Keepers sieht hierbei vor, durch ein Klonen des Schleusensystems einen kompletten Zyklus zu reduzieren. Dabei ergeben sich nun unterschiedliche Restriktionen, was die möglichen Öffnungsperioden der Schleusentore angeht. Nur die Tore IS_1 und OS_2 sowie IS_2 und OS_1 dürfen gleichzeitig eine Verbindung der Netze ermöglichen (vgl. Abbildung 4).

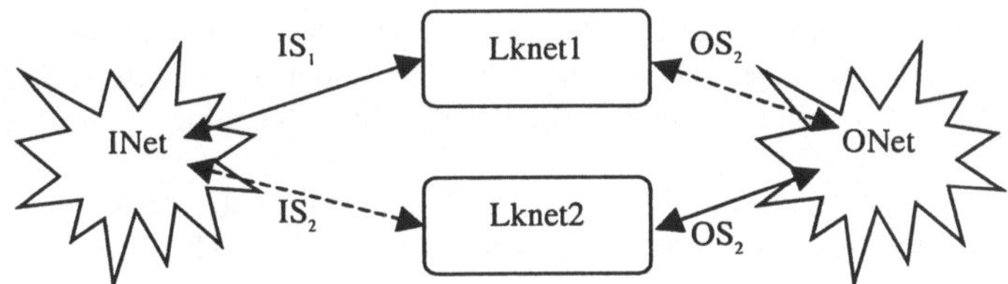

Abbildung 4: Zyklusreduktion durch Lock-Keeper-Verdopplung

4 Zusammenfassung und Ausblick

Moderne Sicherheitsarchitekturen müssen sich am wandelnden und wachsenden Bedarf an elektronischem Datenaustausch orientieren. Vielfältiger und multimedialer Transfer von Informationen zieht jedoch ebenso vielfältig ausgeprägte Angriffsmöglichkeiten nach sich. Durch unterschiedliche Sicherheitslevel lassen sich Anforderungen an die *Quality-of-Service* mit den jeweiligen Sicherheitsbedürfnissen in Einklang bringen. Hierzu ist eine möglichst breit angelegte Palette einsetzbarer Sicherheitskomponenten zu berücksichtigen. Neben klassischen Firewalls stellen so auch Lock-Keeper Infrastrukturen bereit, die Datenaustausch ermöglichen.

Neben der prinzipiellen Funktionsweise dieser Systeme wurde in der vorliegenden Arbeit zudem die Integration in komplexe Sicherheitsarchitekturen gezeigt. Zur Überwindung von zeitlichen Engpässen oder Beschränkungen von Diensten wurden darüber hinaus komplexe Erweiterungsmöglichkeiten skizziert.

Für künftige Ausbaustufen der Schleusentechnologie wird derzeit daran gearbeitet, zeitverzögert auch solche Dienste bereitzustellen, die für gewöhnlich eine unmittelbare Verbindung zwischen den datenaustauschenden Netzen erfordern. Die Einschränkungen im Bereich des Quality-of-Service könnten damit vermindert werden.

Literatur

1. Morrie Gasser: Building a secure Computer System, Van Nostrand Reinhold, 1988
2. William R. Cheswick, Steven M. Bellovin: Firewalls and Internet Security, Addison-Wesley, 5th printing April, 1995
3. P. Gulbins, UNIX Version 7, bis System V.3, Springer-Verlag, 1988
4. B. Costales, E. Allmann: sendmail, O'Reilley and Associates, 2nd edition, 1997
5. David A. Curry: UNIX System Security: A Guide for Users and System Administrators, Addison-Wesley, 1992
6. G. Paul Ziemba et al.: Request for Comments: 1858, Security Considerations – IP Fragment Filtering, October 1996
7. Klaus Brunnstein: Beastware (Viren, Würmer, trojanische Pferde) Paradigmen Systemischer Unsicherheit, Sichere Daten, sichere Kommunikation, Springer-Verlag, 1994, 44-60
8. F. Cohen: Computer Viruses: Theory and Experiments", proceedings of the 7th National Computer Security Conference, Gaithersburg 1984, 240-263
9. P. A. Karger: Limiting the Potential Damage of Discretionary Trojan Horses, Proceedings of the 1987 Symposium on Security and Privacy, IEEE Computer Society, 1987, 32-37
10. J. P. L. Woodward: Applications for Multilevel Secure Operating Systems, proceedings of the NCC 48, 1979, 319-328
11. D. E. Denning: Cryptographic Checksums for Multilevel Database Security, Proceedings of the 1984 Symposium on Security and Privacy, Silver Spring 1984, 52-61

IPSec und IP Multicast

Jörg Schwenk

T-Nova GmbH, Am Kavalleriesand 3,
D-64295 Darmstadt

Zusammenfassung. Die IPSec-Protokollsuite der IETF ist auf dem besten Weg, künftiger de facto-Standard für Netzwerksicherheit zu werden. IPSec bietet unter anderem auch die Möglichkeit, UDP-Ströme zu verschlüsseln und damit Streaming-Anwendungen (Audio-on-Demand, Video-on-Demand) zu schützen. Als letzte wichtige Komponente fehlt dabei noch ein standardisiertes Schlüsselvereinbarungsprotokoll für IP Multicast, um diese Anwendungen effizient absichern zu können. In diesem Artikel werden Vorschläge für solche Protokolle gemacht.

1 Einleitung: Verschlüsselung auf Netzwerkebene

Das OSI-Modell unterteilt eine Kommunikationsbeziehung in 7 Schichten. Diese und eine ungefähre Einordnung der vier Schichten von TCP/IP in das OSI-Modells sind in Abbildung 1 wiedergegeben.

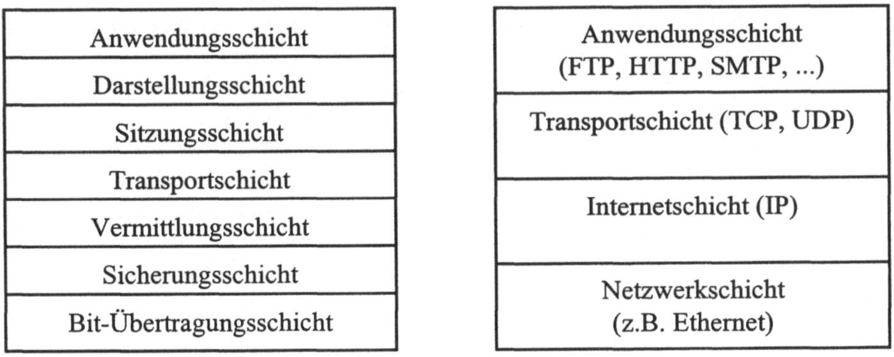

Anwendungsschicht	Anwendungsschicht (FTP, HTTP, SMTP, ...)
Darstellungsschicht	
Sitzungsschicht	Transportschicht (TCP, UDP)
Transportschicht	
Vermittlungsschicht	Internetschicht (IP)
Sicherungsschicht	Netzwerkschicht (z.B. Ethernet)
Bit-Übertragungsschicht	

Abbildung 1: Die 7 Schichten des OSI-Modells und die 4 Schichten von TCP/IP.

Eine Verschlüsselung zum Schutz der übertragenen Daten kann auf verschiedenen dieser Ebenen angesiedelt werden. Daraus ergeben sich jeweils andere Sicherheitseigenschaften.

Auf der Anwendungsschicht (Schicht 7) kann und muß der Nutzer den Einsatz von Verschlüsselung steuern, er ist sich bewußt, Verschlüsselung einzusetzen. Beispiele hierzu sind Dateiverschlüsselung oder Verschlüsselung von E-Mails mittels S/MIME.

Auf der Sitzungsschicht (Schicht 5) werden ganze „Sessions" entweder verschlüsselt oder nicht. Als Beispiel hierfür kann das World Wide Web dienen, in dem man mit ein und demselben Rechner entweder unverschlüsselt mittels http oder verschlüsselt mittels https kommunizieren kann. Bei Wahl der https-Variante wird zu Beginn jeder Sitzung ein SSL-Handshake durchgeführt, bei dem die Verschlüsselungsparameter (verwendete Algorithmen, Sitzungsschlüssel) ausgehandelt und eine partielle Authentikation der beteiligten Instanzen durchgeführt wird. SSL baut auf TCP auf und kann daher nicht für verbindungslose Protokolle wie UDP eingesetzt werden.

Auf Schicht 3 findet man dann die IPSec-Protokollsuite, die in diesem Artikel im Hinblick auf Anwendungen untersucht werden soll, die UDP und IP Multicast verwenden. Mit Hilfe von IPSec läßt sich der gesamte IP-Verkehr zwischen zwei Hosts, aber auch zwischen einem Host und einem LAN oder zwischen zwei LANs verschlüsseln. IPSec arbeitet (genau wie IP) verbindungslos und ist daher für die o.g. Anwendungen geeignet (siehe Abschnitt 3). Auf die Bestandteile von IPSec geht der nächste Abschnitt näher ein.

Unterhalb dieser Schicht findet man noch verschiedene Standards, die PPP-Verbindungen (Schicht 2) über ein IP-Netzwerk verlängern können. Die wichtigsten dieser Standards sind PPTP von Microsoft, L2F von Cisco und als gemeinsamer IETF-Standard der beiden Firmen, L2TP. Von Microsoft stammt dazu der Vorschlag, einen SSL-Handshake auf PPP-Ebene durchzuführen und so einen Sitzungsschlüssel zur Verschlüsselung der PPP-Verbindung abzuleiten.

IP Multicast ist ein wichtiger Ansatz zur Verringerung der zu übertragenden Datenmenge für Anwendungen mit hoher Datenrate wie z.B. Videostreaming. Normalerweise wird für Streaming-Anwendungen für jeden Client eine eigene UDP/IP-Verbindung zum Server geöffnet. Der Server muß somit den gleichen Inhalt gleichzeitig ausspielen und dafür jeweils eine feste Datenrate reservieren. Die verfügbare Bandbreite sinkt dabei proportional mit der Anzahl der Kunden. Auch auf vielen Strecken im IP-Backbone wird so der absolut gleiche Inhalt übertragen.

Bei IP Multicast wird der Inhalt nur einmal ausgespielt und über einen aufspannenden Baum („Spanning tree") im IP-Backbone-Netz zu den Clients geroutet. Es ist Aufgabe der Router, diesen Baum vom Server zu den Clients aufzubauen und den IP-Verkehr in den Routern, die Knoten dieses Baumes sind, zu splitten. Den Clients, die die Streaming-Anwendung empfangen möchten, wird eine zweite IP-Adresse, die sogenannte Gruppenadresse zugewiesen. Diese Adresse muß dem nächsten Router mitgeteilt werden, und der muß eine Anbindung an den nächsten Router im Baum herstellen.

Nicht alle IP-Netze sind Multicast-fähig, aber das MBONE-Netz wächst ständig weiter. Durch die zunehmende Beliebtheit von Streaming-Anwendungen ist hier ein zügiger Ausbau zu erwarten. IP Multicast ist nicht auf das oben beschriebene Point-to-Multipoint-Szenario beschränkt, sondern kann auch mit Gewinn in Multipoint-to-Multipoint-Szenarien wie z.B. Videokonferenzen eingesetzt werden.

2   IPSec

Die IPSec Protokollsuite (RFCs 1828-1829, 2085, 2104, 2401-2412) beschreibt ein vollständiges System zur Verschlüsselung und Authentisierung von Kommunikation auf der IP-Ebene. Sie besteht aus mehreren Blöcken:

-    den Datenformaten Authentication Header (AH) und Encapsulation Security Payload (ESP), jeweils im Transport- und im Tunnelmode,
-    den Sicherheitsdatenbanken Security Policy Database (SPD) und Security Association Database (SAD),
-    dem Internet Security Association and Key Management Protocol (ISAKMP) als Rahmen für den Schlüsselaustausch und aus dem
-    Internet Key Exchange (IKE), einem Diffie-Hellman-basierten Schlüsselvereinbarungs- und Authentisierungsprotokoll.

AH und ESP

Die Datenformate Authentication Header (AH) und Encapsulation Security Payload (ESP) beschreiben das Format, in dem man authentisierte und/oder verschlüsselte IP-Pakete mittels IPSec versenden kann. Das Format AH bietet dabei nur eine Authentikation (dafür aber auch von Teilen des IP-Headers), ESP bietet beides. Da der Schwerpunkt dieses Artikels auf Verschlüsselung liegt, soll hier nur auf ESP näher eingegangen werden.

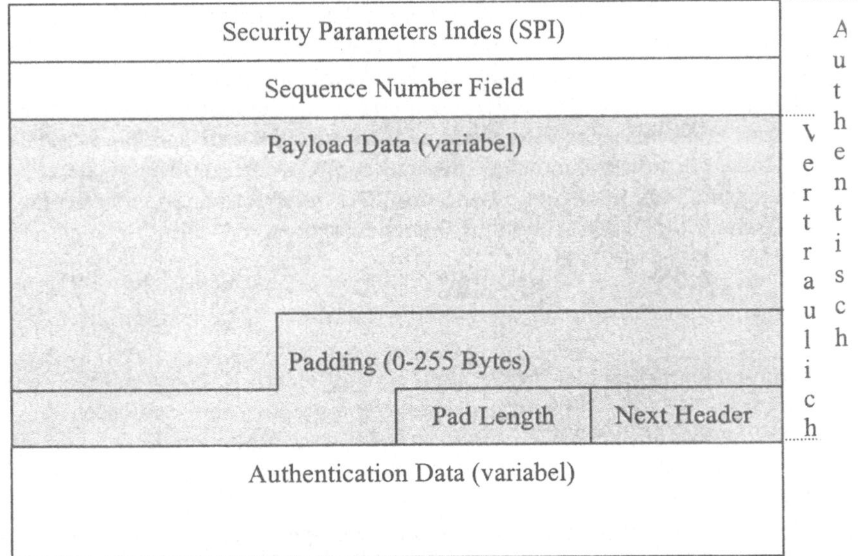

Abbildung 2: Format eines ESP-Pakets.

Abbildung 2 gibt den Aufbau eines ESP-Pakets wieder. Die Nutzlast (Payload) wird durch Anfügen zweier Felder und durch Padding auf eine Anzahl von Bytes gebracht, die durch 4 bzw. die Blockgröße eines Verschlüsselungsalgorithmus (z.B. 8 Byte bei DES und Tripel-DES) teilbar sein muß. Zur Identifizierung der verwendeten Verschlüsselungsparameter wird der Security Parameters Index, ein auf Empfangsseite eindeutiger 32-Bit-Wert eingebracht. Replay-Angriffe werden durch eine Sequenznummer verhindert, und ein Message Authentication Code am Ende des Pakets garantiert die Authentizität.

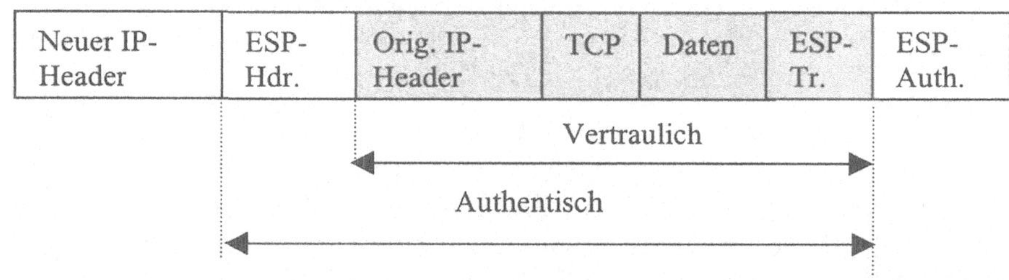

Abbildung 3: Anwendung von ESP im Tunnel-Modus auf ein TCP/IP-Paket.

Die verschlüsselte Nutzlast eines ESP-Pakets kann entweder die Nutzlast des ursprünglichen IP-Pakets sein (d.h. alle Daten nach dem IP-Header, einschließlich TCP- bzw. UDP-Headern), oder sie ist das komplette ursprüngliche IP-Paket (einschließlich des originalen IP-Headers). Im ersten Fall spricht man von Transport Mode; er ist nur zwischen zwei Hosts möglich. Im zweiten Fall handelt es sich um den Tunnel Mode, der immer dann zum Einsatz kommt, wenn ein IPSec-Gateway die Verschlüsselung und Authentikation übernimmt. Die Transformation eines IP-Pakets mit ESP im Tunnel Mode ist in Abbildung 3 wiedergegeben.

SAD und SPD

Ein Host kommuniziert mit einer großen Zahl anderer Hosts. In IPSec hat man daher sehr früh erkannt, daß die Verwaltung der kryptographischen Schlüssel für die einzelnen IP-Adressen ein großes Problem darstellt. Dies führte zur Entwicklung des Konzepts der Security Association (SA).

Eine SA ist dabei ein Eintrag in eine Schlüsseldatenbank, die Security Association Database (SAD), die alle notwendigen kryptographischen Informationen zur Verschlüsselung des IP-Verkehrs von IP-Adresse IP_A zu IP-Adresse IP_B (unidirektional) enthält. (Zwei Hosts kommunizieren also miteinander über zwei verschiedene SA's, für jede Richtung eine.) Auf Sendeseite ist eine SA eindeutig bestimmt durch die IP-Zieladresse und den Security Parameters Index (SPI), auf Empfangsseite eindeutig durch die vom Empfänger gewählte SPI.

Die Verarbeitung von empfangenen IPSec-Paketen ist relativ einfach: Folgt auf den IP-Header ein AH- oder ESP-Feld, so wird das Paket an den IPSec-Prozess weitergeleitet (statt wie sonst an den TCP- oder UDP-Prozess). Anhand der SPI können in der SAD die notwendigen Parameter zur Entschlüsselung und Überprüfung der Authentizität abgerufen werden.

Auf Sendeseite benötigt man eine weitere Komponente: Die Security Policy Database (SPD). In ihr werden Regeln definiert, wie mit einzelnen IP-Paketen, mit einzelnen Domains oder auch Subnetzen zu verfahren ist. Die SPD kann IP-Pakete unverschlüsselt passieren lassen, sie an den IPSec-Prozess weiterleiten, oder sie auch verwerfen. Der IP-Verkehr an eine Zieladresse kann mit Hilfe der verschiedenen SPIs nochmals differenziert behandelt werden.

ISAKMP

Eine Vordefinition von SA's ist nur in sehr kleinen IPSec-Installationen möglich, z.B. bei einer LAN-LAN-Kopplung über das Internet mit Hilfe zweier IPSec-Gateways. Für komplexere Szenarien benötigt man ein Verfahren, um SA's dynamisch aushandeln zu können.

Den Rahmen hierzu bietet das Internet Security Association and Key Management Protocol (ISAKMP), ein UDP-basiertes Protokoll, das den Rahmen zu Aushandlung von Security Associations bereitstellt.

Innerhalb von ISAKMP sind verschiedene Schlüsselaustauschmechanismen für IPSec beschreibbar, und ISAKMP ist auch nicht auf IPSec beschränkt, sondern kann durch Definition einer Domain of Interpretation (DoI) erweitert werden. In der Praxis gibt es aber heute nur eine DoI für IPSec und das IKE-Schlüsselvereinbarungs-protokoll.

IKE

Das Internet Key Exchange-Protokoll (IKE) basiert auf dem klassischen Public-Key-Protokoll schlechthin, der Diffie-Hellman Schlüsselvereinbarung [DH76]. Dieses Protokoll bildete den Kern der Arbeit von Diffie und Hellman aus dem Jahr 1976, in der die moderne Kryptographie begründet wurde. Es soll hier nochmals erläutert werden, da es die Basis für die vorgeschlagene Multicast-Schlüsselvereinbarung bildet.

Das Diffie-Hellman Protokoll hat als öffentliche Parameter eine große Primzahl p und eine Zahl $1<g<p$. Die Zahl g wird als Element der multiplikativen Gruppe Z_p^* betrachtet und muß in dieser Gruppe eine große Ordnung haben. Bei geeigneter Wahl dieser Parameter ist das Problem, den diskreten Logarithmus zu berechnen, praktisch unmöglich. D.h. gegeben eine Zahl $1<h<p$, berechne eine Zahl a so daß $g^a \bmod p = h$ gilt.

Zu diesen öffentlichen Parametern wählt jeder der beiden Teilnehmer A und B in der Diffie-Hellman-Schlüsselvereinbarung einen geheimen Parameter a bzw. b. Dann berechnet er $g^a \bmod p$ bzw. $g^b \bmod p$ und sendet diesen Wert über einen ungeschützten Kanal an den anderen Teilnehmer. Da $g^{ab}\ mod\ p = K = g^{ba}\ mod\ p$ gilt, besitzen beide anschließend einen gemeinsamen Wert, den nur die beiden kennen.

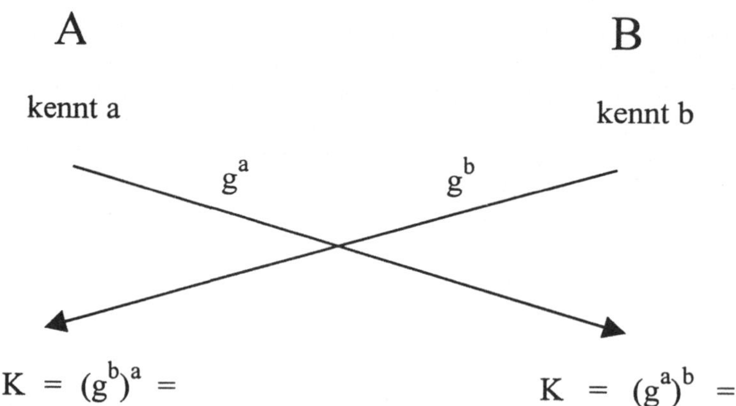

Abbildung 4: Die Diffie-Hellman-Schlüsselvereinbarung

IKE basiert nicht direkt auf dem Diffie-Hellman-Protokoll, sondern auf einer um die Authentikation der Kommunikationspartner erweiterten Version, den Station-to-Station-Protokoll von Diffie, van Oorschot und Wiener [DOW92].

3 IPSec für IP Multicast

Da IPSec wieder auf dem IP-Protokoll aufsetzt, ist die Verschlüsselung verbindungslos und hängt nur von der Security Policy und der Security Association ab. Somit können auch Streaming-Anwendungen über UDP abgesichert werden: Der Streaming-Server verschlüsselt einfach alle ausgehenden Pakete und kümmert sich nicht darum, ob sie ankommen oder ob der Empfänger-Client sie entschlüsseln kann. Sollte es Probleme mit der Entschlüsselung geben, so muß der Client aktiv werden und eine neue Security Association aushandeln.

Um eine IP Multicast-Verbindung zu verschlüsseln werden in allen beteiligten Hosts zwei SA's benötigt: Eine SA zu Senden an die Multicast-Adresse, und eine zum Empfang von der Multicast-Adresse. Wie aber können diese SA's ausgehandelt werden?

Da bei IP Multicast ein TCP-Handshake nicht stattfinden kann, müssen Multicast-Applikationen UDP-basiert sein. ISAKMP ist ein UDP-Protokoll und somit auch Multicast-fähig. Der Rahmen für die Schlüsselvereinbarung muß also nicht geändert werden.

Anders sieht es mit IKE selbst aus. Die Diffie-Hellman-Schlüsselvereinbarung funktioniert nur zwischen zwei Hosts. Der sich ergebende Schlüssel hängt von den Eingaben beider Parteien ab; es ist unmöglich, das Ergebnis so zu steuern, daß sich ein gemeinsamer Gruppenschlüssel für drei oder mehr Parteien ergibt. Es besteht also Bedarf für ein neues, Multicast-fähiges Schlüsselvereinbarungsprotokoll. Dabei muß zwischen den Szenarien Punkt-zu-Multipunkt (z.B. für Video-on-Demand) und Multipunkt-zu-Multipunkt (Videokonferenzen, verteilte Simulationen) unterschieden werden.

Punkt-zu-Multipunkt

In einem Punkt-zu-Multipunkt-Szenario gibt es eine ausgezeichnete Instanz, nämlich die Quelle der Daten (der Server), die auch die Rolle einer Trusted Third Party für die Festlegung des Gruppenschlüssels übernehmen kann. Damit ist das folgende einfache Schlüsselaustauschprotokoll denkbar:
-   Die Clients handeln jeweils bilateral mit dem Server über IKE eine SA aus.
-   Diese SA verwendet der Server dann, um den Clients über ISAKMP gesichert einen Gruppenschlüssel zuzuweisen.

Bei diesem direkten Ansatz lassen sich leicht neue Clients integrieren, aber der Ausschluß eines Clients stellt ein Problem dar: Der Server muß in diesem Fall allen anderen Clients individuell einen neuen Schlüssel zuweisen. Unterstellt man in diesem Szenario z.B. für Video-on-Demand Kundenzahlen, wie sie heute bei Pay-TV im Millionenbereich liegen, so kann dies schnell zu einem Problem werden.

Abhilfe können hier Ansätze schaffen, die auf der Verwendung von Bäumen beruhen. Solche Schlüsselmanagement-Strukturen sind im Bereich von Pay-TV unter dem Namen Conditional Access schon lange im Einsatz [Sch96]. So darf es auch nicht verwundern, wenn etablierte Conditional Access-Anbieter die ersten sind, die marktfähige Produkte zur Sicherung von IP Multicast anbieten [Ird00, NDS98]. Hauptnachteil dieser Lösung sind die benötigten Chipkarten, da die dazu gehörigen Leser nur im Business-Bereich vorhanden sind, nicht im Massenmarkt.

Software-basierte Ansätze zur Verwendung von Baumstrukturen, die eine Schlüsselverteilzentrale umfassen, werden in [CWSP98, MS98] beschrieben. Das strukturierte Schlüsselmanagement mit Hilfe einer Baumstruktur verringert den Aufwand zum Ausschluß eines von n Clients von $n-1$ auf $log_2 n$.

Multipunkt-zu-Multipunkt

Bei einer Punkt-zu-Multipunkt-Verbindung gibt es keine ausgezeichnete Zentrale mehr. Schlüsselvereinbarungsprotokolle für dieses Szenario sollten daher ohne eine solche Zentrale auskommen. Hier bietet sich die Verwendung von erweiterten Diffie-Hellman-Protokollen an.

Der erste Vorschlag für ein solches Protokoll stammt von Ingemarsson et al. aus dem Jahr 1982 [ITW82]. Um einen gemeinsamen Schlüssel der Form $g^{ab...z} \bmod p$ zu erzeugen, werden für n Teilnehmer $2n$ Nachrichten und $n-1$ Runden benötigt.

Eine wesentliche Verbesserung der Performance stellte der Vorschlag von Burmester und Desmedt [BD95] dar. Bei ihrem Protokoll müssen die Teilnehmer in einem logischen Ring angeordnet sein, und mit Hilfe von Multicast-Nachrichten kommt das Protokoll mit nur drei Runden aus. Nachteil dieser Lösung ist, daß zur

Entfernung eines Teilnehmers mindestens $1,5 \cdot n$ Nachrichten gesendet werden müssen [SMS00].

In Arbeiten von Steiner et al. [STW96, STW98, AST98] werden neue Protokolle vorgestellt, in denen ein Teilnehmer dynamisch eine besondere Rolle zugewiesen bekommt. Die Teilnehmer sind linear angeordnet.

4 Verallgemeinerter Diffie-Hellman mit Bäumen

Es bietet sich an, die beiden oben vorgestellten Ansätze zusammenzuführen. Ziel ist es dabei, die Effizienz von Baum-basierten Verfahren mit der Autonomie der Teilnehmer im verallgemeinerten Diffie-Hellman-Ansatz zu verbinden. Grundlage dafür bietet die Technik der iterierten Diffie-Hellman-Schlüsselvereinbarung, die in [BW98] eingeführt und deren Sicherheit auch dort bewiesen wurde. In [SMS00] wird dann ein Rahmen vorgestellt, wie ein solcher Baum ohne Zentrale durch Multicast-Nachrichten aufgebaut und ein gemeinsamer Schlüssel etabliert werden kann.

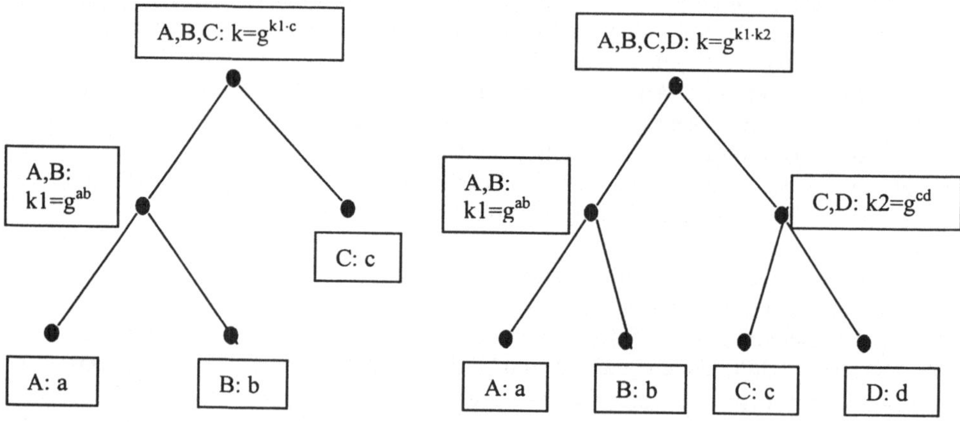

Abbildung 5: Iterierter Diffie-Hellman für drei bzw. vier Teilnehmer.

Um einen solchen Baum autonom wachsen oder schrumpfen zu lassen, kondensieren wir die gesamte Information über die Stellung eines Teilnehmer im Baum in einem n-Bit-Wert, der *VID* (für „Vertex-ID"). Die Wurzel des Baumes hat *VID=1*, und *VID=101* ist z.B. in Abb. 5 der Knoten von Teilnehmer B. Die *VID* kann sehr effizient dazu verwendet werden, Informationen über einen Knote X mit VID_X zu berechnen, z.B. parent$(X)=VID_X$ DIV 2 und level(X)=length(VID).

Algorithmus TREE_KEY_EXCHANGE
1. Jeder Teilnehmer X mit VID_X wählt eine Zufallszahl $1<x<p-1$ und sendet die Multicast-Nachricht (VID_X, $\alpha=g^x \bmod p$).

2. X wartet jetzt, bis er eine Nachricht (VID_Y, β) mit VID_X DIV $2 = VID_Y$ DIV 2 erhält und berechnet dann $k := \beta^x \bmod p$. Er setzt $VID_{NEU} := VID_X$ DIV 2 und $x_{NEU} := k$.

3. Wenn $VID_X > VID_Y$, so wird X passiv und sendet keine eigenen Nachrichten mehr.

4. Nun wiederholt X die Schritte 1-3 (evtl. ohne Senden von Nachrichten) mit x_{NEU} und VID_{NEU}. Dies wird so lange fortgesetzt, bis $VID=1$ erreicht ist. Der so berechnete Schlüssel k ist der Gruppenschlüssel. Alle Zwischenergebnisse, d.h. alle den durchlaufenen Konten zugeordneten Schlüssel, werden vom Teilnehmer gespeichert.

Soll ein Teilnehmer aufgenommen oder ausgeschlossen werden (s.u.), so kann der Algorithmus auch von nur einem Teilnehmer gestartet werden. Die anderen Teilnehmer bleibe dabei so lange passiv, bis eine gesendete VID zur Anfangssequenz ihrer eigenen VID paßt. Danach verwenden sie die gespeicherten Zwischenwerte, um den Schlüsselaustausch zu vervollständigen. Auf diese Art und Weise müssen nur $log_2 n$ Nachrichten ausgetauscht werden.

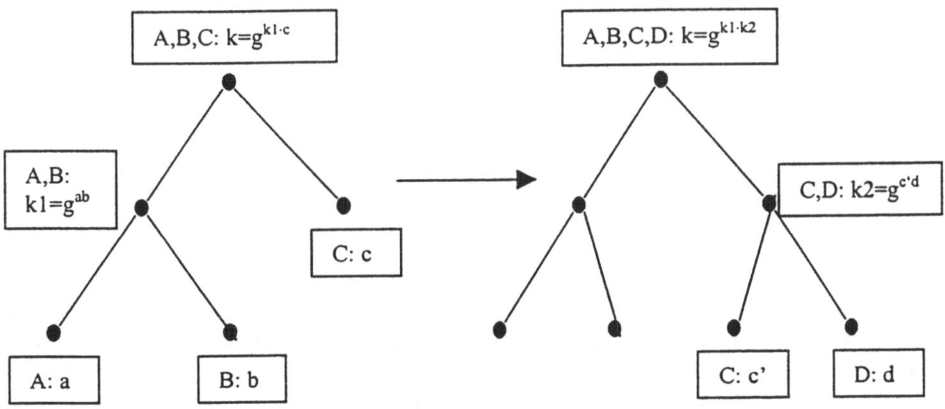

Abbildung 6: Aufnahme eines vierten Teilnehmers.

Algorithmus JOIN

Der Algorithmus JOIN beschreibt, wie ein neuer Teilnehmer in die Gruppe aufgenommen werden kann. Auf diese Art und Weise können sich sichere Multicast-Gruppen autonom formieren.

1. Der neue Teilnehmer sendet seine Identifizierungsdaten an die Gruppe. Er kann sich über ein Publik-Key-Zertifikat ausweisen.

2. Die Gruppenmitglieder antworten auf diesen Request mit einer Multicast-Nachricht, die ihre VID enthält. Diese Antwort erfolgt erst nach einer Verzögerung, die proportional zur Länge der VID ist.

3. Sobald ein Gruppenmitglied eine Antwort eines anderen Gruppenmitglied mit einer kürzeren oder kleineren VID empfangen hat, unterdrückt es die eigene Antwort. Dadurch wird gewährleistet, daß der Baum „Breadth First" aufgebaut wird.

4. Erhält der neue Teilnehmer mehrere Antworten, so wählt er die mit der kleinsten *VID* aus und sendet eine Antwort. Der neue Teilnehmer speichert *VID||1*. („||" steht hier für die Konkatenation der beiden Werte.)
5. Der ausgewählte Teilnehmer speichert seinen neuen Wert *VID||0*. Er initiiert einen neuen Schlüsselaustausch mit *VID||1*.

Algorithmus DELETE

Teilnehmer X mit $VID_X = VID'||b$ soll entfernt werden. Dann muß lediglich sein Nachbar, Teilnehmer Y mit $VID_Y = VID'||(1-b)$, einen neuen Schlüsselaustausch mit VID' initiieren.

5 Anwendungen

Pay-per-Streaming: Die Übertragung von Streaming-Daten im Internet hat bereits heute beachtliche Ausmaße angenommen. So kann man, um ein aktuelles Beispiel zu zitieren, das BigBrother-Haus von RTL II aus 18 verschiedenen Live-Kameras im Internet betrachten.

Werden solche Live-Streams wie heute üblich im IP Unicast-Modus übertragen, so muß für jeden Zuschauer eine eigene IP-Verbindung etabliert werden. Die erzeugt in Spitzenzeiten eine enorme Last am Video-Server und reduziert die für den Einzelnen zur Verfügung stehende Bandbreite. Außerdem fällt auf den Hauptstrecken des IP-Backbone redundanter IP-Verkehr an. Beim Einsatz von IP Multicast kann die Anzahl der gleichzeitigen Verbindungen, die der Server verwalten muß, auf eine konstant kleine Anzahl gesenkt werden, und das Backbone wird entlastet.

Bei der Übertragung von Streaming-Daten im Pay-Bereich oder für geschlossenen Benutzergruppen (z.B. berufliche Weiterbildung) muß eine Verschlüsselung des Contents erfolgen.

Video-on-Demand: Auch Video-on-Demand kann aufgrund verbesserter Video-Codecs (MPEG-4, MPEG-7) im Internet durchaus Realität werden. Hier muß für Spitzenereignisse wie den Internet-Start eines neuen Kinofilms (Sportveranstaltungen fallen eher in den Bereich des Pay-per-Streaming) mit hohen Belastungen gerechnet werden, die durch IP Unicast nicht aufgefangen werden können.

Durch geringfügige Verzögerungen bei der Ausspielung der Filme (z.B. durch Trailer variabler Länge) kann auch hier ein Multicast-Szenario konstruiert werden, bei dem nach vorgegebenen Kriterien (maximale Wartezeit, minimale Anzahl von Gruppenmitgliedern) Kunden zu IP Multicast-Gruppen „gebündelt" werden, um anschließend den Inhalt verschlüsselt ausgespielt zu bekommen. Die benötigte Übertragungsbandbreite kann so den vorhandenen Kapazitäten angepaßt werden.

Literatur

[AST98] G. Ateniese, M. Steiner and G. Tsudik, Authenticated group key agreement and friends. 5th ACM Conference on Computer and Communication Security, November 1998.
[B96] A. Ballardie, Scalable multicast key distribution. IETF RFC 1949, May 1996.

[Ber91] S. Berkovits, How to broadcast a secret. Eurocrypt'91, Springer LNCS, pp. 536-541.

[BW98] C. Becker and U. Wille, Communication complexity of group key distribution. ACM Conference on Computer and Communication Security, November 1998.

[BD94] M. Burmester and Y. Desmedt, A secure and efficient conference key distribution system. Eurocrypt'94, Springer LNCS, pp. 275-288.

[BD96] M. Burmester and Y. Desmedt, Efficient and secure conference key distribution. Cambridge Workshop on Security Protocols, Springer LNCS 1189, pp 119-129 (1996).

[CWSP98] Germano Caronni, Marcel Waldvogel, Dan Sun, Bernhard Plattner, Efficient Security for Large and Dynamic Multicast Groups.proceedings of the Seventh Workshop on Enabling Technologies, (WET ICE '98), IEEE Computer Society Press, 1998. http://www.skip-vpn.org/wetice98/HacknSlash.html .

[DH76] W. Diffie und M. Hellman, New Directions in Cryptography, IEEE Transactions on Information Theory, IT-22(6):644-654, November 1976

[DOW92] W. Diffie, P.C. van Oorschot and M. J. Wiener, Authentication and authenticated key exchanges. Designs, Codes and Cryptography, 2, 107-125 (1992)

[HMR96] H. Harney, C. Muckenhirn and T. Rivers, Group key management protocol (gkmp) architecture. IETF Draft, 1996.

[IPSec] IP Security Protocol (ipsec): http://www.ietf.org/html.charters/ipsec-charter.html and http://ietf.org/ids.by.wg/ ipsec.html.

[Ird00]   http://www.mindport.com/irdetoaccess/IAProductCyphercast.htm.

[ITW82] I. Ingemarsson, D. Tang and C. Wong, A conference key distribution system. IEEE Transactions on Information Theory, September 1982.

[MS98] McGrew, David A., and Alan T. Sherman, "Key establishment in large dynamic groups using one-way function trees," submitted to IEEE Transactions on Software Engineering (May 20, 1998). http://www.cs.umbc.edu/~sherman/Rtopics/Crypto/oft.html

[Multicast] The MBONE Information Web, http://www.mbone.com.

[NDS98] Amit Kleinmann, Scenarios and Requirements for Business-Oriented Multicast Security. http://www.ipmulticast.com/community/smug/

[O98] H. Orman, The OAKLEY key determination protocol. IETF RFC 2412, November 1998.

[SaS95] K. Sakurai and H. Shizuya, Relationships among the Computational Powers of Breaking Discrete Log Cryptosystems. EUROCRYPT'95, Springer LNCS 921, pp.341-355.

[Sch96] J. Schwenk, Establishing a Key Hierarchy for Conditional Access without Encryption. Proc. IFIP Communications and Multimedia Security 1996, Chapman & Hall, London.

[SMS00]   J. Schwenk, T. Martin and R. Schaffelhofer, *Tree based Key agreement for Multicast*. Submitted.

[STW96] M. Steiner, G. Tsudik and M. Waidner, Diffie-Hellman key distribution extended to groups. ACM Conference on Computer and Communication Security, pp 31-37, March 1996.

[STW98] M. Steiner, G. Tsudik and M. Waidner, CLIQUES: A new approach to group key agreement. IEEE International Conference on Distributed Computing Systems, May 1998.

The Evolution of Mobile IP Towards Security

Matthias Hollick

GMD - German National Research Center for Information Technology
Institute IPSI, Dept. MOBILE - Mobile Interactive Media

Dolivostrasse 15, D-64293 Darmstadt
Phone 49.6151.869.60195

`matthias.hollick@darmstadt.gmd.de`

Abstract. Mobile IP provides a framework for transparent host mobility in the Internet. This paper identifies the most important security related issues coupled to Mobile IP, mirroring the current and past development process in related IETF working groups. A short introduction on how Mobile IP works leads to a brief discussion of the integrated security mechanisms of Mobile IP. As special focus the integration of Mobile IP and IP Security (IPSec) is described and the related state-of-the-art architecture is presented and classified. Thereafter several outstanding security issues in the area of Mobile IP and the problems concerning Mobile IP and IPSec will be clarified. Summarizing, and to introduce ideas to make Mobile IP applicable for the future, I describe ongoing approaches in the field of authentication, authorization and accounting (AAA).

1 Introduction

The advent of cellular phones can be seen as milestone for the rapidly changing communication paradigm throughout the recent years. Today's exponential growth in number of networked computer systems and telecommunication networks is likely to accelerate in the next years, based on estimations on user- and system mobility. A realistic future scenario comprises nearly ubiquitous network access in large areas of the world to allow for nomadic and mobile use of different services.

Which problems arise in this context? Even nowadays cellular phones provide instant access to data networks – with the drawback of low bandwidth at high costs. Short Message Service (SMS) can be regarded as emerging mailing system for the cellular world and we expect an evolution for mobile systems, which will start with simple text-based applications and are on the way to multimedia capable systems, comparable to the Internet's history. The answer can be given by exploring today's users' needs. Users raise the demand to network structures, which can equally deal with data and voice, with the special focus on mobility and seamless interoperability with the Internet. Moreover the rapid transition from by monopolistic telecommunication companies dictated structures towards a highly dynamic Internet, and such IP-based heterogeneous network infrastructure, will accelerate the advent of flexible networks ready to support different services from speech over data towards multimedia applications.

For the scenario mentioned above the standardization of Mobile IP was a significant step towards enabling mobile user access to the Internet. However, Mobile IP never had been a success or was widely deployed within the Internet. Company and market considerations, different approaches to deal with mobility on the application-layer and with the highest influence the performance and security related issues hindered Mobile IP to be a successful protocol to provide real and transparent mobility to extend the Internet to mobile participants. Nevertheless I expect that mobility support in the Internet can only be introduced using a network-layer-based approach.

The remainder of this paper comprises three sections. To provide an overview of the Mobile IP protocol section 2 explains the basic function of Mobile IP. Section 3 provides the major part of this contribution and classifies the different problem domains. Following, the approaches, concepts and solutions to build a security conscious Mobile IP framework are described and analyzed. Moreover the actual IETF development, which is coupled to Mobile IP security, is tackled in this part of the work. Section 4 concludes this paper and draws some closing remarks related to my own work and future research plans.

2 History and Function of Mobile IP

The above described grow in usage of mobile communication services raised the demand to allow for mobility support in the Internet. The TCP/IP protocol suite was developed for stationary use and in the beginning of the 90s there was significant effort to develop mobility support for Internet users. It turned out that a carefully designed transparent mobility approach on the network-layer would provide seamless interoperability with the existing Internet infrastructure. In 1996 the Mobile IP working group within the IETF proposed a standard way to support mobile users, the Mobile IP protocol [17], [18], [19].

Mobile IP is built upon the existing Internet framework and makes some additional design considerations. The mobility-enabled Internet comprises three core components, the mobile node (MN), a home network which hosts a home agent (HA) and a foreign network which provides a foreign agent (FA) or which allows for visiting nodes to act as their own foreign agent. The goal is to allow the MN to continue sending and receiving packets, even if on the move. Architectural Mobile IP can be divided in a control plane and a data plane. The control plane consists of in-band messages that enable a mobile node to roam between networks and achieve IP-mobility; the data plane takes care of forwarding the data to the MN's actual point of attachment [17].

Normally IP addresses are topologically significant, but with a mobile user the Internets routing fabric would have to take care of all the hosts on the move and therefore require a lot of processing and memory overhead. While abroad the mobile node visits foreign networks and detects his movement by receiving agent advertisements, which are periodically sent by the FAs and can be forced by solicitations sent from the MN. Upon discovering a FA, the MN registers with his HA via means of the FA and for the lifetime of this registration the MN can be reached via the address of the FA (foreign agent care-of address) or via a dedicated care of addresses assigned by means of PPP or DHCP configuration options (collocated care-of address) [15], [16], [17].

Following, the MN is reachable via his home network where the HA intercepts data sent by a correspondent node (CN) meant for the MN and tunnels them to the registered care-of address. This is comparable a postal forwarding request for a recipient who has moved. The MN should answer directly to the correspondent node, the so-called triangular routing takes place [17].

Beneath the forward tunneling there is the possibility for the MN to tunnel packets reverse to the HA, which then forwards them. Reverse tunneling is needed to allow a MN away from home to join multicast groups and transmit multicast packets such that they emanate from its home network. A second issue is related to the Time-To-Live (TTL) of the packet, if sending to other hosts in the home network and not using a reverse tunnel, the packets may be discarded because of the TTL reaching zero. The use of reverse tunneling can be requested via means of registering procedures. At this point the direct- or the encapsulating-delivery style has to be chosen [8], [21].

Since Mobile IP builds upon the IP protocol (without major changes to the current Internet infrastructure) it per se assumes some prerequisites and defines only very few, security related issues. So, Mobile IP was build upon an open Internet model, which allows for reachability of each node via routers. This applies if the MN's home address and the care-of address are routable in the public Internet [17].

With security issues taken into account, in nowadays Internet the situation and thus the base for Mobile IP changed significant. Network operators and administrative stuff takes care of security e.g. by hiding internal network infrastructure with private address schemes and network address translation. Firewall systems on network- and/or application-layer intercept and inspect packets and only forward them if these packets are not suspect to be dangerous for the network.

The following section focuses on studying the implications of security conscious network design and user behavior vs. the mobility support introduced by Mobile IP.

3 Mobile IP evolves towards security

As mentioned in the introduction the security related points hindered the large-scale deployment of Mobile IP. Therefore it is necessary to protect both, the control plane and the data plane, in terms of authentication, integrity and nonrepudiation. Moreover it is necessary to embed Mobile IP in a security conscious environment without weakening the security mechanisms in place. In this section we will focus on security related issues in Mobile IP regarding the core standard specification, additional add-ons and security approaches. The chapter will end by discussing AAA infrastructures related to Mobile IP.

Especially for mobile hosts there is the danger to compromise security in either way. Common network security threats like eavesdropping, sniffing, Man-in-the-

Middle attacks, rerouting, IP address spoofing, password-based attacks, compromised-key attacks, Denial-of-Service attacks or application-layer attacks have to be well thought-out if talking about Mobile IP and security [4], [14], [20]. Figure 1 draws a picture to illustrate some problem domains in respect to Mobile IP.

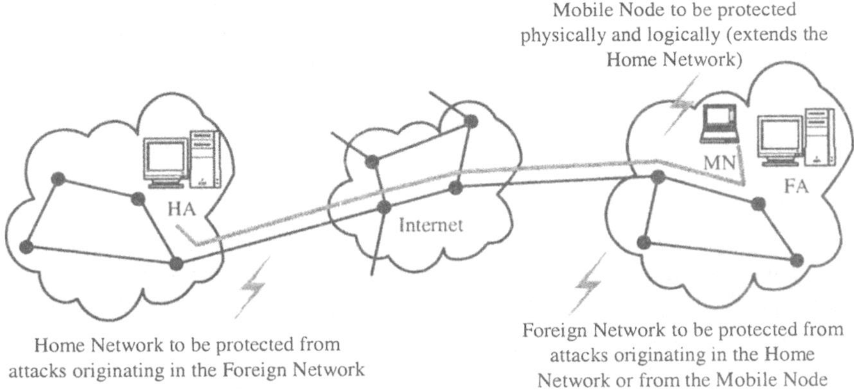

Fig. 1. Security Related Problem Domains of Mobile IP

Mobile IP integrated security

During the initial part of the Mobile IP protocol interaction, the agent discovery or solicitation is unsecured because it relies on per se not authenticated protocols like the Address Resolution Protocol (ARP). The rest of the Mobile-IP control plane was designed with basic security means in mind, in particular for securing the registration request and registration reply since establishing or changing the binding between the different nodes (MN, HA, FA) is key part of the protocol and deals with establishing new routing paths [17].

The registration request, which is delivered within an UDP packet, provides information about home agent, home address of the mobile node and identification while the authentication extension has a Security Parameter Index (SPI) and an authenticator (possible for each pair out of MN, FA, HA). The authentication related security issues are described in [17] and [13] in greater detail. As essence Mobile IP is only allowed to function if the registration messages between a MN and its HA are authenticated with the MN-HA authentication extension. This authentication relies on MD5 with manual key distribution as default algorithm and may be extended to other algorithms and key distribution methods. Additionally there are strong means of replay protection for the registration request, relying on timestamps or nonces [17], [28].

Having explained the basic means of security related to Mobile IP there are some concerns about the problematic triangular routing in Mobile IP. For normal operation Mobile IP involves forward tunnels that shuttle packets towards the mobile node. These tunnels start at the HA, and end at the MN's care-of address (and vice versa for reverse tunnels). This tunneling of packet causes significant overhead and thus the protocol suggests the MN to directly send packets to the correspondent node using his home address. Mobile IP assumes packets to be routed based on the destination address, but to deal with firewalls the source and destination IP address in a packet must be topologically correct [4], [17], [21], [22].

The forward tunnel complies with this, as its endpoints (home agent address and care-of address) are properly assigned addresses for their respective locations. On the other hand, the source IP address of a packet transmitted by the MN does not correspond to the network prefix from where it emanates [8], [21].

The work to allow for topologically correct reverse tunnels was done in [8] and [21]. This solution uses reverse tunneling back to the HA plus decapsulating and sending from the HA. It is clear that reverse tunneling issues even more performance restrictions.

Essentially, creation of both forward and reverse tunnels involves an authentication procedure, which reduces the risk for attack. Because firewall administrators normally get in "panic" if forced to allow tunnels through, one have to very carefully examine the interoperability of firewalls and Mobile IP in respect to tunneling and reverse tunneling.

A remaining issues of the core standard concerning tunneling is for example to hijack a reverse tunnel and inject malicious packets into the network, which are decapsulated at the end of the tunnel and maybe forwarded beyond the local network. A further problem arises if an existing tunnel is re-directed to a malicious node. The best way to protect against these attacks is by employing the MN-FA and FA-HA authentication extensions [8], [21].

Summarized Mobile IP presents obvious security leaks and concentrates on control plane security while it does not take care of the security during the data transfer. The use of reverse tunnels can solve some network design related problems but also allows for malicious attacks. Problems arising with the reverse tunnel and tunnels in general are that firewalls may throw away IP-in-IP packets and will not let tunnels trough the firewall being established.

Development of Mobile IP integrated security
The evolution of the Mobile IP core protocol is documented in the revised protocol specification [13]. Beneath minor changes concerning syntax errors, editorial mistakes and misc. Protocol items there are some security related issues worth to be mentioned. The major security related changes since RFC2002 occurred in the area of reverse tunneling which now has to be supported by FA's and HA's. Moreover the computation of the authentication algorithm now uses the SPI of the MN-HA authentication extension as influencing data. Another approach was started to deal with Denial-of-Service problems. [13] specifies that the FA may configure a maximum number of pending registrations that it is willing to maintain (typically 5). The foreign agent should then reject additional registrations [13], [17].

Interoperability Mobile IP and IPSec

The agent discovery, registration request and registration reply are followed by the data exchange between CN and MN via encapsulated packets, which should be protected as well.

Since Mobile IP can be viewed as network layer mobility approach it seems useful to use at least mechanisms on the same layer to secure the traffic. The IPSec Framework specified in numerous Internet Standards provides means to do so and is now discussed in detail covering the relationship to Mobile IP [23], [24], [25].

The first approach to bring Mobile IP and IPSec together was undertaken in [22]. Herein are the specifications to allow a mobile node out on a public sector of the network to negotiate access past a firewall, and construct a secure channel into its home network. The negotiation protocol was chosen to be SKIP (Simple Key Management for Internet Protocols). Goal of the approach was to give the same level of connectivity and privacy to mobile nodes, as IPSec is able to provide within the home network [22]. It worked out that there are at least four different scenarios, which differ in terms of the scope of encryption and authentication between the peers.

1. Encryption and authentication only outside of private network
2. End-to-End encryption and authentication
3. End-to-End encryption, intermediate authentication
4. Encryption and authentication inside and outside of private network

In the first approach the traffic is encrypted between the mobile node out on the Internet, and the home networks firewall external interface. This can be seen as minimal security required – and results in encryption overhead only on the public network [22]. Within the second approach after establishing the tunnel, the firewall can be seen as a simple packet relay, which essentially is tunneled. This approach is probably unrealizable because authentication is carried out by the home agent but not by the firewall, and the former security is assumed to be much weaker than the latter [22].

The third alternative is to integrate the firewall to be one party of the security association. Essentially, the SKIP approach is used to provide intermediate authentication with end-to-end security. After verifying authentication (IPSec Authenticating Header (AH) Mode), the firewall forwards the encrypted packet (IPSec Encapsulating Security Payload (ESP) Mode) to the home agent [22].

The forth approach depicted in figure 2 includes encrypted and authenticated traffic on the public and the private part of the network. On the public network a security association between the MN and the firewall carries out IPSec. On the private network a security association between the HA and the firewall has to be established [22].

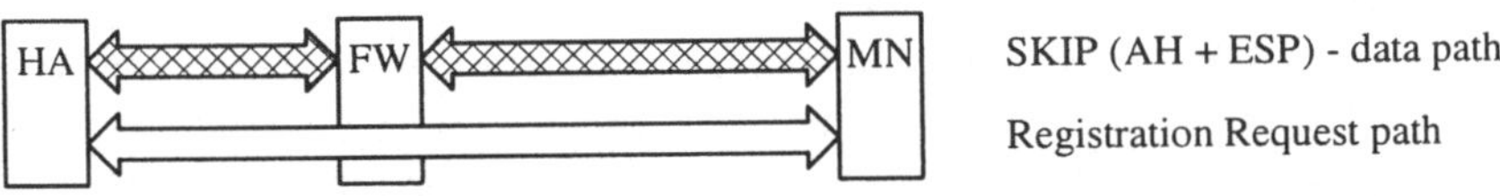

Fig. 2. Encryption and Authentication Inside and Outside of the Private Network[22]

As conclusion approach 1 can be viewed as minimal security needed whereas Option 2 above is not agreeable to security and system administration guidelines. Option

3 on the other hand will show somehow unsavory to the end user. Option 4 can provide the same security to the public part of the network as option 1 does and should be used if the home network security is a concern [22].

The Mobile IP plus SKIP Framework is able to extend the secure home network to the mobile node, thus the mobile host itself must also take responsibility for securing the private network, because it extends its periphery. As conclusion the MN must have some firewall capabilities, otherwise any malicious individual that gains access to it will have gained access to the private network as well.

Beneath the SKIP approach to deal with firewalls there was work done to use ISAKMP as key management protocol. [29] proposes ISAKMP as a mechanism for negotiating the use of IPSec protection, a procedure for establishing the resulting IPSec tunnels and the encapsulating packet format. The use of the IPSec ESP tunnel protocol can protect the redirected packets against both passive and active attacks launched. Since [29] doesn't deal with firewall related problems and ISAKMP merged into IKE as a key exchange standard the approach will not be described in more detail.

The most recent approach to tie Mobile IP together with IPSec describes the usage of IKE as key distribution protocol [9]. The draft proposes some concepts how IP Security can be used to provide an security framework for Mobile IP communications but only shows rough ideas and is not as detailed as [22], from which it nevertheless borrows ideas. [9] and [29] aim to protect the network and esp. the MN from various forms of attack including: Session hijacking (a hostile node can steal a session from a mobile node by having packets redirected to it), spoofing of identity to obtain access to the network and eavesdropping and stealing of data during sessions [9].

The core goal is - alike the IPSec approaches mentioned before – to secure the data plane of Mobile IP. [9] proposes four Security Associations (SAs) following below for securing Mobile IP communication.
1. Between the Mobility Control Message Gateway Function (MCMGF) server in the visited/foreign domain and the MCMGF server in the home domain.
2. Between the MN and the serving FA in the visited domain.
3. Between the MN and the HA.
4. Between the MN and the CN for end-to-end security.

To provide these associations [9] introduces the concept of a Mobility Control Message. These messages are controlled by a Mobility Control Message Gateway Function and in essential will be provided in form of AAA components in future networks [9]. However SA3 may be optional if there exists some other link layer security mechanism and SA4 is optional and is established only if policies at the MN require it [9].

Since SKIP can be regarded as proprietary, the corresponding approach cannot be seen as state of the art. On the other hand the IKE approach in combination with Mobile IP is only described theoretical and thus not proven by implementation nor does it take care to deal with firewalls. Summarizing the ongoing IPSec and Mobile IP integration it is clear that IPSec can be viewed as state of the art solution. However, the possibility of authenticated but compromised tunnels through firewalls leaves a lot of space for future work.

Additional Mobile IP development coupled to security

Having explained the most important security issues concerning Mobile IP the following ongoing work is tightly coupled to security and will influence the future development process of Mobile IP.

The IETF's Mobile IP working group works on the route optimization problem and smooth handoff since the early days of RFC2002. Route optimization is related to the triangular routing problem, as mentioned earlier, while smooth handoff means that a mobile node tells the old FA where to be reached and therefore allows for resending packets to the new FA [11], [12].

Both methods need binding updates to be performed, which need authentication. [11] specifies registration keys to deal with the establishment of the security associations needed.

Essential for the function is the key distribution method. Since common usable public key infrastructures are not in place yet there are different possibilities to create security associations. For example the reuse of previous established SA's between MN and FA. If FA and HA trust each other already, they can exchange new keys this way. Trusting FA's can use the same (old) key by transferring key information. More possibilities include FA's or MN's public key which can be included in the registration message and thus allow the HA or FA to choose a registration key. The last point mentioned in [11] refers to a key exchange method using elliptic curves or Diffie-Hellman key exchange. Once the registration key is established, the smooth handoff method described in [12] can be used.

There is a lot of other ongoing work influencing security, which is too specific for this contribution. Just to give an idea, a very specific security problem may arise if a mobile node uses the MN – FA authentication extension. Under certain circumstances it can be possible to send a bogus replay message to the MN that causes the MN to act as if its Registration Reply were rejected. To deal with this problem [3] defines an extension to allow for challenge response interaction between MN and FA to authenticate the mobile node [3], [6], [12].

Actual requirements for Authentication, Authorization, Accounting (AAA)

Actual the Mobile IP community provides input for the Authentication, Authorization and Accounting (AAA) Working Group within the IETF, which focuses on the development of requirements for authentication, authorization and accounting in relation to network access. Requirements are also gathered from the Network Access Server Requirements Working Group (NASREQ) and the Roaming Operations Working Group (ROAMOPS). The common goal of the AAA approach is to define ways of establishing trust relationships between the roaming, mobile or moving hosts and access servers distributed in home and foreign networks to allow for service usage from foreign domains. The actual work underway in the AAA working group is to shootout between different proposed AAA-protocols like DIAMETER, COPS, SNMPv3 or extended RADIUS vs. the predefined requirements to match the needs of the input working groups [1], [5], [30].

There are different AAA structures underway influencing Mobile IP. Within the Internet a client belonging to one administrative home domain sometimes needs to use resources provided by another administrative domain (foreign domain). An agent in the foreign domain that attends to the client's request (attendant) is likely to require that the client provides some credentials that can be authenticated before access is permitted [5], [30].

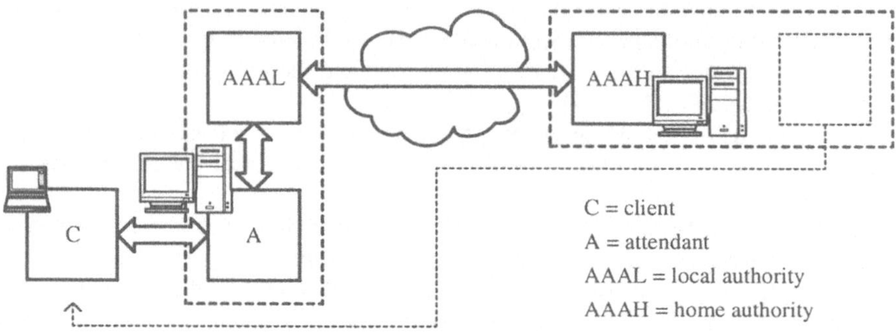

Fig. 3. AAA Infrastructure in Home and Local Domains [5]

The attendant is expected to contact an authority to verify the credentials of the client. The following verification of the credentials authorities lies in the responsibility of the local authority (AAAL), which should be configured with sufficient security relationships. Once the local authority has obtained the authorization and the authority has notified the attendant about the successful negotiation, the attendant can provide the requested resources to the client [5].

The security model implicit in the above figure is crucial. For correct function, first there need to be a security association between the client and his AAAH. Second AAAL and AAAH have to share a security association to rely on the exchanged data. In the easiest way this can be manually configured (but then will not scale) but AAA also defines more convenient ways to do so. It is also clear that the attendant shares a security association with the AAAL. There are some additional security consideration like intervening nodes must not be able to learn about the secret information between the client and his home network, which cannot be covered in greater detail at this place. Without the security association mentioned first it would be technically infeasible to do so [5].

The general AAA model shown above is compatible with the needs of Mobile IP. In AAA the FA gets a translation agent between the Mobile IP registration protocol and AAA. However, some basic changes are needed. The initial pure AAA transactions are handled without need for the HA, but Mobile IP requires every registration to be handled between the HA and the FA. This means that during the initial registration home and foreign agent have to perform subsequent Mobile IP registrations [5], [10].

Moreover AAA should be able to interact with Firewall systems in the same administrative domain systems to overcome the existing problems in relation to Mobile IP.

Consideration of the scalability of the security associations leads to the possibility of introducing third party components between AAAL and AAAH to help them arbitrate secure transactions [5], [30].

More sophisticated and scalable AAA models are underway, as example there may be the possibility to have common brokers to minimize the number of security trusts as the number of AAA authorities increases. For better scalability even a hierarchy of brokers may be feasible. In respect to AAA there is a lot of work going on and to point out some open issues esp. the accounting part and performance (concerning latency of requests) are under heavily research [30].

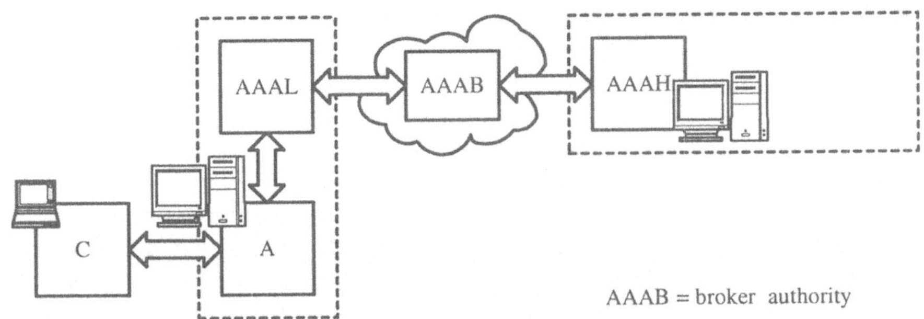

Fig. 4. AAA Servers Using a Broker [30]

The AAAB in figure 4 is the broker's authority server, which acts as a central point of contact for many service providers and enterprises. The AAAB enables the local and home domains to cooperate without requiring each of the networks to have a direct trust relationship with all the other networks. Thus, the needed scalability for Internet use can be provided [30].

As with any security proposal, adding more entities that interact using security protocols creates new administrative requirements for maintaining the appropriate security associations. In the case of the AAA services however, these administrative requirements are natural and already well understood, because comparable to today's dial up network access structures [30].

Having introduced the basic AAA functionality there is work underway coupling AAA and Mobile IP e.g. to specify AAA registration keys with Mobile IP. These extensions are necessary for Mobile IP to interact with upcoming AAA infrastructure. Also, to uniquely identify a mobile node, AAA needs to obtain the Network Access Identifier (NAI). This can be accomplished by the MN's NAI extension to the Mobile IP registration, which is specified in [10], [26], [27].

Summarizing, the Mobile IP - AAA interaction will result in mobile nodes being able to establish secure connections to their home network. In Detail a MN registers with a MN-AAA authentication extension. The answering AAA Server also generates keys for the MN, encodes the keys according to its own security association with the MN and sends the key or keys along with the registration reply. Upon receipt of the reply the MN decodes the key, which then is used to establish the mobile node's security association with its home agent and to authenticate the MN-HA authentication extension and/or the MN-FA authentication extension.

4 Conclusion

This paper presents the evolution and implications concerning Mobile IP and security. There are different well-known security architectures to deal with special problems of Mobile IP. It was shown that Mobile IP in combination with IPSec provides powerful means of securing communication. Concerning firewalls there is work to be done to extend the SKIP based concepts to provide secure integration of Mobile IP and firewalls. Moreover the design of network infrastructures, which are able to deal with mobile users and can securely provide resources, should be investigated thoroughly. The work in the field of AAA will provide an infrastructure to solve the problems to establishing trust relationships via the Internet and thus push large-scale Mobile IP deployment one step nearer. Finally, reaching the goal of hassle free secure mobility will always be a trade-off between mobility vs. security considerations.

Work is going on to integrate Mobile IP based mobility support in the next generation Internet, which will build upon IPv6. Unlike Mobile IPv4, Mobile IPv6 utilizes IP Security for all security requirements (sender authentication, data integrity protection, and replay protection) for binding updates (which serve the role of both registration and route optimization in Mobile IPv4) and solves a lot of security related problems. With the tight integration of security mechanisms in IPv6 there is additional need for a cost and bandwidth effective authentication, authorization and accounting. It has to be mentioned that IPv6 is not as well understood as IPv4 today and that security implications related to Mobile IPv6 are likely to appear and impact mobility [2], [7].

Having shown the security issues concerning Mobile IP in current IPv4 networks, future work will concentrate on tackling problems in the area of secure service discovery plus provision to mobile nodes and in optimizing security related issues in the field of Mobile IP and Mobile IPv6. Future all-IP networks (often referred as 4th Generation), which can provide internetworking capabilities even in very heterogeneous networks, have the chance to unify today's different networks types - if security and mobility are taken into account.

References

[1] J. Arkko; Requirements for Internet-Scale Accounting Management; INTERNET-DRAFT draft-arkko-acctreqlis-00.txt; August 1998; (work in progress)
[2] N. Asokan, P. Flykt, T. Eklund, C. Perkins, AAA for IPv6 Network Access, INTERNET DRAFT draft-ietf-perkins-aaav6-00.txt, March 2000
[3] P. Calhoun, C. Perkins; Mobile IP Foreign Agent Challenge/Response Extension; INTERNET DRAFT; draft-ietf-mobileip-challenge-11.txt; June 2000; (work in progress).
[4] D. B. Chapman and E. Zwicky, Building Internet Firewalls, O'Reilly & Associates, Inc., 1995.
[5] S. Glass, T. Hiller, S. Jacobs, C. Perkins; Mobile IP Authentication, Authorization, and Accounting Requirements; INTERNET DRAFT draft-ietf-mobileip-aaa-reqs-03.txt; March 2000; (work in progress).

[6] E. Gustafsson, A. Jonsson, C. Perkins; Mobile IP Regional Registration; INTERNET DRAFT draft-ietf-mobileip-reg-tunnel-02.txt; March 2000; (work in Progress).

[7] D. Johnson, C. Perkins; Mobility Support in IPv6; INTERNET DRAFT, draft-ietf-mobileip-ipv6-12.txt; April 2000; (work in progress).

[8] G. Montenegro, Editor; Reverse Tunneling for Mobile IP, revised; INTERNET DRAFT draft-ietf-mobileip-rfc2344-bis-01.txt; March 2000; (work in progress).

[9] B. Patil, R. Narayanan, E. Qaddoura; Security Requirements/Implementation Guidelines for Mobile IP using IP Security; INTERNET-DRAFT draft-bpatil-mobileip-sec-guide-00.txt; June 1999; (work in progress).

[10] C. Perkins, Pat R. Calhoun; AAA Registration Keys for Mobile IP; INTERNET DRAFT draft-ietf-mobileip-aaa-key-01.txt; January 2000; (work in Progress).

[11] C. Perkins, D. Johnson; Registration Keys for Route Optimization; INTERNET DRAFT draft-ietf-mobileip-regkey-01.txt; February 2000; (work in progress).

[12] C. Perkins, D. Johnson; Route Optimization in Mobile IP; INTERNET DRAFT draft-ietf-mobileip-optim-09.txt; February 2000; (work in progress).

[13] C. Perkins, editor; IP Mobility Support for IPv4, revised; INTERNET DRAFT draft-ietf-mobileip-rfc2002-bis-01.txt; January 2000; (work in progress).

[14] ISO; Security Architecture for open Systems interconnection for CCITT Applications; Recommendation X.800; 1991

[15] G. McGregor; The PPP Internet Protocol Control Protocol(IPCP); RFC 1332; May 1992.

[16] W. Simpson, The Point-to-Point Protocol (PPP), RFC 1661 , Jul. 1994.

[17] C. Perkins, Editor; IP mobility support; RFC 2002; October 1996.

[18] C. Perkins; IP encapsulation within IP; RFC 2003; October 1996.

[19] C. Perkins; Minimal encapsulation within IP; RFC 2004; October 1996.

[20] J. Solomon; Applicability Statement for IP Mobility Support; C. Perkins; RFC 2005; October 1996.

[21] G. Montenegro, Editor; Reverse tunneling for Mobile IP; RFC 2344; May 1998.

[22] G. Montenegro, V. Gupta; Sun's SKIP Firewall Traversal for Mobile-IP; RFC2356; June 1998.

[23] Kent, Atkinson; Security Architecture for the Internet Protocol; RFC 2401; November 1998

[24] Maughan, Schertler, Schneider, Turner; Internet Security Association and Key Management Protocol (ISAKMP); RFC 2408; November 1998

[25] D. Harkins, D. Carrel; The Internet Key Exchange (IKE); RFC 2409; November 1998.

[26] B. Aboba, M. Beadles; The Network Access Identifier; RFC 2486, January 1999.

[27] P. Calhoun, C. Perkins; Mobile IP Network Access Identifier Extension for IPv4; RFC 2794; March 2000.

[28] Bruce Schneier; Applied Cryptography: Protocols, Algorithms, and Source Code in C; John Wiley; New York, NY, USA; 1994.

[29] J. Zao, M. Condell; Use of IPSec in Mobile IP, INTERNET DRAFT draft-ietf-mobilep-IPSec-use-00.txt; November 1997; (work in progress).

[30] J. Vollbrecht, P. Calhoun, S. Farrell, L. Gommans, G. Gross, B. de Bruijn, C. de Laat, M. Holdrege, D. Spence; AAA Authorization Framework; INTERNET DRAFT draft-ietf-aaa-authz-arch-00.txt; October 1999

A Survey of Requirements and Standardization Efforts for IP-Telephony-Security

Christoph Rensing[1], Utz Roedig[1], Ralf Ackermann[1], Ralf Steinmetz[1,2]

[1] Darmstadt University of Technology, Merckstr. 25, D-64283 Darmstadt, Germany
[2] GMD IPSI, Dolivostr. 15, 64293 Darmstadt, Germany
{Christoph.Rensing, Utz.Roedig, Ralf.Ackermann, Ralf.Steinmetz}
@KOM.tu-darmstadt.de

Abstract. Security as a dimension of trustworthiness in IP-Telephony systems and protocols is a main condition for the commercial success of IP-Telephony. In this work, we present a survey of security requirements and show how various standardization efforts address these requirements. We describe the basic tasks and elements of IP-Telephony systems and compare them to Telephony via PSTNs to derive some possible attacks for example. We classify the security preconditions to achieve trustworthiness of users and providers in this systems. We list weighty criteria for further evaluation of security mechanisms which can fulfil these requirements. After this, we describe the integration of security mechanisms in current IP-Telephony protocols and figure out work areas which have to be solved in future.

1 Introduction

Trustworthiness of service users and service providers in applications and systems is a necessary condition for commercial success of IP-Telephony also called "Voice over IP" and for the total replacement of Public Switched Telephone Networks (PSTN) by IP-Networks for Voice Communication, as it is predicted sometimes.

Trustworthiness in Information Technology Systems generally has different dimensions: correctness, availability and security. In this paper we are focusing on security, which is concerned about ensuring that a system resists potential attacks that can compromise the secrecy, integrity, or availability of data and services. To achieve security in IP-Networks is more sophisticated than in PSTNs. The risk to be attacked using IP-Telephony Infrastructure is higher than using PSTNs for a telephone call due of the differences of the networks and system architecture: IP-Networks are not centrally managed or controlled. In IP-Telephony voice transmission and signaling is done over the same IP-Networks. Active elements of an IP-Network, like routers or network-servers, are, by design, accessible from the network they control. Endpoints of IP-Networks, personal computers and servers, can be used to attack the network.

Single aspects of IP-Telephony security only are content of related work and IP-Telephony standards most times. The goal of this paper is, to give a complete survey of the risks of IP-Telephony, the resulting requirements and how they are addressed and possibly solved in the existing standards. In addition, we list some criteria which should be noted choosing security mechanisms.

2 IP-Telephony basic Tasks and their Security Requirements

PSTNs and IP Networks exist separately from each other for long days. In the last years voice and data networks are converging more and more. Three different kinds of convergence can be distinguished:

- Telecommunication Providers use IP-Access to configure and manage the PSTN components like exchanges or databases storing the operational Information for e.g. billing or charging.
- The service user request is triggered via an IP-Network, but the service is provided by the PSTN as transport infrastructure. The PINT-Working Group of the IETF [1] is concerned with this scenario.
- Voice transfer and signaling is done via one IP-Network. This is called *IP-Telephony* or "Voice over IP".

2.1 IP-Telephony basic Tasks

IP-Telephony should rather be a reengineering of existing PSTN services in the Internet but to implement new value added services. This is getting more and more important because the cost reduction argument for investigating in IP-Telephony will not be a strong argument in future [2]. Nevertheless, IP-Telephony systems and protocols have to carry out three basic tasks like in the old PSTNs. These basic tasks are the same in every scenario and have to be done for providing every service:

- *Signaling* addresses the set up and tear down of calls, including the setup and maintaining of databases and processors used for call routing and number translation.
- *Transmission* is the carrying of the audio and / or video data.
- *Operation* implies the provision, configuration and maintenance of all services which are used by providers and different users, like location services or charging- and billing services.

We distinguish these basic tasks in order to reduce the complexity of defining the security requirements and the mechanisms possibly used to fulfil these requirements.

2.2 IP-Telephony Infrastructure and Protocols

The current IP-Telephony Infrastructure is based on a decentral organized and managed architecture. Inside this, some islands e.g. in company networks are administered in a centralistic structure. The main signaling and operational functions are distributed over intelligent end systems and network servers in IP-Telephony architectures. In PSTNs, they are located in central nodes controlled by the providers in contrast. The end systems are either especially for IP-Telephony build computers, IP-Phones, or normal computers with software implemented phones like MS-Netmeeting. On the other side, there are network servers used for maintaining the signaling information and for operational functions. A common characteristic of these network servers is the decentral setup and maintenance.

Currently, two major different protocol families for IP-Telephony exist. The ITU approach is described in the ITU H.323 umbrella standard [3]. H.323 is supported by the most existing systems and applications. In contrast, the IETF approach is based on the Session Initiation Protocol [4] for signaling. It is not in the focus of this paper to explain the different protocols and system architecture. They are described in detail in [5,6]. The appearing of network servers like named above is common in both architectures. In H.323 they are called Gatekeeper or Gateways. Proxy Server, Redirect Server, Registrars and Gateways are satisfying almost the same tasks in the IETF architecture.

2.3 Characteristics of IP-Telephony

The risk to be attacked using IP-Telephony Infrastructure is higher than using PSTNs for a telephone call due to the differences of underlying networks and system architecture:

- For IP-Telephony signaling, the same IP-Network as for audio transmission is used. This increases the options for fraud, because a user can maybe forge signaling informations like IP-addresses or user-IDs.
- IP-Telephony network elements are configured via the IP-Network in contrast to the PSTN, where the network servers are managed centrally. So, in IP-Telephony, these elements are accessible for users (and attackers) and have to be secured.
- In IP-Telephony, more functions are located in the decentral end-systems and network servers. This results in a higher effort to administrate these systems in a secure way and to achieve a high security level, than in an environment, where function is provided more centralized.
- In IP-Networks, mechanisms, to access data on different nodes of the network and to use them remote by the users (and possibly attackers) of the network, are available in general. Vulnerabilities of IP-Networks and end-systems (operating systems) are documented and people are more skilled with this. This increases the risk of an attack.
- Tapping in PSTNs is difficult, since the attacker needs a physical access to the wire the audio is transmitted. In an IP-Network the attacker only needs physical access to the network anywhere, when he gets logical access to a router or network server on the route from endpoint to endpoint.
- Most of the end systems in IP-Telephony are computers, which use and provide general network services in addition to telephony specific services. These computers and services can be attacked and can be used to compromise the entire telephone system.

In this work we only look at IP-Telephony related risks in depth and not at the risks of general network services or risk resulting by integration of new IP-Telephony services in existing IP-Networks.

2.4 Attacks on the basic Services

We show in the following some different workable attacks on the three basic tasks defined above, to clarify the listed risks.

Eavesdropping with a packet sniffer is the simplest *attack on the transmission service* in a non switched network. The attacker can listen the conversation. This attack can be done by everyone who has access to a general network node on the way from end system to end system. These can also be IP-Telephony related network servers like proxies or gateways, whose providers maybe can not be trusted.

Attacks on the signaling service can be used to fraud attacks. The caller ID or called ID can be changed and the attacker can use services he is not authorized to or without payment, when the service is with costs, for example. The signaling servers like gatekeepers or proxies and redirect servers can be attacked also. An invader can change the entries in the database for instance, so that all calls are rejected or forwarded to his own voice mail box. This can be done by direct access on the systems, which is not part of this work, or by sending a forged request to the signaling server. Traffic analysis is an other kind of attacks. It can be realized by eavesdropping the signaling informations. Especially service providers may not ignore this problems due of legal regulations.

Attacks on the operational services can result in wrong accounting, no provisioning of services an so on. They can be done on the one hand by direct attacks on the systems, these services are located on, or, on the other hand, by forged configuration or management commands in the same way.

Additionally, *general network attacks*, which are not especially IP-Telephony related, can be used. Such attacks are name server attacks or denial of service attacks for example.

2.5 Required Security Services

Five different security services are distinguished in principle. We are using the X.800 security services defined in [7] for future use. These are authentication, access control, confidentiality, integrity and non-repudiation. They are necessary for the IP-Telephony tasks transmission, signaling, operation and other not especially IP-Telephony related services in principle. We illustrate how these essential services are used for IP-Telephony, to figure out which services are essential.

Communication security is the part of security, this work is related with. It includes all security mechanisms which have to be integrated in the IP-Telephony specific protocol stack for signaling and transmission. Encryption of voice data respectively RTP-Streams and some signaling information is necessary for confidentiality. Encryption of voice data protects against some attacks on the transmission service. Authorization of service users, especially callers, has also to be part of signaling. It protects for misusing services. Authentication is a elementary requirement. Different kinds of authentication (end-system to end-system, end-system to network-system, network-system to network-system and hop by hop authentication) are needed. Hop by hop authentication is necessary, because a call can be forwarded via different domains with not trusted proxies or gatekeepers. End-system to network-system authentication is used, when an end-system registers at a network-system. Caller ID, Called ID and "who we thought we are calling"-ID are the informations that have to be authenticated at least. Authentication protects from many attacks on signaling and operational services.

It is not possible to describe all security requirements in detail in this work. In addition to the above categories, the following table shows an executive summary of the requirements, whereby the essential requirements are marked in grey.

Table 1: Security requirements for basic IP-Telephony tasks

	Signaling	Transmission	Operation
Authentication/ Integrity	end to end hop by hop end to network		end to end (a network servers in this context is a end system)
Non-Repudiation	especially for services which are liable for costs	not for simple calls, for special services e.g. voice information on call	outside IP-Telephony related services e.g. Billing
Confidentiality	for anonymity reasons for protection from traffic analysis	end to end (end to gateway)	for data protection reasons
Access Control	for particular service requests	not IP-Telephony specific but for used services e.g. QoS admission	for every management request
Key Management	end to end hop by hop	end to end (end to gateway)	outside IP-Telephony specific protocols

Key management is not a fundamental security requirement, but it is necessary for many cryptographic security mechanisms, used to ensure the other requirements. So, it is part of the table, though it is not clear, whether it is part of the IP-Telephony specific signaling itself or part of an external key exchange protocol.

Other security aspects has to be observed by manufactures and system administrators, using IP-Telephony solutions in addition to the communication security. We mention it in this work, because it is also essential form a security view.

Systems security covers well known requirements. Many manufacturers are developing new end systems like IP-Phones and network servers like Gatekeepers and Gateways. They can be combined with existing PBXs mostly. They are integrated in the corporate IP-Network on the other hand, since they are specialized computers in a distributed heterogeneous environment. The same security requirements have to be achieved for these systems like for existing computer systems and applications. Our observations from a big field trial [8] are, that many systems unfortunately do not meet the requirements. We will present our results after the vendors had time to fix the problems in detail.

The support of additional telephony services in an IP-Network should not result in new security risks for the environment, the IP-Telephony systems are integrated in. This can not be guaranteed in any case, because many existing security mechanisms are not designed for supporting IP-Telephony communication. The access from and to a corporate IP network is controlled via a firewall for example. Firewalls do often network address translation in addition. Both, existing firewall mechanisms like packet filters or proxies and network address translation, represent a problem for IP-Telephony protocols vice versa. This problem is described in [9] in detail. To enable IP-Telephony over existing firewalls, the security level has to be reduced in many cases. Therefore, new approaches for firewall architectures, as described in [10], or the support of firewalls by the IP-Telephony protocols, are necessary. The IETF SIP Working Group has addressed this problem as open task. First starting points are described in [11,12].

Laws and regulations have to be observed at the end. This leads to new requirements which are sometimes contradictionary to users requirements. For example lawful interception is a must in many cases.

2.6 Evaluation Criteria for Security Mechanisms

Many cryptographic mechanisms do exist. They are solving most requirements in principle, but not every solution can be used in every scenario. At this point, we list different criteria to evaluate the different mechanisms:

- Quality of service is a major concern for realtime IP-Telephony services. It must match or exceed that of PSTNs [13]. Different measures should be considered.
  The call setup delay is one significant aspect. The integration of cryptographic mechanisms can result in a bigger delay, especially if public-key mechanisms are used. The work overhead per sending and receiving packet for encryption and decryption is an other criteria. Asymmetric encryption of the coded audio data can not be done in realtime by simple end-systems. The bandwidth overhead, incurred by inflating the data packets via cryptographic transformations, should also be considered from the communication network point of view.
- Scalability is the second major concern. For commercial use, the implemented mechanisms have to work in large environments and not only in a testbed. Scalability can be observed on the different levels. The verification of a certificate or the number of different domains are examples.
- A precondition for choosing mechanisms is the general availability and operationality of the infrastructure, used by the cryptographic mechanisms inside the IP-Telephony protocols. Per-user public keys and the integration of Certification Authorities in the architecture are necessary for using public key mechanisms for example. An other example is the broad implementation of IPSec if it should be used.
- Reliability of security mechanisms is a further criteria. No single point of failure may exist.

- The grade of security the mechanisms provide is an other criteria. A reasonable grade has to be choosen. But, it is difficult to quantify the degree of security. For algorithms for example it depends on how hard they are to break [14].

The evaluation of security mechanisms is a difficult tasks, because all aspects do not have to be considered isolated. It is only necessary to address this task for the purpose of this paper.

3 Security Mechanisms in IP-Telephony Standards

Security mechanisms have to be part of the IP-Telephony standards due to meet the mentioned requirements and to achieve compatibility and operability between different IP-Telephony systems. We will describe where security is part of the standards and show where the requirements are realized in the following section. Our focus is on the main security requirements marked in Table 1.

3.1 Transmission Services

Confidentiality of the media streams is the primary requirement for transmission services. RTP [15] and RTCP are the underlying protocols used for transmission services in both IETF and ITU architecture. To realize confidentiality, the data streams have to be encrypted. This can be done after coding and segmenting the data by the sender. The encrypted segments can be sent as RTP data units and decrypted by the receiver. The RTP-Headers are not encrypted. The use of symmetric encryption is necessary, due to the bad performance of asymmetric encryption. The ITU suggests the encryption of the media streams in this way in H.235 [16]. The encryption capabilities of the systems can be negotiated during signaling. DES, Triple DES and RC2 are intended as encryption algorithms. SIP covers only the signaling, but the encryption of the media streams is possible in the same way. RTCP security is not done so far.

The use of symmetric encryption results in the necessity, to exchange session keys between the partners. The key management is not part of the transmission service (RTP) itself. It is part of the H.245 signaling in the ITU world and not defined in SIP. So the key management has to be part of the SIP message body.

3.2 Signaling Services

Authentication, confidentiality and in addition key management are the two major security requirements for signaling. The realisation of this security services differs in the two approaches.

ITU H.235. Recommendation H.235 retains the security aspects within the H.323 protocol family. Authentication and call authorization is necessaryly done during call establishment and sometimes before the call is accepted. TLS [17] or IPSec [18] on transport or network layer are the only possibilities to realize this. Authentication of users is supported during call control. It is done either during the initial call connection in the process of securing the signaling-channel (H.245) by support of challenge response mechanisms or by exchanging certificates on the H.245 channel. H.245 [19] supports the negotiation of the necessary parameters. Hop by hop authentication is provided by using this mechanisms only. End to end authentication is not provided.

In H.235 two security profiles are defined. The simple security profile and the signature profile. Both profiles do not cover the confidentiality of the signaling information, except using TLS or IPSec. The key management is part of the profiles. The exchange of certificates and a Diffie Hellmann key exchange are supported. But the key management only covers the exchange of certificates, not the criteria by which they are mutually verified and accepted.

SIP. Security support is inside the SIP protocol. There is a hard discussion about which problems should be solved in the Working Group actually. From this, we can only describe the existing RFC.

SIP requests may be authenticated using the Authorization header field to include a digital signature of certain header fields, the request method and version number and the payload. For authentication PGP or HTTP authentication are intended. Not all header fields can be authenticated, because they have to be changed possibly by proxies. So, end to end authentication is not achieved completely. On the other hand, hop-by-hop authentication can be provided. It is not specified which mechanism should be used on the underlying layers. IPSec and TLS are discussed.

SIP supports three complementary forms of encryption to protect confidentiality. End-to-end encryption of the SIP message body and certain sensitive header fields; hop-by-hop encryption to prevent eavesdropping that tracks who is calling whom; hop-by-hop encryption of Via fields to hide the route a request has taken. Not all header fields can be encrypted because they are used for call routing. Additionally SIP requests and responses may also be protected by security mechanisms at the transport or network layer, maybe IPSec or TLS. The specification of using a particular mechanism is not part of SIP signaling. It has to be specified outside of the signaling.

3.3 Operational Services

Many different protocols have to be surveyed for securing operational services. The security requirements are strongly related to systems security most times, if the services are maintained and configured by closed groups, e.g. by the providers of the services. This is in contrast to the management of signaling information. In this case, well known mechanisms for authentication and authorization can be used. Due to this characteristic, we will not focus the operational aspects so far.

3.4 Summary

The major security requirements are covered in the standardization efforts, as shown in Table 2. Many additional requirements, like non repudiation, are not performed. Eventually, this prevents the evaluation of new commercial services. An other disadvantage is the use of mechanisms which are not spreaded, like IPSec or the use of public key certificates. We do not believe, that every user of an IP-Phone holds a public key certificate. Also, some other criteria we defined, are not accomplished. The verification of certificates during call establishment grows up the setup delay. Also, such mechanisms maybe do not scale in large environments. The evaluation of the mechanisms in detail by using the criteria listed above, is for future work.

Table 2: Security support in the IP-Telephony protocols

	Signaling	Signaling	Transmission	Transmission
	ITU (H.323)	IETF (SIP)	ITU (H.235)	IETF (SIP)
Authentication/ Integrity	hop by hop	end to end apart from some header fields; hop by hop by TLS or IPSec	not supported	not supported
Non-Repudiation	part of signature security profile	not supported	not supported	not supported
Confidentiality	only by TLS or IPSec	end to end apart from some header fields; hop by hop by TLS or IPSec	end to end RTP encryption	end to end RTP encryption
Access Control	not supported	by authentication of SIP requests	not supported	not supported
Key Management	different mechanisms	not defined	part of H.245 signaling	part of SIP message body

4 Conclusion and future work

IP-Telephony Security was given less or no attention in recent years. Nowadays, when IP-Telephony becomes a commercial available service and many vendors implement systems, it is necessary to support security mechanisms by the protocols and to build secure systems and applications. This demand is recognized by the standardization bodies during the last months. ETSI-TIPHON has founded a new working group "TIPHON Security" at End of 1999 [20]. The IETF-SIP Working Group has consensus to make security a WG effort. An informal design team has the goal, to clarify the SIP specification with respect to security and to describe practices and mechanisms for interaction with other security systems. The discussion started at the 47th IETF meeting in March 2000 [21].

Much work has to be done, we think. Especially, many security mechanisms, which are discussed in the different groups, like IPSec, are not in widespread use. Additionally, it is insufficient to define the standards, they have to be implemented. No commercial implementation, supporting confidentiality of transmission, exists to our knowledge. It is useful to point out the security aspects. Therefore, we give a review of the different requirements, evaluation criteria and standardization efforts in this paper. Our main focus of future work will be on integration of authentication mechanisms in signaling protocols, systems vulnerability and firewall mechanisms for multimedia communication in general.

References

1 H. Lu, M. Krishnaswamy, L. Conroy, S. Bellovin, F. Burg, A., DeSimone, K. Tewani, P. Davidson, H. Schulzrinne, K. Vishwanathan: "Toward the PSTN/Internet Inter-Networking-- Pre-PINT Implementations" RFC 2458, November 1998

2 C. A. Polyzois, K. H. Purdy, P. Yang, D. Shrader, H. Sinnreich, F. Ménard and H. Schulzrinne: "From POTS to PANS -- A Commentary on the Evolution to Internet Telephony," IEEE Network, vol. 13, no. 3, pp. 58--64, May/June 1999.

3 ITU-T Recommendation H.323 V.2 "Packet-Based Multimedia Communication Systems", Februar 1998.

4 M. Handley, H. Schulzrinne, E. Schooler, J. Rosenberg: "SIP: Session Initiation Protocol" RFC 2543, März 1999.

5 I. Dalgic, H. Fang: "Comparsion of H.323 and SIP for IP Telephony Signaling" In Proceedings of Photonics East, Boston, Massachusetts, September 20-22, 1999.

6 B. Douskalis: "IP Telephony - The Integration of Robust VoIP Services" Prentice Hall, 2000.

7 ITU: "X.800, Security Architecture for Open Systems Interconnection for CCITT Applications" 1991.

8 KOM, TU Darmstadt; http://www.kom.e-technik.tu-darmstadt.de/~rac/personal/ IPTEL_FRONTPAGE/iptel_field_trial.html

9 Utz Roedig, Ralf Ackermann, Ralf Steinmetz: "Evaluating and Improving Firewalls for IP-Telephony Environments" In Proceedings of the 1st IP-Telephony Workshop (IPTel2000), ISSN 1435-2702, GMD-Forschungszentrum Informationstechnik GmbH, April 2000

10 U. Roedig, R. Ackermann, C. Rensing and R. Steinmetz: "DDFA Concept" Technical Report KOM-TR-1999-04, KOM, December 1999

11 B. Biggs: "A SIP Application Level Gateway for Network Address Translation" Internet Draft, draft-biggs-sip-nat-00.txt.

12 J. Rosenberg, D. Drew, H. Schulzrinne: "Getting SIP through Firewalls and NATs", Internet Draft, draft-rosenberg-sip-firewalls-00.txt.

13 T. Eyers and H. Schulzrinne, "Predicting Internet Telephony Call Setup Delay," in Proceedings of the 1st IP-Telephony Workshop (IPTel 2000), ISSN 1435-2702, GMD-Forschungszentrum Informationstechnik GmbH, April 2000

14 B.Schneier: "Applied Cryptography" John Wiley & Sons, New York, 2. Auflage, 1996.

15 H. Schulzrinne, S. Casner, R. Frederick, V. Jacobson: "RTP: A Transport Protocol for Real-Time Applications" RFC 1889, IETF, Jan. 1996

16 ITU-T Recommendation H.235 "Security and Encryption for H. Series (H.323 and other H.245 based) Multimedia Terminals", Februar 1998

17 T. Dierks and C. Allen: "The TLS Protocol Version 1.0", RFC 2246, Januar 1999.

18 R. Thayer, N. Doraswamy und R. Glenn: "IP Security Document Roadmap" RFC 2411, November 1998.

19 ITU-T Recommendation H.245, Version 3 "Control Protocol for Multimedia Communication" September 1997

20 ETSI TIPHON: "15 meeting report (Leipzig October 4 – 8, 1999)", http://docbox.etsi.org/tech-org/tiphon/Document/tiphon/03-permanent/(99)23.doc

21 http://www.softarmor.com/sipwg/teams/sipsec/index.html

The Challenges of CORBA Security

A. Alireza[1], U. Lang[2,3], M. Padelis[4], R. Schreiner[3], and M. Schumacher[4]

[1] T-Nova Deutsche Telekom Innovationsgesellschaft mbH - Technologiezentrum
[2] University of Cambridge
[3] technoSec Ltd.
[4] Darmstadt University of Technology
`ameneh.alireza@telekom.de`
`ulrich.lang@cl.cam.ac.uk`
`padelis@ito.tu-darmstadt.de`
`ras@technosec.com`
`schumacher@ito.tu-darmstadt.de`

Abstract Large, distributed applications play an increasingly central role in today's IT environment. The diversity and openness of these systems have given rise to questions of trust and security. It is the aim of the project *Secure TINA* to examine exactly these questions and try to find possible solutions. The focus lies on OMG's *Common Object Request Broker Architecture* (CORBA) as a basis technology for developing distributed systems and on the Security Service specified for it, since this seems to be the most promising technology in the field. The followed approach is thereby twofold. At first, a thorough analysis of the specification itself and known implementations thereof is performed, based also on experiences in the broader area of distributed systems security. At a second, more practical stage, the attempt to develop an own, prototypical implementation of CORBA Security is undertaken, with the main objective of gaining as much practical experience as possible and experimenting with possible alternatives to find a solution to the problems encountered.

1 Introduction

Today, many applications are re-engineered to use Internet technologies. Much attention has been devoted recently to security issues and it is apparent that a high level of security is a fundamental prerequisite for Internet-based transactions, especially in the business-to-business area.

In our collaborative research project *Secure TINA* we address security aspects of distributed, heterogenous systems, especially for the *Telecommunications Information Networking Architecture* (TINA) platform. The basic idea of TINA is to logically separate applications and the communication infrastructure from each other. Another very important issue is to integrate management and control functions into a unified, logical software architecture supported by a single distributed computing platform [Lap98].

As CORBA is the distributed computing platform of choice, we decided to focus on the CORBA Security Service (*CORBAsec*). One of the expected results of this bottom-up approach is, to answer whether or not TINA components can use CORBAsec and to show how CORBAsec can be integrated into TINA.

In this paper we begin with a brief introduction on CORBA and CORBAsec. In the next section we discuss problems that we identified during the analysis of the specification and given CORBAsec products. With the introduction of the project *Mico Security* we describe our approach to filling the gaps between theory (the specification) and real world implementation, as well as gathering practical experience with the application and the implementation of CORBAsec.

2   CORBA and the CORBA Security Service

The technological advances in recent years have led to a situation where large, distributed applications that cooperate with each other are becoming an essential part of IT technology. As a consequence, the need for standard architectures and frameworks for developing such applications has arisen. The Object Management Group (OMG, [OMG00a]) has specified the OMA (Object Management Architecture) in response to these needs; at the heart of OMA lies the CORBA specification ([OMG99], [HV99]).

2.1   CORBA in a Nutshell

The CORBA specification allows programmers to design and implement distributed applications in a standardized manner that guarantees portability and interoperability, following the object-oriented paradigm. The central component in the CORBA architecture is the Object Request Broker (ORB), as depicted in figure 1.

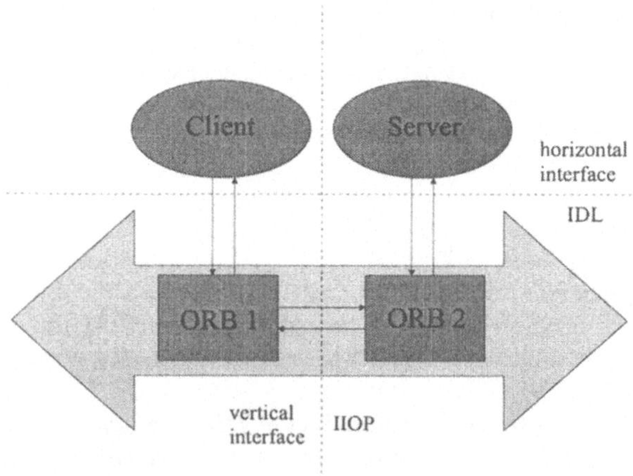

Figure1. Interfaces of the CORBA Architecture

We can distinguish between two distinct interfaces in this architecture. The first is the horizontal interface, which is defined between the application and the ORB. At this interface the application interacts with the underlying CORBA infrastructure. On the server side, the application implements objects, which provide services to clients in the network. These services are specified in a programming language independent fashion, using the CORBA-specific Interface Definition Language (IDL). On the client side, the application can use the services provided by a server by accessing the appropriate (application-specific) stub. Any programming language can be used for the implementation, as long as an appropriate language mapping from IDL exists. Furthermore, any platform (operating system) can be used for which an ORB system is available. This way, CORBA achieves portability of the application code and reusability for legacy systems.

The second interface is the vertical interface, which is the interaction point of ORB systems installed at different nodes in the network. At this point, a standardized protocol is used by any compliant ORB product. For the normal case of TCP/IP-based networks, this is the Internet Inter-ORB Protocol (IIOP). In this way, interoperability between installations of CORBA products of various vendors (corresponding to independent technological domains) is guaranteed. In a nutshell one could describe the ORB as a software bus, that enables and manages the communication between clients and servers.

The ORB specification represents the backbone of the CORBA architecture and forms the foundation for providing portability, reusability and interoperability. Nevertheless, in many cases it does not provide enough support for developers of distributed applications. When developing distributed applications, one has to cope with several common tasks, such as finding services, guaranteeing transactional processing and/or providing asynchronous communication. These are not done inside the ORB, as this was designed to provide only the core functionality. For this reason, the OMG has specified so-called object services, which reside outside of the ORB core. Examples for CORBA services are the naming service, the trading service, the transaction service, the event service, and the security service; this latter service (i.e. CORBAsec) is the topic of the next chapter.

2.2 Overview of CORBA Security

As described above, the objective of the CORBAsec ([OMG00c], [Bla00]) is to provide security in the ORB environment in the form of an object service. The focus lies hereby on confidentiality, integrity, and accountability. Technically these services are provided through the specification (by the OMG) and the implementation (by a CORBAsec product vendor) of objects, which exhibit a series of interfaces described in CORBA IDL that define precisely the necessary functionality. A high-level overview of these interfaces/ functionality together with the underlying design principles will be given in this chapter.

Terminology and Main Components. In CORBAsec, actors (the users of the system) are described with the term *principals*. Each principal is associated with a *credential*, which collects his *security attributes* (e.g. privileges). Another important term in CORBAsec is that of a *domain*. The most security relevant type of domains in CORBAsec are the *security domains*, which denote a part of the system, where a specific set of *security policies* (rules) is valid.

CORBAsec includes interfaces that define services for the following well-known areas of computer security: *Authentication*, *Message Protection* (including encryption for guaranteeing confidentiality as well as integrity), *Access Control, Auditing*, and *Non-repudiation*[1]. The latter two provide means to achieve some degree of accountability. In addition, CORBAsec describes interfaces that can be used for coping with the tedious, but very crucial task of security management/administration (e.g. assigning policies to domains). Furthermore they take care of specific problems with object-oriented (security) systems, such as the delegation of rights.

Design Principles. In order to meet its objectives, CORBAsec's design is based on some general principles. The most important ones are *transparency, scalability, flexibility*, and *interoperability*, presented in the following.

The functionality of CORBAsec is provided in three distinct *levels* of increasing functionality. The bottom Level 0, which is not part of the specification in the beginning, but was added later on, just integrates SSL into CORBA. Level 1, provides all the above-mentioned security measures except for non-repudiation. This is done in such a way that the applications running on top of the CORBA system are not aware of the security features provided underneath. Level 1 thus covers the *security unaware* applications. On the contrary Level 2 deals with those applications that are *security aware* and that are consequently in a position to interact with CORBAsec in order to specify the exact security features used. For these security aware applications non-repudiation is also relevant.

Note that CORBAsec itself does not provide any security mechanisms (e.g. cryptography). Instead, CORBAsec provides only a standardized architecture and interfaces that can be used to integrate security in a CORBA distributed objects scenario. The concrete security mechanisms (implementations) must be provided separately. Security mechanisms that have been considered so far are Kerberos, SPKM, SESAME, and SSL. It is considered beyond the scope of this paper to give an introduction to all these technologies; the interested reader may refer to the extensive literature in this area, cf.[Gol99] for an introduction. Of course, the actual functionality provided through CORBAsec is mostly determined by the underlying technology. For example, SSL, although extremely popular, is not very powerful, as discussed in more detail in the next chapter. In some cases, as with digital signatures (used for non-repudiation), a more elaborated security infrastructure is needed, such as a Public Key Infrastructure (PKI).

Interoperability is one of the most important design principles of CORBAsec. First is the issue of interoperability between ORB products and CORBAsec products, often described as *security replaceability* and achieved through a well-defined and standardized interface between ORB and CORBAsec. In the current stage of development this interface is defined by *interceptors*, but the work in this field is not completed yet. Second is the interoperability between different CORBAsec implementations. This is similar to the case of interoperability between different ORBs. The solution is also similar: a special standardized communication protocol, SECIOP (Secure Common Inter-ORB Protocol) in our case, is defined. This whole area is covered by the *Common Secure*

---

[1] This is optional and available only for Level 2 (see below), as non-repudiation makes sense only for security-aware applications.

Interoperability (CSI) part of the specification. In addition to these major notions of interoperability there are a range of other aspects of interoperability, such as interoperability between security domains or underlying security mechanisms.

3 Problems and Weaknesses of CORBA Security

In this section we discuss major problems that have been identified in the current phase of *Secure TINA*. Based on an extensive analysis[2] of the CORBAsec specification and detailed investigations of available implementations of CORBAsec, we found that those issues are not only of a technical, but also of a non-technical nature.

3.1 Application Layer of CORBA Security

Architecture. CORBAsec was initially developed for static applications in restricted environments and cannot be easily adapted to new requirements and trust relationships of Internet-based applications, for example because the code base of CORBAsec is too big, and because firewalls block messages passed between objects. The OMG firewall draft [OMG00d] and the (however proprietary) integration of SSL into CORBA are first attempts to bring CORBAsec to the Internet.

In theory the architecture of CORBAsec follows a *layered approach*, the security functionality can be achieved at the level of the ORB or at the application layer. However, often it is unclear where and how a given security feature should be implemented. For example encryption can often be done most efficiently outside of the CORBA system, if there are no additional security requirements.

More specific weaknesses of the architecture are *covert channels*, e.g. via object references (IORs), which can contain security sensitive data like object keys or names of internal servers. Beside that it is possible to scan a network for unknown objects as an "access denied" exception explicitly discloses the existence of a server.

Authentication and Authorization. Before client and server can exchange messages in a secure way, they must know the identity and other security attributes of the communication peer. The predefined attributes of CORBAsec are limited and cannot describe all properties of a principal, and many security mechanisms do not provide sufficient security attributes.

The authorization model of CORBAsec has several weaknesses [Lan99], such as the predefined access rights that have only limited validity and do not fit to all application scenarios. Thus, many vendors introduce their own access control models, which are not interoperable by nature. Therefore, the only reasonable way to achieve access control seems to be to implement it within the applications.

Note that some problems or conflicts described in this paper are not CORBAsec related, but are a consequence of inherent difficulties and trade-offs in distributed, object-oriented systems; for example, authentication versus delegation, or access control versus inheritance.

---

[2] Carried out by technoSec Ltd.

Security Audits. The audit service of CORBAsec can be the basis for a reasonable audit mechanism if the following weaknesses are addressed and eliminated: firstly, the specification of the audit functionality is not complete, e.g. security for audit records, effective filtering means, or interfaces for an appropriate analysis are missing. Furthermore, there is no standardized format for audit records or audit trails, so it is impossible to achieve a centralized audit processing. For portability only the attributes of the corresponding CSI level should be used. Unfortunately, this affects the flexibility of the audit service dramatically.

Non-Repudiation. The specification of the non-repudiation service in CORBAsec is also incomplete, requiring components like *delivery authority*, *adjucator* and *secure storage*. The specification refers to other services and standards, but does not mention details of service integration and standards availability explicitly. Even worse, there are no products that implement the *ISO Non-Repudiation Framework* [ISO97] which is the basis for the CORBAsec non-repudiation service, nor a prototype implementation for the referred standard is available.

Besides that, the supported interfaces offer only a subset of the different kinds of evidence. It is only possible to prove that a message was sent or received, but not successfully executed; only a trusted non-repudiation service on the ORB-level can achieve this.

As there is no standard format for non-repudiation evidence tokens, it is impossible to achieve interoperability. The main reason for this may be that there is no proposal for an agreed upon technology.

The non-repudiation service has been announced as a *stand-alone replaceable service*, but in fact it is highly dependent on other components, such as the CORBA Time-Service. Both asymmetric and symmetric cryptography can be used, i.e. these methods are replaceable, not the service itself.

Apart from that, there are several other reasons why products that implement the CORBAsec non-repudiation service are not available today. Firstly the CORBAsec non-repudiation service relies on CORBA security level 2 and there are only a few implementations on the market. Secondly it is not mandatory to implement non-repudiation, as it is only declared as an optional extension. Finally, severe legal restrictions prevent the usage of non-repudiation.

Policy Management. The *SecurityAdmin* interfaces provide a rudimentary definition of how policy objects can be accessed and how they can be used. The actual version of the specification does not address many important issues like management of underlying security mechanisms, management of policies at the application layer, support for conflicting policy rules, policy federations, etc. For more sophisticated management of policies the specification refers to *management services* that are part of the CORBA Common Facilities. Again, there is no agreed upon standard, but only an "initial submission" for a *Security Domain Membership Management Service* [OMG00f].

Assurance. In contrast to stand-alone systems, it is very difficult to establish trust in distributed systems, as there are many different components and mechanisms involved.

In addition, trust relationships change frequently, which makes an analysis for assurance very difficult. The CORBAsec specification introduces the notion of a *Distributed Trusted Computing Base* that includes all security-critical components, such as application objects that enforce security, the ORB kernel, object adapters, security interceptors, security mechanisms, hardware, etc. In practice, often only a partial analysis of all components is possible as many components are not under control of the service provider, e.g. client side software.

3.2 Implementation Layer

Interoperability. One of CORBA's most important strengths is its platform and programming language independence, where distributed applications can ideally run on different computers, even on top of different ORBs. In theory the same should be true for secure CORBA. However, practical experience shows that there are obstacles that prevent the interoperability of CORBAsec solutions. As written in [Sch00b] it is up to the ORB vendors to push interoperability, as only they have the chance to move CORBAsec in that direction.

Portable Integration. A portable integration of CORBAsec can be achieved in several ways, through either additional ORB source code, pluggable protocols, or interceptors.

The first approach has the advantage of a straightforward integration, as all required information of the ORB can be accessed directly. On the other hand this always requires the source code of the ORB, therefore third party implementations for most commercial products are not very likely.

Pluggable protocols [KOSP99] represent an abstraction of the ORB's transport mechanisms. This allows for a comfortable way of replacing the transport mechanisms used by the ORB, so that SSL for SSLIOP instead of TCP for IIOP can be plugged in. Pluggable protocols are a convenient way to implement security features like message protection, but unfortunately they are currently not standardized, i.e. each ORB that provides pluggable protocols implements proprietary interfaces.

Interceptors play an important role with regard to an integration of CORBAsec into an ORB, especially if there is no source code available.They are also required to implement other services that have to manipulate individual messages, such as the Transaction Service. In the past, each ORB manufacturer implemented proprietary interceptor interfaces. As this resulted in poor interoperabilty capabilities, the OMG addressed this with a Request for Proposals (RFP) for *Portable Interceptors* [OMG00e]. Unfortunately the agreed submission does not define message level interceptors, which are (amongst other things) required to implement message protection. As a consequence the situation with interoperabilty has not changed at all.

Using any of these approaches, SECIOP can be implemented[3], which is responsible for establishing the *security context* between client and server, as well as protection of subsequent messages between them. It is a very powerful protocol, for example it makes it possible to have multiple secure associations over a single TCP connection,

---

[3] Alternatively DCEIOP or SSLIOP.

but consequently it is complex and difficult to implement. Besides that it is very demanding on its environment, e.g. both client and server have to be multi-threaded. On the other hand, most of SECIOP's functionality is already provided on other layers of the CORBA protocol stack, and therefore, compared to the complexity of SECIOP, the benefits seem to be minimal. This may be the reason why only a few vendors offer an implementation of SECIOP. As a consequence, a more lightweight approach has been proposed to the OMG [OMG00b].

External Dependencies. CORBAsec cannot be seen in isolation, because it is dependent on external services and additional security infrastructure, such as *NamingService*, *EventService* or *Persistent Object Service*. In the field of CORBA Security, some concepts are quite new and therefore stable interfaces to external components cannot be expected immediately. Besides that it is not always easy to determine how new proposals should fit into the existing CORBAsec architecture, such as the CORBA PKI draft [DST00] and the CORBA firewall draft [OMG00d].

3.3 Non-technical Issues

Misleading Advertisement. An often neglected problem of CORBAsec comes from misleading discussions about the objectives and features of the architecture that are discussed below.

Just as OSF's Distributed Computing Environment (DCE) [Ope00], the predecessor of the CORBAsec architecture (ICL's DAIS Security) was originally developed for huge company intranets that are static by nature.

Since around 1997 CORBAsec has been applied to Internet applications that have different security requirements and trust relationships than intranet applications. Very soon the limitations of the architecture in this new environment were revealed, for example by the lack of support for firewalls or mobile code. In other words, various important features were missing.

Maybe it is an unrealistic concept to define and implement a security service for all possible application scenarios. The approach to introduce different conformance levels does not help, as it was intended for a phase-by-phase adoption of security and not for the support of different types of applications. It could be useful to have subsets of CORBAsec for specific application domains, such as company intranets, electronic commerce, telecommunications or health-care. The current discussions in the OMG on *CORBAsec Light* indicate that this may be the right way to go.

CORBAsec should by no means be seen as a panacea for all security problems, as it essentially does not define any new security functionality. CORBAsec also cannot solve the fundamental difficulties associated with distributed systems security, the architecture suffers under the same problems and conflicting objectives as other solutions for distributed object-oriented systems, such as the conflict of flexibility and guaranteed security.

The usage of CORBAsec per se does not result in a secure system - both the developers and operators of a distributed application have to know what they are doing, and security specialists have to analyze on a case-to-case basis to ensure the effectiveness of the security enforcement. In summary, it is a more realistic viewpoint to consider CORBAsec as a powerful toolkit for secure, distributed applications rather than a plug-in that automatically secures CORBA systems.

Lack of Experience. CORBAsec was the first security system for object-oriented middleware. It has been developed from scratch with very little previous experience to draw on, and as a result the specification is not mature at this time of writing.

One of the major issues is that the architects of CORBAsec had a wrong estimation of the market trends with respect to future security technologies. During the development of CORBAsec, SESAME [Cla00], the most powerful security mechanism available at that time, has served as a paragon, therefore the basic concepts of SESAME are found in CORBAsec. Unexpectedly the weaker SSL became more widely used than SESAME. Consequently, CORBAsec on top of SSL is not as powerful as CORBAsec on SESAME, and many features simply no longer match.

Based on the fact that there are only a few implementations of CORBAsec that offer the full functionality, most CORBA developers lack experience with regard to the utilization of most advanced CORBAsec features. The only way to solve this problem is to gather practical experience and to adapt CORBAsec to today's requirements.

4 Project: MICO Security

Consequently of the lack of usable CORBAsec products, it was decided to implement a CORBAsec prototype for MICO [PR00] as part of *Secure TINA*. The main goal of MICOsec (MICO Security Service) was to gain practical experience with securing CORBA applications, in particular already existing applications which need to be secured a posteriori.

4.1 Why MICO?

The main objective of MICO (MICO Is CORBA) is to provide a freely available and fully compliant implementation of the CORBA standard. The clear micro-kernel based architecture allows for extensibility and customization for different environments. Note that MICO has been branded as CORBA compliant by the OpenGroup, thus demonstrating that open-source software can indeed produce industrial strength software.

As outlined in [Sch00a], open-source software is a good way to achieve reliability and secure IT systems supporting the business needs of many companies. In fact, a source code analysis of MICO with ITS4 [VBKM00] revealed that MICO does not contain very security critical code.

As MICO provides only a C++ language mapping, we decided to show interoperability of the MICOsec prototype with another CORBAsec product. Adiron's ORBAsec SL2 [Adi00], which is based on Java, was chosen as the peer security service implementation to which interoperability should be established as part of the project. Both implementations are based on SSL and Adiron has also signaled an interest in participating in such an experiment.

4.2 Prototype Implementation

The long-term goal of the MICOsec prototype project is to implement as much of the CORBAsec Level 2 functionality as possible to gain experience with this new technology and to identify potential pitfalls. An incremental approach to implementing the various parts of the Level 2 functionality was chosen, and at the current stage of the project the basic functionality for authentication and message protection is implemented. SSL was chosen as the basic security mechanism, firstly because various open-source SSL implementations are available, and secondly because most other CORBAsec products are based on it.

The IDL interfaces used for MICOsec are currently based on the CORBAsec 1.7 draft [OMG00c] which also closely resembles the ORBAsec SL2 interfaces. The findings of an extensive CORBAsec analysis carried out at an earlier stage of *Secure TINA* are also taken into account during the implementation, in particular with respect to the access control model and the representation of security attributes.

As a proof of concept, our MICOsec prototype will be used to secure an online auctioning system that will make use of all implemented parts of the security service. The auctioning application, which is implemented in C++, will be accessible through many platforms supported by MICO, such as Tcl/Tk based clients written for Windows or Linux. In addition, it is planned to integrate mobile devices like the Palmpilot [Pud00] at a later stage of the project,.

At the time of this writing, the basic authentication and message protection functionality has been implemented and tested. Subject to the successful completion of *Secure TINA*, the full MICOsec implementation is anticipated to be completed around mid-2001[4] and will include some of the following security functionality: CORBAsec Level 2 access control and auditing, a PKI interface both at the ORB and application layers based on the upcoming OMG PKI standard, as well as a limited non-repudiation service.

5 Conclusions

Despite all the problems mentioned in this paper, we believe that CORBAsec has a lot of potential, especially when looked at its features in a more realistic way. It is important to understand that CORBAsec is only a (powerful) security toolbox and not the solution to all security problems. In order to move the specification into the right direction, the various inherent problems of its architecture have to be further analyzed.

We recommend the following approach to securing CORBA systems with the current version of CORBAsec:

- Take into account the security of the entire system, not just the CORBAsec components. It is always necessary to look at the system as a whole and at the interplay of its various components.
- Detect and solve weaknesses of CORBAsec, e.g. the management of users or domains.

---

[4] Please contact the authors if you are interested in the MICOsec distribution.

- Develop creative solutions when needed, such as making the firewall ORB-friendly when it isn't.
- Ignore absurd issues in the specification, such as the predefinition of the TCP ports for IIOP/SSLIOP[5].

Competing technologies like DCOM/COM+, DCE, and EJB don't provide the functionality of CORBA and its independence from languages and platforms. They are more immature than CORBA, especially in the field of security. There is no alternative to CORBA for large-scale, distributed and heterogenous applications.

References

[Adi00]   Adiron. Orbasec SL2 and Control. http://www.adiron.com, 2000.

[Bla00]   Bob Blakley. *CORBA Security: An Introduction to Safe Computing with Objects.* Addison Wesley, 2000.

[Cla00]   Joris Claessens. A Secure European System for Applications in a Multi-vendor Environment. https://www.cosic.esat.kuleuven.ac.be/sesame/, 2000.

[DST00]   DSTC. Public Key Infrastructure RFP. ftp://ftp.omg.org/pub/docs/ec/99-12-03.pdf, 2000.

[Gol99]   Dieter Gollmann. *Computer Security.* Wiley, 1999.

[HV99]   Michi Henning and Steve Vinoski. *Advanced CORBA Programming with C++.* Addison Wesley, 1999.

[ISO97]   ISO. Iso 10181-4: Information Technology - Security Frameworks for open Systems: Non-repudiation Framework, 04 1997.

[KOSP99]   Fred Kuhns, Carlos O'Ryan, Douglas C. Schmidt, and Jeff Parsons. The Design and Performance of a Pluggable Protocols Framework for Object Request Broker Middleware. http://www.cs.wustl.edu/ schmidt/PfHSN.ps.gz, 1999.

[Lan99]   Ulrich Lang. Distributed Access Control. http://www.cl.cam.ac.uk/ ul201/proposal.pdf, 1999.

[Lap98]   Martine Lapierre. *TINA.* Prentice Hall Europe (Academic), 1998.

[OMG99]   Object Management Group. CORBA/IIOP 2.3.1 specification. http://sisyphus.omg.org/technology/documents/corba2formal.htm, 1999.

[OMG00a]   Object Management Group. Website. http://www.omg.org/, 2000.

[OMG00b]   OMG. Common Secure Interoperability V2 RFP. http://www.omg.org/ /techprocess/meetings/schedule/Common_Secure_Interop._V2_RFP.html, 2000.

[OMG00c]   OMG. Corba Security Service Specification v1.7 (Draft). ftp://ftp.omg.org/pub/docs/security/99-12-02.pdf, 2000.

[OMG00d]   OMG. Joint Revised Submission CORBA/Firewall Security. ftp://ftp.omg.org/pub/docs/orbos/98-05-04.pdf, 2000.

[OMG00e]   OMG. Portable Interceptors RFP. http://www.omg.org/techprocess/meetings/schedule/Portable_Interceptors_RFP.html, 2000.

[OMG00f]   OMG. Security Domain Membership RFP. http://www.omg.org/ /techprocess/meetings/schedule/Security_Domain_Membership_RFP.html, 2000.

[Ope00]   Opengroup. DCE Portal. http://www.opennc.org/dce/, 2000.

[PR00]   Arno Puder and Kay Römer. *MICO: An Open Source CORBA Implementation.* Morgan Kaufmann Publishers, 2000.

---

[5] As they are assigned to privileged ports, a talented attacker could easily gain root access.

[Pud00]   Arno Puder. Mico for the Palmpilot. http://www.mico.org/pilot/index.html, 2000.

[Sch00a]   Rudolf Schreiner. Open Source Software Security. http://www.technosec.com/ /whitepapers/open_source/open_source_security.html, 2000.

[Sch00b]   Rudolf Schreiner. Sicherheitsbedürfnis. *iX - Magazin für professionelle Information-stechnik*, page 14, June 2000.

[VBKM00] John Viega, J.T. Bloch, Tadayoshi Kohno, and Gary McGraw. ITS4 : A Static Vul-nerability Scanner for C and C++ Code. *ftp://ftp.rstcorp.com/pub/papers/its4.pdf*, 2000.

Eine Sicherheitsinfrastruktur für das Virtuelle Projektbüro

Rolf Reinema[1], Marie-Luise Moschgath[2], Mario Hoffmann[1]

[1] GMD Institut für Sichere Telekooperation (GMD-SIT)
{reinema, hoffmann}@darmstadt.gmd.de
[2] Institut für Informationssysteme, ETH Zürich
moschgath@inf.ethz.ch

Kurzfassung. Die Arbeitswelt der Zukunft wird durch ein hohes Maß an Vielfalt, Dynamik und Flexibilität geprägt sein, die weit über das hinausgeht, was man derzeit vorfindet. Virtuelle Organisationen mit organisationsübergreifenden, räumlich verteilten und mobilen Teammitgliedern sind Beispiele für neu zu erwartende Arbeits- und Organisationsformen. Das Projekt VPO (Virtual Project Office) verfolgt das Ziel, durch die Bereitstellung einer integrierenden Kooperationsplattform verteilt agierende Teams auf Basis offener Dienste und Standards in ihrer Zusammenarbeit zu unterstützen. Neben dem Internet als Kommunikationsplattform sowie Multimedia- und CSCW-Werkzeugen zur Gruppenarbeit spielt eine inhärente und modulare Sicherheitsinfrastruktur eine wesentliche Rolle. Diese beinhaltet einen Security Policy Manager, eine Public Key Infrastruktur, einen digitalen Dienstausweis sowie mehrseitige Sicherheitsdienste, welche verschiedene Sicherheitsfunktionen für das Arbeiten über offene Netze, wie das Internet, zur Verfügung stellen, um eine sichere Ende-zu-Ende-Kommunikation zu garantieren.

1. Einleitung

Unternehmen und Organisationen unterliegen derzeit einem starken Wandel. Die Bildung von „virtuellen Teams", welche aus geographisch verteilten Mitgliedern bestehen, ist in vielen Unternehmungen bereits heute anzutreffen. Obwohl derartige Teams mit modernsten Kommunikationsmitteln miteinander verbundenen sind, werden sie mit größeren Schwierigkeiten konfrontiert und benötigen ein größeres Maß an Flexibilität und Unterstützung durch moderne Informations- und Kommunikationstechnik, als heutzutage üblicherweise zur Verfügung stehen. Neue Paradigmen, Technologien, Informationssysteme und Kommunikationsinfrastrukturen sind notwendig, um virtuelle Teams mit einer optimalen, und vor allen Dingen sicheren Arbeitsumgebung auszustatten. Virtuelle Teams benötigen Arbeitsumgebungen, die einerseits Zusammenarbeit und Zusammengehörigkeitsgefühl im Team fördern, die aber andererseits auch jedem einzelnen Teammitglied genügend individuelle Entfaltungsmöglichkeit lassen. Diese Arbeitsumgebungen müssen sich zusammen mit ihren Werkzeugen und Diensten schnell und in äußerst flexibler und dynamischer Weise an die spezifischen Bedürfnisse eines Teams und seiner Mitglieder anpassen lassen.

Mit dem Projekt VPO (Virtual Project Office) wird das Ziel verfolgt, inter- und intraorganisationale Geschäftsprozesse und –anwen

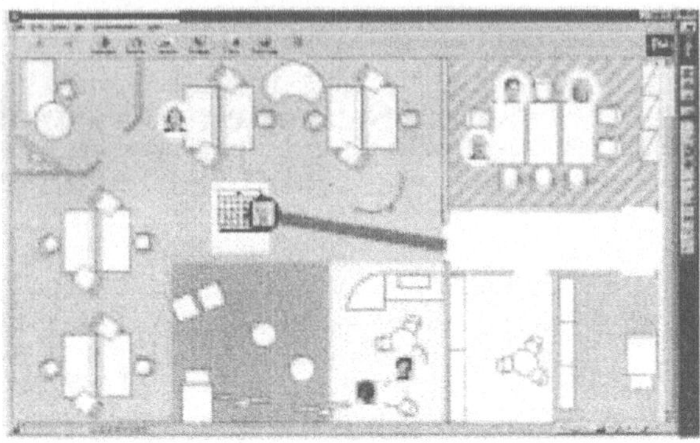

Abb. 1: Das Virtuelle Projektbüro

dungen in virtuellen Teams und Organisationen auf Basis einer sogenannten Kooperationslandschaft zu unterstützen [8][9][10]. Diese setzt sich aus einer Kooperationsplattform sowie einer ausgewählten Menge darauf aufsetzender spezifischer Kooperationsanwendungen und Geschäftsprozesse zusammen.

Ausschlaggebend für den Erfolg einer jeden Internet-basierten Kooperationsplattform ist neben der einfachen und intuitiven Handhabung des Systems dessen Sicherheit. Dazu zählen neben einer sicheren Ende-zu-Ende-Kommunikation (gegenseitige Authentisierung, Integrität und Vertraulichkeit) auch die Autorisierung (Access Control), Nicht-Abstreitbarkeit (Non-Repudiation), Auditing sowie die flexible Definition von Sicherheitspolitiken. Im Rahmen wählbarer Sicherheitspolitiken erlaubt das VPO, Personen eindeutig zu identifizieren, ortstransparent zu adressieren sowie die Authentizität und Vertraulichkeit kommunizierter Nachrichten und gespeicherter Daten zu gewährleisten. Innerhalb eines derartigen Teams kann offen kommuniziert und Betriebsmittel, wie Archive und Programme, gemeinsam genutzt werden. Gegen die Außenwelt wird das Team jedoch in definierbarer Weise abgeschottet.

Dieser Beitrag ist wie folgt aufgebaut: Abschnitt 2 enthält einen Überblick über die Sicherheitsinfrastruktur des VPO. In den Abschnitten drei bis sechs werden die vier wichtigsten Komponenten der Sicherheitsarchitektur des VPO, der Security Policy Managers, die Public Key Infrastruktur (PKI), der digitale Dienstausweis und die mehrseitigen Sicherheitsdienste beschrieben.

2. Die Sicherheitsinfrastruktur

Ziel des VPO Projekts ist es, eine Plattform zur Verfügung zu stellen, welche die Integration verschiedenster Kooperations- und Kommunikationsdienste in einem heterogenen Umfeld in ein Internet-basiertes System erlaubt. Dies stellt für die Sicherheitsarchitektur eine besondere Herausforderung hinsichtlich Skalierbarkeit, Flexibilität und Modularität dar, da sowohl auf der Client- wie auch auf Serverseite unterschiedlichste Technologien und Standards unterstützt werden müssen.

Die Kooperation in wechselnden Gruppen, deren Mitglieder in der Regel unterschiedlichen Organisationen angehören, erfordert unilaterale, bilaterale und multilaterale Sicherheits-Technologien, um die Authentisierung der Mitglieder, deren Autorisation, die vertrauenswürdige Kommunikation untereinander sowie die Integrität und Vertraulichkeit aller Projekt-Dokumente zu gewährleisten. Ein weiteres Problem stellen die unterschiedlichen organisationsabhängigen Sicherheitspolitiken dar, die aufeinander abgestimmt bzw. berücksichtigt werden müssen.

Obige Beziehungen werden im folgenden anhand der ableitbaren Schutzziele sowie der zur Realisierung notwendigen Schutzmechanismen mit Bezug auf das Virtuelle Projektbüro erläutert. Die Sicherheitsarchitektur des VPO besteht aus den folgenden Hauptkomponenten:

1. Einem Security Policy-Manager, welcher Funktionen zur Definition von projektbezogenen Sicherheitspolitiken bereitstellt.
2. Einer Public Key-Infrastruktur inkl. einem digitalen Dienstausweis als Träger von Sicherheitstoken.
3. Inhärenten mehrseitigen Sicherheitsdiensten, die verschiedene Sicherheitsfunktionen, wie beispielsweise Verschlüsselung, Authentifizierung und digitale Signatur zur Verfügung stellen, sowie einem Access Control System, das jeden Zugriff auf Ressourcen und Dienste auf Autorisation überprüft, inklusive integrierter Auditing-, Accounting- und Nichtabstreitbarkeits-Funktionalität.

Der Security Policy-Manager ist dabei Teil des VPOs. Die PKI und die mehrseitigen Sicherheitsdienste sind eigenständige Komponenten. Sie können durch organisationsinterne Sicherheitssysteme realisiert werden. Ausschlaggebend dabei ist die Integrationsfähigkeit und Interoperabilität der unternehmensinternen Systeme ins VPO über definierte Schnittstellen.

3. Security Policy-Manager

Eine Sicherheitspolitik oder Sicherheitsstrategie (security policy, SP) ist nach dem auch unter dem Namen *Orange Book* bekannten *Trusted Computer System Evaluation Criteria* eine „Sammlung von Gesetzen Regeln und Praktiken, die den Umgang, den Schutz und die Verbreitung von sensitiven Informationen in einer Organisation festlegen" [1]. Sicherheitspolitiken benötigen zu ihrer Durchsetzung sowohl konkrete Sicherheitsmechanismen (siehe Abschnitt 6) zur Erfüllung von bestimmten Sicherheitsanforderungen, wie Authentifikation, Zugriffskontrolle, Vertraulichkeit, Integrität, Nicht-Abstreitbarkeit (Non-Repudiation), Delegation und Auditing, als auch einen Akteur (sogenannter Referenzmonitor), welcher deren Einhaltung realisiert, überwacht und garantiert.

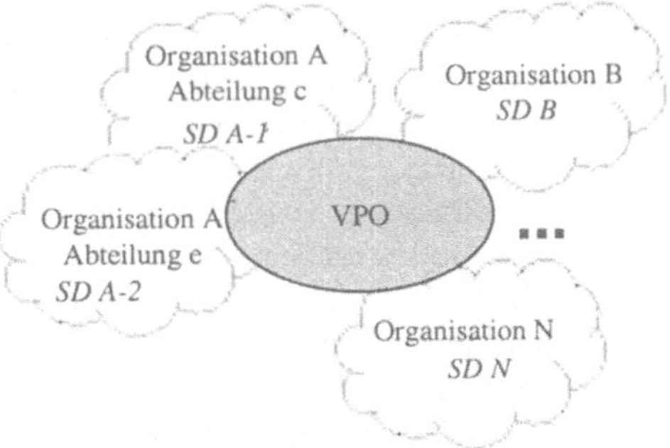

Abb. 2: Sicherheitsdomänen

Eine Sicherheitspolitik definiert auch den Bereich, die sogenannte Sicherheitsdomäne (SD), in der sie Gültigkeit besitzt.

Sicherheitspolitiken werden meist zum besseren Verständnis und Lesbarkeit informell beschrieben. Eine präzise Formulierung beispielsweise in Form von temporalen Logiken oder Prädikatenlogiken wird Sicherheitsmodell genannt und bildet die Grundlage für formale Nachweis- und Zertifizierungsverfahren. Bekannte Modelle sind beispielsweise Bell/La Padula, Biba, Clark/Wilson oder Chinese-Wall, die aber alle auf eine entsprechende Sicherheitspolitik zugeschnitten sind [12][13][14].

Bei der Festlegung einer Sicherheitspolitik für das VPO wird schnell deutlich, daß das Konzept einer „einfachen" Sicherheitpolitik nicht ausreichend ist. Das übergeordnete Ziel ist es, eine einheitliche Plattform für verteilte Teams zu bieten, deren Mitglieder sowohl innerhalb einer größeren Organisation (beispielsweise zwischen verschiedenen Abteilungen) wie auch organisationsübergreifend zusammenarbeiten (Abb. 2). Die zugrundeliegenden IT-Systeme liegen somit in unterschiedlichen Sicherheitsdomänen, so daß verschiedene SPs koexistieren, die die jeweiligen Sicherheitsanforderungen mit unterschiedlichen Granularitätsstufen festlegen und durch verschiedene Sicherheitsmechanismen realisiert werden. Es ist daher ein zentrales Problem innerhalb eines VPO, eine einfache, flexible und weitgehend automatisierte Möglichkeit zur Festlegung einer SP für das jeweilige Projekt sowie eine Abbildung auf die SPs der beteiligten Organisationen zu finden.

In der Literatur existieren hierzu im wesentlichen zwei Ansätze: die Interoperation und die Kombination. Bei der Interoperation darf die übergeordnete Sicherheitspolitik die Sub-SPs nicht verletzen und muß deren Autonomie garantieren [3]; bei einer Kombination kann die übergeordnete SP Inkonsistenzen zu den Sub-SPs beinhalten, muß jedoch die Sicherheit im vorliegenden Kontext garantieren [4]. Da bei virtuellen Teams in der Regel nicht nur zwei Organisationen oder Abteilungen beteiligt sind, diese von Projekt zu Projekt variieren und einer hohen Dynamik unterliegen, ist nur eine Kombination möglich.

Wird für ein virtuelles Team ein VPO eingerichtet, ist für dieses Projekt eine unabhängige Sicherheitspolitik festzulegen. Die Berücksichtigung der darunterliegenden SPs der beteiligten Organisationen erfolgt dadurch, daß über weitgehend automatisierte Verhandlungsstrategien eine Mappingfunktion zwischen der Team-SP und den jeweiligen Sub-SPs gesucht wird.

Die Regeln zur Auflösung von Konflikten und Akzeptanzgrenzen werden über eine Metapolitik festgelegt. Dies ist jedoch nur möglich, wenn eine universelle Spezifikationssprache zur Verfügung steht, die nicht auf ein einheitliches Sicherheitsmodell zugeschnitten ist. Wir verfolgen daher einen Ansatz auf Basis von XML [10]. XML ist plattformunabhängig, leicht in die Internet-Welt zu integrieren und bietet die Möglichkeit, die Lücke zwischen Politikspezifikation und Implementierung zu überbrükken und somit automatisierte Verhandlungsstrategien zu ermöglichen.

Zur Festlegung einer SP für ein neu konzipiertes Projekt steht ein Werkzeug zur Verfügung, das aufbauend auf einem Repository eine Benutzungsoberfläche bereitstellt, mit der sich kontextabhängige Zugriffsregeln, die Rollen innerhalb des Teams, die Subjekte, die Objekte, die Zugriffs- und weiterführende Rechte, Lokationen etc. festlegen lassen. Über einen Regel-Manager werden die Sicherheitsregeln definiert

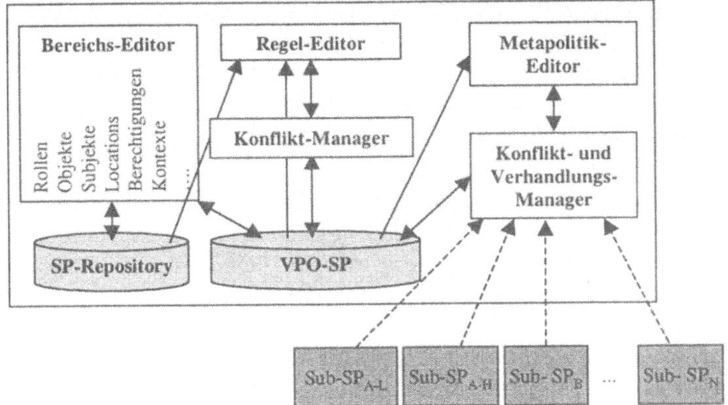

Abb. 3: Policy-Editor

und von einem Konflikt-Manager auf Konflikt- und Widerspruchsfreiheit überprüft. Die Metapolitik wird über den Metapolitik-Editor festgelegt, über den Konflikt- und Verhandlungsmanager auf interne und SP-übergreifende Konflikte überprüft und diese soweit wie möglich aufgelöst (Abb. 3).

4. Public Key-Infrastruktur

Voraussetzung für die Absicherung von Kommunikationsverbindungen zwecks Wahrung von Vertraulichkeit, Integrität, Authentifikation und Nichtabstreitbarkeit (Non-Repudiation) sind asymmetrische Kryptographieverfahren mit privaten und öffentlichen Schlüsseln und damit verbunden eine Public Key-Infrastruktur (PKI).

Eine PKI ist eine Kombination aus Hard- und Softwareprodukten, Richtlinien und Prozeduren. Sie besteht im wesentlichen aus folgenden Komponenten:

- Sicherheitsrichtlinien (SR): Die SR legen einen einheitlichen Sicherheitsstandard fest und garantieren die Sicherheit für den Einsatz und die Verwaltung der PKI.
- Krypto-Token: Das Krypto-Token dient der Speicherung des privaten Schlüssels (siehe hierzu Abschnitt 5).
- Zertifikationsinstanz (Certification Authority, CA): In der CA werden die Schlüsselzertifikate durch die Verknüpfung von Benutzer-Identitäten mit dem öffentlichen Schlüssel erzeugt, mit einer Gültigkeitsdauer verknüpft und verwaltet. Aus Performanzgründen und auf Grund von Speicherplatzproblemen erfolgt im aktuellen PKI-Szenario die Erstellung des asymmetrischen Schlüsselpaares ebenfalls in der CA. Ziel ist es jedoch, die Erzeugung der Schlüssel in die Chipkarte zu verlagern, die als Krypto-Token eingesetzt wird (siehe Abschnitt 5).
- Registrierungsinstanz (Registration Authority, RA): Die RA bildet die Schnittstelle zum Benutzer. Sie garantiert die Identität des Benutzers gegenüber der CA.
- Verzeichnisdienst für Zertifikate: In einem Verzeichnisdienst werden die öffentlichen Schlüssel allen Benutzern frei zugänglich gemacht, damit deren Korrektheit und Gültigkeit überprüft werden kann.

- Sperrlisten: Sperrlisten sind Datenstrukturen des Verzeichnisdienstes, die Informationen wie den Sperrzeitpunkt und -grund von gesperrten Zertifikaten enthalten, deren Gültigkeitsdauer noch nicht abgelaufen ist.
- Zeitstempel-Service: Der Zeitstempel-Service beglaubigt das Vorliegen von digitalen Daten zu einem bestimmten Zeitpunkt. Dieser Dienst bildet die Grundlage für den Non-Repudiation-Service.

Da zu erwarten ist, daß in Zukunft jedes Unternehmen über eine eigene interne PKI verfügt, ist diese Komponente als externe VPO-Komponente zu betrachten. Für eine organisationsübergreifende Nutzung von internen Public Key-Infrastrukturen ist die Interoperabilität zwischen den verschiedenen auf dem Markt erhältlichen Produkten notwendig. Dies stellt derzeit (zumindest teilweise) noch ein Problem dar.

Als PKI-Produkt wird im VPO Projekt derzeit Secude [2] eingesetzt. Secude erstellt Zertifikate nach dem internationalen Standard X.509 in den Versionen X.509v1 oder X.509v3, unterstützt deren Widerruf, pflegt Sperrlisten, verwaltet Benutzer und führt ein Logbuch.

5. Der digitale Dienstausweis

Eine sichere Speicherung der von einer CA erstellten PSE (personal security environment oder dt. Persönliche Sicherheitsumgebung) ist nur in einer Chipkarte möglich. Die Speicherung auf einem Rechner entspricht weder heutigen Sicherheitsanforderungen und –standards, noch ist sie im Zeitalter von Mobilität und modernen Arbeitsformen mit nicht territorialen Arbeitsplätzen (sog. desk-sharing) praktikabel.

Die verwendete Chipkarte sollte nicht nur zur Speicherung der Zertifikate für Verschlüsselung und Signatur eingesetzt werden, sondern auch als digitaler Dienstausweis mit Zusatzapplikationen für den innerbetrieblichen Ablauf wie Zugangskontrolle, Single-Sign-On, Bezahlkarte oder Bibliotheksausweis. Aus diesem Grund bot sich das Konzept der sogenannten „Office Identity Card" an [1].

Die Office Identity Card (OIC) wird zur Zeit in einer Untergruppe der TeleTrust Arbeitsgruppe 2 spezifiziert und voraussichtlich im dritten Quartal 2000 der Öffentlichkeit zugänglich gemacht werden. Auslöser hierzu war die Absicht des Bundesministerium des Inneren (BMI), einen Dienstausweis auf Basis einer multi-funktionalen Chipkarte für die gesamte Bundesverwaltung einzuführen, mit dem Ziel der Einführung gesetzeskonformer digitaler Signaturen, Interoperabilität und Austauschbarkeit. Die Spezifikation der OIC legt folgende Funktionen fest:

- Herkömmliche Ausweisfunktion: der Ausweis soll sowohl optisch wie auch elektronisch prüfbar sein. Dabei müssen die elektronisch gespeicherten Daten mit den optischen, auf dem Kartenkörper aufgebrachten Daten vollständig übereinstimmen und auf Echtheit prüfbar sein.
- Erzeugung digitaler Signaturen nach dem Signaturgesetz.
- Authentisierungsfunktion: die OIC unterstützt verschiedene Authentisierungsverfahren wie TLS, Kerberos mit der Erweiterung PKINIT und CV-basierte Terminalauthentisierung.

- Schlüsselgenerierung und -management: Signatur- und Authentisierungsschlüssel werden in der Karte erzeugt und verwaltet.
- Zusatzanwendungen sind möglich, jedoch nicht Bestandteil der Spezifikation.

Für den Einsatz im VPO wurde eine OIC mit folgenden Zusatzapplikationen realisiert: Zertifikat-basiertes Authentisierungs- und Autorisierungssystem für Daten und Dienste, Single-Sign-On sowie datenschutzgerechte Zeiterfassung. Weitere, für die OIC entwickelte Anwendungen, sind Zutrittskontrolle zu Gebäuden und Räumen, Bibliotheksfunktionen sowie kontextbasierte Bezahlfunktionen.

Da die entwickelte OIC standardisierte Schnittstellen, wie beispielsweise PKCS#11 und eine Crypto-API bereitstellt, ist die Integration in Sicherheitsapplikationen möglich. So wird beispielsweise die OIC für die Authentisierung bei der sicheren Kommunikation über das SSL-Protokoll verwendet. Die Verschlüsselung einer Sitzung zwischen Client und Server erfolgt anschließend ohne weiteren Zugriff auf die Chipkarte.

6. Inhärente Mehrseitige Sicherheitsdienste

Die vom VPO bereitgestellten mehrseitigen Sicherheitsdienste [5] [6] sind als inhärente Dienste realisiert, d.h. die Teammitglieder können sich auf ihre eigentliche Projektarbeit konzentrieren, da die jeweiligen Sicherheitsmaßnahmen transparent im Hintergrund laufen. Zu den integrierten Sicherheitsdiensten gehören: Authentisierung der Projektmitglieder mit Hilfe des digitalen Dienstausweises, Vertraulichkeit und Integrität von Kommunikationsinhalten, Dienst- und Dokumenten-Zugriffskontrolle sowie die Zurechenbarkeit von Projektvorgängen zu Teammitgliedern.

Authentisierung der Projektmitglieder

Als erstrangiges Schutzziel hinsichtlich einer vertrauenswürdigen Kommunikation unter den registrierten Projektmitgliedern, gilt die eindeutige und überprüfbare Authentisierung jedes einzelnen Projektmitglieds. Dabei wurde ein 2-stufiges Authentisierungsverfahren realisiert. Hierbei erfolgt zunächst die klassische Authentisierung gegenüber der VPO-Clientsoftware, die über ihre graphische Benutzungsschnittstelle für eine geeignete Visualisierung des persönlichen Projektbüros sorgt und gegebenenfalls die für die Projektarbeit benötigten integrierten Dienste und Werkzeuge aufruft. Im Verlauf der individuellen Projektarbeit erfolgt eine weitere Authentisierung gegenüber der VPO-Serversoftware bei jedem Eintritt in eine spezifische Projektumgebung.

Die sogenannte *Single-Sign-On*-Identifikation gegenüber der VPO Systemsoftware ermöglicht, durch Verwendung des im vorigen Kapitel eingeführten *Dienstausweises*, die einmalige Bestätigung der Identität sowie ihre transparente Verwendung für die gesamte Zeit einer Arbeitssitzung. Für jede serverseitige Verbindungsaufnahme während einer solchen Arbeitssitzung wird, zum Zwecke der Zuteilung individueller, von der Projektidentität abhängiger Berechtigungen, die Gültigkeit der Identität mit Hilfe einer vertrauenswürdigen Zertifizierungsinstanz verifiziert (siehe *Dienst- und Dokumenten-Zugriffskontrolle*).

Nach erfolgreicher Authentisierung kann die Arbeit im persönlichen Arbeitsumfeld beginnen. Dazu gehört ein persönliches Büro mit Zugriff auf alle gespeicherten persönlichen Daten und die Eintrittsmöglichkeit in die VPOs der jeweiligen Projekte. Die Kontaktaufnahme zum jeweiligen Projektserver erfolgt mit Hilfe der Authentisierungsinformationen ebenso transparent wie die Zuteilung der individuellen Projektberechtigung abhängig von der Gruppenidentität (siehe Dienst- und Dokumenten-Zugriffskontrolle).

Vertraulichkeit und Integrität von Kommunikationsinhalten

Angelehnt an die Schichten des OSI-Modells unterscheiden wir bei der Realisierung von Vertraulichkeit und Integrität von Kommunikationsdaten zwischen Maßnahmen in der Anwendungsschicht und darunter. Unsere Bestrebungen, das Virtuelle Projektbüro durch Sicherheitstechniken in einem vertrauenswürdigen Umfeld für virtuelle Teams einzusetzen, betreffen zunächst die Anwendungsschicht. Eigenentwicklungen, wie beispielsweise der digitale Dienstausweis, und kryptographische Verfahren in Dritt-Anbieter-Software, wie beispielsweise Web-Browser, unterstützen bereits zahlreiche Mechanismen zum Verschlüsseln, Signieren und Authentifizieren. Ein konfigurierbarer flexibler Einsatz dieser Verfahren ermöglicht somit allen Teammitgliedern, abhängig von der jeweiligen Team-Sicherheitspolitik, die vertrauliche Kommunikation und Kooperation und sichert deren Integrität.

Voraussetzung für die erfolgreiche Integration in VPO ist, daß die Anwendungsprogramme die zu verwendenden Verfahren unterstützen, was oftmals eine Anpassung der eingesetzten Software erfordert. Nicht jede Applikation eignet sich gleichermaßen für den integrierten Einsatz im VPO. Außerdem können Informationen, die in tieferen Schichten relevant sind (z.B. Absender- und Empfängeradressen), in der Anwendungsschicht nicht verschlüsselt werden, was beispielsweise für Verkehrsflußanalysen ausgenutzt werden könnte [7].

Vertraulichkeit und Integrität der übermittelten Daten unterhalb der Anwendungsschicht wird im VPO deshalb zusätzlich durch die Verwendung bekannter Verschlüsselungsprotokolle garantiert. SSL-erweiterte Projektserver sorgen beispielsweise für eine verschlüsselte Ende-zu-Ende-Übertragung von TCP-basierten Diensten. UDP-basierte Dienste, die nicht durch SSL unterstützt werden - wie beispielsweise IP-Telephony -, erfordern eine Verschlüsselung unterhalb der Transportschicht in der Vermittlungsschicht. Zu diesen Verfahren zählt IPSEC (integriert in IP Version 6). IPSEC erweitert das herkömmliche IP-Protokoll um einige Bestandteile. Im Gegensatz zu SSL kann IPSEC auch für Teilstrecken zwischen zwei Routern eingesetzt werden und eignet sich daher auch für die Errichtung virtueller privater Netze (VPN), auf deren Basis abhängig von den Sicherheitsanforderungen auch Virtuelle Projektbüros ihre Dienste bereitstellen können [7].

Dienst- und Dokumenten-Zugriffskontrolle

Die für die Verschlüsselung von Kommunikationsdaten vorgestellten Verfahren eignen sich ohne Abstriche auch für den Transport von digitalen Dokumenten und die sichere Nutzung der angebotenen Projektdienste. Der autorisierte Zugriff auf Dokumente in der projekteigenen Dokumentenablage sowie auf die für das jeweilige Projekt bereitgestellten Dienste erfolgt hingegen durch Assoziation der einzelnen Projektmitglieder mit bestimmten projektabhängigen Rollen, die durch dessen Sicherheitspolitik festgelegt sind.

Das VPO unterscheidet unterschiedliche, systemspezifische, projektunabhängige Rollen - wie z.B. Projektmanager, Administrator, Gruppenmitglieder und Gäste - sowie projektspezifische Rollen - wie z.B. Autoren, Editoren, Graphiker, Verleger. Abhängig von diesen Rollen erfolgt während der Anmeldung an einem VPO-Server die Zuweisung der entsprechenden Rechte, beispielsweise zur Wartung des Systems. Innerhalb des Virtuellen Projektbüros sind durch die Auswertung der zugeordneten Rechte nur bestimmte Dienste erreichbar sowie der Zugriff auf projektbezogene Dokumente reglementiert.

Zurechenbarkeit von Projektvorgängen

Die Unterstützung kooperativer, koordinierter Arbeit an digitalen, multimedialen Dokumenten in verteilten Teams erfordert, einzelne Projektvorgänge nachvollziehbar und in letzter Konsequenz als nicht-abstreitbar zu realisieren. Zu diesem Zweck wird der Zugriff auf Dienste und Dokumente zusätzlich zur Berechtigungsprüfung datenschutzgerecht protokolliert und gegebenenfalls ausgewertet.

Gesichert wird die Integrität und Zurechenbarkeit der Dokumente durch Signieren der Dokumente bzw. der durchgeführten Änderungen. Neben dem Namen werden zusätzlich Datum und die Uhrzeit in einer Dokumenten-Historie gespeichert. Zum beidseitigen Nachweis erhält der Benutzer schließlich eine Quittung über die Änderungen und Aktionen auf dem digitalen Dokument.

Die Protokollierung bildet außerdem die Grundlage für die Abrechnung in Anspruch genommener Dienste. Auf diese Weise können beispielsweise die Kosten für Dienste von Dritt-Anbietern einzelnen Projektmitgliedern oder Projektvorgängen zugeordnet werden.

7. Zusammenfassung

Ein wesentlicher Aspekt der im Rahmen von VPO entwickelten Sicherheitsinfrastruktur ist, daß sie die Zusammenarbeit in verteilten Teams unterstützt. Deren Teammitglieder sind weltweit verteilt, gehören verschiedenen Organisationen an, die wiederum eigene Sicherheitspolitiken und -infrastrukturen haben. Die Einrichtung eines Virtuellen Projektbüros bedeutet folglich die Integration vorhandener Infrastrukturen und standardisierter Sicherheitstechniken. Für jedes einzelne Virtuelle Projektbüro können spezifische Sicherheitspolitiken definiert werden. Dadurch kann der Zugang zu den einzelnen Zonen innerhalb eines Virtuellen Projektbüros und der Zugriff auf die zugehörigen Dokumenten und Dienste kontrolliert werden.

Der bereitgestellte Security-Policy Manager bietet die Möglichkeit, unterschiedliche Sicherheitspolitiken für die einzelnen Virtuellen Projektbüros, je nach Team und

Projekt, flexibel und dynamisch zu konfigurieren und anzupassen. Sicherheitsregeln lassen sich über einen Regeleditor definieren und von einem Konflikt-Manager auf Widerspruchsfreiheit überprüfen. Als Basis für die Public Key-Infrastruktur wird Secude eingesetzt. Der entwickelte digitale Dienstausweis dient dabei als Träger von Sicherheitstoken. Die vom VPO bereitgestellten mehrseitigen Sicherheitsdienste sind als inhärente Dienste realisiert. Diese unterstützen die Authentisierung der Projektmitglieder, sichern die Vertraulichkeit und Integration von Kommunikationsinhalten, bieten Dienst- und Dokumentenzugriffskontrolle und unterstützen die Zurechenbarkeit von Projektvorgängen.

Literatur

[1] TTT-AG2: German Office Identity Card. TeleTrust. Spezifikation (work in progress). Version 0.71, 14.12.1999.

[2] Stephan André, Andreas Berger, Ute Faltin, Jochen Dückminor, Harald Giehl, Petra Glöckner, Susanne Hennecke, Thomas Hetschold, Detlef Hühnlein, Markus Nüsseler, Wolfgang Schneider, Hans Schupp, Oliver Schwarz, Thomas Surkau, Ursula Viebeg: SECUDE-5.0 Documentation. Darmstadt, Oct. 1996. Siehe auch www.secude.de.

[3] L. Gong and X. Qian: Computational issue in secure interoperation. IEEE Transactions on Software Engineering. 22(1):pp. 43-52. Jan. 1996.

[4] D. E. Bell: Modeling the Multipolicy Machine. In: Proceedings of the New Security Paradigm Workshop. Aug. 1994.

[5] Hannes Federrath, Andreas Pfitzmann: Bausteine zur Realisierung mehrseitiger Sicherheit, In: Mehrseitige Sicherheit in der Kommunikationstechnik, G. Müller, A. Pfitzmann (Hrsg.), Addison-Wesley, 1997.

[6] Rüdiger Grimm: Sicherheit für offene Kommunikationsnetze, In: Mehrseitige Sicherheit in der Kommunikationstechnik, G. Müller, A. Pfitzmann (Hrsg.), Addison-Wesley, 1997.

[7] Klaus Schmeh: Safer Net - Kryptographie im Internet und Intranet, dpunkt.Verlag, 1998.

[8] R. Reinema, K. Bahr, M. Baukloh, H.-J. Burkhardt, G. Schulze: Cooperative Buildings - Workspaces of the Future; In: Callaos, C.; Omolayole, O.; Wang, L. (Eds.), Proceedings of the World Multiconference on Systemics Cybernetics and Informatics (SCI'98), Orlando, Florida, Vol. 1, pp. 121-128., Jul. 1998.

[9] R. Reinema, K. Bahr, H.-J. Burkhardt, L. Hovestadt: Integrating Virtual and Real Work Environments; In: Proceedings of IEEE Conference on Software in Telecommunications and Computer Networks (SoftCOM '99), Split, Rijeka, Croatia, Trieste, Venice, Italy, Oct. 1999.

[10] R. Reinema, K. Bahr, H.-J. Burkhardt, L. Hovestadt: Cooperative Rooms - Symbiosis of Real and Virtual Worlds; In: Proceedings of 8th International Conference on Telecommunication Systems, Modelling and Analysis, Nashville, Texas, Mar. 2000.

[11] W3C: Extensible Markup Language (XML) 1.0 10.02.1998. http://www.w3c.org/TR/RECxml.

[12] D. E.Bell, Leonard J. La Padula. Secure Computer Systems: Mathematical Foundations and Model. MTR 2547, Vol. 2. Bedford, MA: MITRE, Nov. 1973.

[13] D. D. Clark, D.R. Wilson: A Comparison of Commercial and Military Computer Security Policies; pp. 184-194 in Proceedings of the IEEE Symposium on Security and Privacy. Los Alamitos, CA: IEEE Computer Society Press. 1987.

[14] D. Brewer, M. Nash: The Chinese Wall Security Policy; pp. 206-214 in Proceedings of the IEEE Symposium on Security and Privacy. Los Alamitos, CA: IEEE Computer Society Press. 1989.

A Framework for
Comparing and Querying
Certification Practice Statements

Stephan Grill

Institute for Applied Information Processing and Communications
Graz University of Technology
A-8010 Graz, Austria
sgrill@acm.org

Abstract. Public Key Infrastructures are gaining importance in today's IT environment for managing certificates and keys. Much effort is devoted to understand and standardize protocols to mange this infrastructure. However it is equally recognized, that the quality and trustworthiness of certificates depend to a large extend on the practices and procedures a certification authority applies when issuing certificates. These procedures are documented in so called Certification Practice Statements (CPS), which are generally text-based documents and therefore cannot be processed by machines. This paper describes a framework based on knowledge representation techniques that addresses this situation. Subsumption will be used to compare and query CPS. Based on a case study of modeling a real CPS some features of this framework will be described. Learnings and an outlook of future work conclude this paper.

1 Introduction

Public Key Infrastructures are emerging as an important cornerstone of today's communications systems. X.509 certificates are envisioned to provide a wealth of services ranging from electronic ID cards, digital signature, authorization schemes, etc. Processes and protocols to manage and use private keys and certificates are well understood and corresponding standards [1] are currently in the process of being defined.

The degree to which a certificate user can trust the binding embodied in a certificate depends on several factors (e.g. practices followed by the CA in authenticating the subject, the subjects obligations in protecting the private key, the legal obligations of a CA, etc.).

X.509 provides two means to bind this kind of information to certificates:

– Certificate Policy and
– Certification Practice Statement

A Certificate Policy (CP) essentially is a unique, registered Object Identifier, which can be included in the certificate. A Certification Practice Statement (CPS) may be published or referenced by a CA and may contain a more detailed description of the practices a CA follows when issuing certificates. The objectives and the contents of a CP and a CPS are described in RFC 2527 [2].

Both formats have weaknesses:

- A CP is based on numbers (OID), which only support equality-comparisons. However it is not possible to retrieve specific detail information related to a CP/CPS and it is also not possible to apply relational operators other then equality (e.g. is a CP/CPS more trustworthy than another).
- A CPS is based on textual descriptions, which cannot be automatically processed by machines. End-Users have to read each CP/CPS and judge whether associated certificates are trustworthy or not. However the length of a CPS will usually lead users to refrain from reading and understanding it when receiving a certificate.

A framework to improve this situation will be suggested in the following sections. Section 2 will discuss requirements for a structured and formal representation of information typically contained in a CP and CPS (from now own denoted by CP/CPS). Section 3 will explain the general approach that was taken to address this problem. Section 4 will highlight some examples based on a case study that was performed by modeling real CP/CPS. Section 5 will provide a summary with learnings and an outlook for future work.

2 Requirements for the Representation of a CP/CPS

To define requirements for a CP/CPS representation cases for using these models will be discussed first:

- Relying parties should be enabled to *retrieve* specific aspects of a CP/CPS of a received certificate (e.g. they want to check where the associated private key of a certificate is generated and stored)
- Relying parties might want to *specify conditions or policies* a CP/CPS of a certificate must match in order to be accepted (e.g. they want to specify that only certificates are accepted, if the associated private key is generated and stored on a smart-card).
- These comparisons might be based on equality comparisons but also on other *comparison operators* which might be applicable for the quality of certificates (e.g. practices described in a CP/CPS might indicate that associated certificates are more trustworthy than certificates issues according to another CP/CPS - e.g. a certificate for an associated private key that is generated and stored on a smart-card might be more trustworthy than a certificate whose associated private key is generated in software and stored on a hard disk).
- Certification Authorities (CA) might be interested to better investigate CP/CPS of another CA when engaging in cross-certification.

From these possible use cases a set of requirements can be derived:

- A representation of a CP/CPS exists primarily in the realm of the internet. Hence it must support the flexible nature of the internet. It must be possible to construct a CP/CPS from existing definitions. It must be possible to derive a new CP/CPS from an already existing CP/CPS. Building blocks of a CP/CPS can be shared and might be stored in a distributed manner.
- Current text-based CP/CPS describe complex objects and complex practices. A formal model must support this complexity. The representation has to support *<attribute, value>* pairs, which might be organized in a hierarchical structure, and where *value* by itself might be a complex object. A wide range of data types must be supported.
- The representation must allow to define a metric and/or classification scheme to support not just equality comparisons, but also additional relational operators.
- The representation must be declarative (opposed to a procedural representation) in order to support operations on this representation.
- Based on the possible uses of a CP/CPS representation described above operations like *projection*, *equality comparison*, and *relational comparison* ought to be possible.

3 Solution-Approach

A two-phased approach was chosen to address this problem. In the first phase a possible semantic representation is investigated, and in the second phase the syntactical representation of the defined semantics is defined.

3.1 Semantic Representation using Description Logics

Based on the identified requirements regarding the possible complexity of the models that must be represented, it appeared natural to use known techniques from the Knowledge Representation community. After reviewing different representation paradigms (procedural, logic-based, frame-based/object-oriented) the decision was taken to use a Description-Logics-based model. Description Logics combine the strengths of a logic model, which is formally well understood, and the object-oriented model, which provides good means of structuring the modeling domain.

Formal Knowledge Representation was first pursued using Semantic Networks and Frames. However, both of these techniques do not provide sufficient formal semantics. KL-ONE [3] tried to add a formal semantics to frames and semantic networks and initiated research in what was subsequently called Description Logics (DL) - or terminological systems. Consequently several systems were devised and studied: KRYPTON [4], NIKL, BACK, LOOM, CLASSIC, KRIS, etc. Hence, capabilities and restrictions of DL-based systems are in the meantime well understood.

Description Logics Overview: A thorough discussion of DL goes beyond the scope of this paper and can be found in others [5], but in order to subsequently describe the case study a very brief overview of the architecture and capabilities is given.

The core of a DL-based system is a *concept language*. The major constructs of this language are *concepts*, *roles*, and *individuals*. *Concepts* are used to represent classes as sets of individuals. *Roles* describe properties (attributes) of concepts in form of binary relations between classes. *Individuals* are instances of classes. From now on *Concepts* and *Classes*, *Individuals* and *Instances* will be used synonymously.

Example: The following DL statement defines the concept FatherOfGirls as the set of individuals that are parents (belongs to the class Parents), are male (belongs to the class Male) and all of whose children are female (the individuals have the property CHILD, and all values of this property are individuals that belong to the class Female).

```
FatherOfGirls ≡ Parent ∩ Male ∩ ∀CHILD.Female
```

It can be seen that the structure of a DL statement is based on first-order logic and a formal semantic of DL statements can be given. The most commonly used connectives in DL are:

Concept definition	$\equiv$
Conjunction	$\cap$
Disjunction	$\cup$
Negation	$\neg$
Universal Quantification	$\forall$
Existential Quantification	$\exists$
Number Restriction	$(<= n), (>= n)$
Enumeration of Individuals	$\{ a_1, a_2, \ldots, a_n \}$

DL Reasoning Services: Besides being able to explicitly define concepts DL provides interesting reasoning services, i.e. new information can automatically be derived from explicit specifications:

- *Concept Satisfyability* - given a concept C and given a set of individuals I, check if there are any individuals that belong to C (based on their described properties).
- *Equivalence Checking* - given two concepts C and D, check whether their descriptions are equivalent.
- *Subsumption* - given two concepts C and D, check if D subsumes C, i.e. if all individuals that belong to C also belong to D (intuitively it could be said that D is a super class of C). Subsumption supports the definition of a partial ordering scheme, where the underlying ordering relationship is Generalization-Specialization.
- *Instance Checking* - given a concept C and an individual I, check if I is an instance of C.

There are additional reasoning services available, but they will not be used in the following paragraphs. Because of the formal foundation of DL these reasoning services also can be formally investigated to verify their correctness and completeness [6].

These reasoning services provide the required means to implement the operations mentioned as requirements previously:

- Equivalence Checking can be used to determine if two descriptions of a CP/CPS are equal
- Subsumption and Instance Checking can be used to determine the relationship of two CP/CPS descriptions.

The strength of the subsumption reasoning service is, that, in contrast to commonly used object-oriented class-definition the super-class/sub-class relationship needs not to be specified manually, but can be derived automatically from the given class definitions and instance descriptions.

A case study that has been performed will show how this can be used on a real CP/CPS.

3.2 Syntactic Representation

Currently an investigation is ongoing to identify means to represent a model in a DL-based language suited to the environment where certificates are used. Currently the focus lies on studying the Resource Description Framework [7] of the W3C.

4 Case Study

To verify the applicability of this approach some CP/CPS have been modeled using an implemented DL-system.

The CP/CPS chosen are

- Certificate Policies for the Government of Canada (GoC) Public Key Infrastructure [8], and
- SEIS Certificate Policy [9]

The GoC PKI Policies actually defines eight different policies - four designed for Digital Signature certificates, and four designed for Confidentiality certificates. These four policies cover different assurance levels: rudimentary, basic, medium, high. In the following examples these policies will be identified with the prefixes `GocSign[1234]` and `GocConf[1234]` respectively.

The reason for choosing these policies was, that both are based on the framework suggested in RFC 2527 - and therefore provide some possibility to make them comparable.

The DL system chosen was NeoClassic [10]. NeoClassic is one of the more widely used DL systems.

First the syntax of NeoClassic is briefly shown. Then the methodology for performing the case study is described and finally some examples are shown and explained.

4.1 NeoClassic

NeoClassic implements the following connectives:

Concept definition	$\equiv$
Conjunction	$\cap$
Universal Quantification	$\forall$
Existential Quantification	$\exists$
Number Restriction	$(<= n), (>= n)$
Enumeration of Individuals	$\{ a_1, a_2, ..., a_n \}$

Syntactically the above DL statement

```
FatherOfGirls ≡ Parent ∩ Male ∩ ∀CHILD.Female
```

is represented as:

```
( createConcept FatherOfGirls
    ( and Parent
          Male
          ( all CHILD Female ) ) )
```


4.2 Methodology

One of the objectives to formally represent a CP/CPS is to make them better comparable. Therefore it is necessary to use a common structure: the same topics have to be described, the same attributes have to be used and the same sets of values have to be used, etc.

Consequently a reference description had to be defined first. This description is based on RFC 2527. It defines concepts and individuals, which can be refined and combined by subsequent CP/CPS descriptions using specialization and the definition of new concepts respectively. These concepts and individuals define a core terminology, which ought to be accepted as a common framework. In practice it will possibly be the case that several of such reference frameworks will be developed and a combination of these frameworks will be possible. This approach is quite similar to the definition of classification schemes in Library Science [11].

During the definition of such frameworks it is also possible to define some primitive taxonomies, which will then support the creation of more complex taxonomies. This will be exemplified further below.

Based on the established reference ontology (RFC 2527) specific CP/CPS (GoC, SEIS) have been modeled.

4.3 Examples

The following examples will show this approach more specifically.

Asymmetric Key Sizes: The first example is rather simple - as it is using the predefined properties of the build-in concept `Integer`.

The core terminology based on RFC 2527 requires to describe the minimal length of the used keys:

```
( createConcept Rfc2527AsymmetricKeySizes
    ( all keyLength Integer ) )
```

Concept `Rfc2527AsymmetricKeySizes` has one role (attribute) named `keyLength`, which is of type/concept `Integer` (a primitive NeoClassic Concept).

The Government of Canada PKI CP/CPS defines the following restrictions on the above concept:

```
( createConcept GocSign1AsymmetricKeySizes
    ( and Rfc2527AsymmetricKeySizes
          ( all keyLength ( minimum  512 ) ) ) )
```

Concept `GocSign1AsymmetricKeySizes` is a sub-class of `Rfc2527AsymmetricKeySizes` with the additional restrictions that all values of the attribute `keyLength` must be greater-equal 512.

```
( createConcept GocSign2AsymmetricKeySizes
    ( and Rfc2527AsymmetricKeySizes
          ( all keyLength ( minimum 1024 ) ) ) )
```

```
( createConcept GocSign3AsymmetricKeySizes
    ( and Rfc2527AsymmetricKeySizes
          ( all keyLength ( minimum 1024 ) ) ) )
```

```
( createConcept GocSign4AsymmetricKeySizes
    ( and Rfc2527AsymmetricKeySizes
          ( all keyLength ( minimum 2048 ) ) ) )
```

The SEIS policy is denoted as:

```
( createConcept SeisAsymmetricKeySizes
    ( and Rfc2527AsymmetricKeySizes
          ( all keyLength ( minimum  1024 ) ) ) )
```

Using the built-in properties of NeoClassic's type `Integer` an ordering scheme is predefined: `Rfc2527AsymmetricKeySizes` defines a class of instances with the attribute `keyLength`, which may take all integers as value; `GocSign1AsymmetricKeySizes` restricts the values to greater equal 512; `GocSign[23]AsymmetricKeySizes` restricts the values to greater equal 1024; `GocSign4AsymmetricKeySizes` restricts the values to greater equal 2048. Because of the properties of `Integer` the application of the subsumption reasoning service results in the following ordering:

− `Rfc2527AsymmetricKeySizes` subsumes `GocSign1AsymmetricKeySizes`

- which in turn subsumes `GocSign[23]AsymmetricKeySizes`
- which in turn subsumes `GocSign4AsymmetricKeySizes`

NeoClassic also automatically finds that

- `GocSign[23]AsymmetricKeySizes` is equivalent to `SeisAsymmetricKeySizes`

If the only requirement would be to compare numeric values the general subsumption mechanism would not be necessary - PICS [12] does something similar. However, not all properties described in a CP/CPS can be represented by numeric values, which can be seen in the next examples.

Activation Actions: Often constructs comparable to object enumeration are required. Enumerations (`oneOf`) do not define any order relationship.

RFC 2527 recommends specifying how a private key can be activated, i.e. accessed by the user:

```
( createConcept Rfc2527MethodOfActivatingPrivateKey
  ( and
    ( all activationAgent   Rfc2527Agents )
    ( all activationActions Rfc2527ActivationActions)
    ( all activationPeriod  Rfc2527ActivationPeriod )))
```

The above concept definition creates a concept with three properties describing who may activate (`agent`), how the activation is done (`action`) and how long the activation may be valid (`period`) with respective types.

An agent can be the *end-entity*, *RA*, *CA*, or the *directory*.

```
( createConcept Rfc2527Agents
    ( oneOf ENDENTITY RA CA DIRECTORY ) )
```

Activation-actions are defined below:

```
( createConcept Rfc2527ActivationActions
    ( oneOf POWER-ON LOGIN INSERT-TOKEN
            PIN AUTOMATIC ) )

( createConcept GocSign2MethodOfActivatingPrivateKey
    ( and Rfc2527MethodOfActivatingPrivateKey
          ( all activationActions ( oneOf PIN ) ) )

( createConcept SeisMethodOfActivatingPrivateKey
    ( and Rfc2527MethodOfActivatingPrivateKey
          ( all activationActions ( oneOf PIN ) ) )
```

NeoClassic would determine that `GocSign2MethodOfActivating-PrivateKey` and `SeisMethodOfActivatingPrivateKey` are equivalent.

Key Pair Generation: In order to support comparison operations it is necessary to define an order relationship amongst newly defined concepts.

Example: a key pair generated in HW might be trust worthier than a key pair generated in SW.

```
( createConcept Rfc2527Hw       Rfc2527ModuleTypes )
( createConcept Rfc2527HwOrSw Rfc2527Hw )
( createConcept Rfc2527Sw       Rfc2527HwOrSw )
```

Above statements define that

- `Rfc2527Hw, Rfc2527HwOrSw, Rfc2527Sw` are sub-classes of `Rfc2527ModuleTypes`
- `Rfc2527Hw` subsumes `Rfc2527HwOrSw`
- `Rfc2527HwOrSw` subsumes `Rfc2527Sw`.

This subsumption relationship can be associated with an interpretation of *Trustworthiness*: module types whose concept descriptions subsume other are trust worthier than the module types associated with the subsumed concepts.

Using this taxonomy `Rfc2527KeyGeneration` can be defined with two attributes: `caKeyGen` and `eeKeyGen`. Both of which require values that belong to the concept/class `Rfc2527ModuleTypes`.

```
( createConcept Rfc2527KeyGeneration
    ( and ( all caKeyGen Rfc2527ModuleTypes )
          ( all eeKeyGen Rfc2527ModuleTypes ) ) )
```

The Government of Canada Policy can be specified as:

```
( createConcept GocSign2KeyGeneration
    ( and Rfc2527KeyGeneration
          ( all caKeyGen Rfc2527HwOrSw )
          ( all eeKeyGen Rfc2527HwOrSw ) ) )

( createConcept GocSign3KeyGeneration
    ( and Rfc2527KeyGeneration
          ( all caKeyGen Rfc2527Hw       )
          ( all eeKeyGen Rfc2527HwOrSw ) ) )

( createConcept GocSign4KeyGeneration
    ( and Rfc2527KeyGeneration
          ( all caKeyGen Rfc2527Hw       )
          ( all eeKeyGen Rfc2527Hw       ) ) )
```

NeoClassic will determine that `GocSign4KeyGeneration` subsumes `GocSign3KeyGeneration`, which subsumes `GocSign2KeyGeneration`. This can then in turn be interpreted in such a way that certificates associated with CP `GocSign4` are more secure than certificates associated with CP `GocSign2`.

The SEIS policy can be described as:

```
( createConcept GocSign2KeyGeneration
    ( and Rfc2527KeyGeneration
          ( all caKeyGen Rfc2527HwOrSw )
          ( all eeKeyGen Rfc2527HwOrSw ) ) )
```

NeoClassic will recognize `GocSign2KeyGeneration` as being equivalent to `GocSign2KeyGeneration`.

5 Summary

In this paper it was shown how techniques from the area of formal knowledge representation could be used to better represent the information contained in Certificate Policies and Certification Practice Statements. It has been discussed how subsumption can be used in order to compare the quality and trustworthiness of certificates.

Performing the case study of modeling different CP/CPS the following observations have been made:

- The definition of a core terminology in form of an ontology is necessary. RFC 2527 actually provides some kind of framework that can be followed to specify such a reference terminology.
- It also became clear that CP/CPS that follow RFC 2527 are difficult to compare because this framework leaves too much room for interpretation and expressing different aspects.
- This shows that users who want to compare the quality of certificates actually do face a major problem, as existing CP/CPS are difficult to compare.

Planned work comprises the specification how a DL-based language like NeoClassic can best be syntactically represented in an environment where certificates are being used.

While performing this work it also became apparent that different domains are using different models to represent authorizations, capabilities, rights, etc. These different representations in turn require domain-specific processing models. It seems promising to study how a DL-based system can be used as a unifying scheme for a generic policy specification.

References

1. Housley, R., Ford, W., Polk, W., Solo, D.: Internet X.509 Public Key Infrastructure: Certificate and CRL Profile, IETF RFC 2459, 1999.
2. Chokhani, S., Ford, W.: Internet X.509 Public Key Infrastructure: Certificate Policy and Certification Practices Framework, IETF RFC 2527 (1999)
3. Brachman, R. J., Schmolze, J. G.: An Overview of the KL-ONE Knowledge Representation System, Cognitive Science 9(2) (1985) 171-216
4. Brachman, R. J., Pigman-Gilbert, V., Levesque, H. J.: An Essential Hybrid Reasoning System: Knowledge and Symbol Level Accounts in KRYPTON, In Proc. of the 9th Int. Joint Conf. on Artificial Intelligence (IJCAI-85) (1985) 532-539
5. Donini, F. M., Lenzerini, M., Nardi, D., Schaerf, A.: Reasoning in Description Logics, CLSI Publications, Principles of Knowledge Representation and Reasoning, (1994) 193-238

6. Borgida, A., Patel-Schneider, P. F.: A Semantics and Complete Algorithm for Subsumption in the CLASSIC Description Logic, Journal of Artificial Intelligence Research 1, (1994) 277-308
7. Lassila, O., Swick, R.: Resource Description Framework (RDF): Model and Syntax Specification, W3C Recommendation, (1999)
8. Treasury Board of Canada, Secretariat: Digital Signature and Confidentiality Certificate Policies for the Government of Canada Public Key Infrastructure", Version 3.02 (1999)
9. Secured Electronic Information in Society: SEIS Certificate Policy SeisS10-1: 1.0, High assurance general ID-certificate with private key protected in an electronic ID-card, Version 1.0 (1998)
10. Brachman, R. J., McGuinness, D. L., Patel-Schneider, P. F., Resnick, L. A., Borgida, A.: Living with CLASSIC: When and How to Use a KL-ONE-Like Language, Ed. John F. Sowa, Principles of Semantic Networks - Explorations in the Representation of Knowledge, Morgan Kaufmann Publishers (1991) 401-456
11. Nabil, A., Yelena, Y.: Strategic Directions in Electronic Commerce and Digital Libraries: Towards a Digital Agora, ACM Computing Surveys, Vol. 28, No. 4 (1996) 818-835
12. Krauskopf, T., Miller, J., Resnick, P., Treese, W.: PICS Label Distribution Label Syntax and Communication Protocols, W3C Recommendation (1996)

Mit Sicherheit Schutz vor dem bekannten Feind

Reinhard Bertram

Siemens Business Services GmbH & Co OHG
Reinhard.Bertram@mch20.sbs.de

Zusammenfassung: Sicherheit im Unternehmen und die Absicherung von unternehmenskritischen Infrastrukturen, Medienströmen und Geschäftsprozessen beginnt primär mit einer Verwurzelung von Sicherheitsaspekten in das Design der Infrastrukturen und die Entwicklung der eingesetzten Protokolle und Applikationen. Es hat sich in der Praxis bewährt, frühzeitig an die potentiellen Einsatzszenarien von Sicherheitsinfrastrukturen, Sicherheitskomponenten, wie beispielsweise Firewalls, und E&M-Business-Anwendungen im laufenden Betrieb in Unternehmen unterschiedlicher Größe zu denken. Hierbei findet man unter Verwendung geeigneter Denkansätze oftmals Schwächen, die sich am "grünen Tisch" nicht offenbaren. Der vorliegende Text gibt solche Denkansätze, allerdings ohne Lösungen aufzuzeigen. Ein motivierter Angreifer wird sich ebenso kreativ verhalten, wie ein von der Praxis der Sicherheit inspirierter Wissenschaftler.

1   Einleitung

Die traditionelle Form der Gefahrenabwehr verwendet häufig die Annahme, dass es Schwachstellen in Informationssystemen gibt, die von Tätern ausgenutzt werden, die unterschiedliche Gründe haben, einem Unternehmen Schaden zuzufügen. Man kann nun versuchen ein Täterprofil zu erstellen, um so das Risiko frühzeitig zu erkennen. Auf dieser Basis werden Mitarbeiter von besonders sicherheitsrelevanten Aufgaben entbunden.

Andererseits ist gerade bei der Gefahrenabwehr nicht unbedingt das Täterprofil ausschlaggebend, um herauszufinden, ob man sich einer Gefahr aussetzt, sondern die mögliche Motivation für einen Angriff. Hierbei geht man davon aus, dass beliebige Täter einen Angriff durchführen können. Im Zusammenspiel mit den Schwachstellen des Informationssystems setzt man sich einer Gefährdung aus, die erst bei fehlenden Schutzmechanismen zum Tragen kommt. Der vorliegende Text geht davon aus, dass eine Gruppe hochmotivierter Angreifer es darauf abgesehen hat, dem Unternehmen Schaden zuzufügen, wobei es unerheblich ist, wer diese Täter tatsächlich sind. Diese Tätergruppe stellt die Gesamtheit aller potentiellen Angreifer dar. Der Schaden, den diese Gruppe zufügen möchte, kann einen Gewinn für einen Täter darstellen. Es gibt dementsprechend nicht nur materielle, sondern auch ideologische Motive.

Versucht man nun das individuelle Risiko zu bewerten, damit man geeignete und optimale - auch im Sinne von kostengünstig - Schutzmaßnahmen einführen kann, so wird oft versucht die Minimierung des Risikos durch finanzielle Größen auszudrücken. Da die Einführung von Schutzmaßnahmen im ersten Schritt meist mit Kosten verbunden ist, die gegenüber den Kaufleuten eines Unternehmens gerechtfertigt werden müssen, wurden Methoden entwickelt, die es erlauben sollen, das Risiko vor und nach der Einführung einer Schutzmaßnahme finanziell zu bewerten. Typische Methoden basieren darauf, dass die Schwachstellen eines Systems ermittelt werden und die Eintrittswahrscheinlichkeit des Ausnutzens dieser Schwachstellen geschätzt wird. Zusammen mit den potentiellen Verlusten beim Eintritt eines Schadensfalles wird versucht das Risiko zu bemessen. Zu diesem Zweck wurden vielfach Risikobewertungs- und managementverfahren entwickelt.

Für die Darstellung der Gefährdung und der damit verbundenen Angriffs- und Abwehrmethoden ist es sinnvoll, davon auszugehen, dass jedes technische, wie auch organisatorische System mit Schwachstellen behaftet ist. Die Problematik bei der Behandlung von Schwachstellen stellt nicht die Existenz der Schwachstellen an sich, sondern vielmehr die Unkenntnis über deren Vorhandensein dar. Diese Unkenntnis wirkt oftmals gepaart mit einem bewussten Vertuschen von Schwachstellen, so dass korrigierende Gegenmaßnahmen oftmals gar nicht eingeleitet werden.

2 Täterprofile

In der Verbrechensaufklärung werden Täterprofile erfolgreich eingesetzt. Hier kennt man meist die Umstände der Tat und kann aus Indizien eine Abfolge nachstellen. Diese spezielle Abfolge oder die Umstände der Tat lassen es zu, dass man versuchen kann, ein Persönlichkeitsprofil möglicher Täter zu erstellen. Diese Methodik ist geeignet, den oder die Täter einer ganz speziellen Tat zu ermitteln. Die Täterprofile dienen dazu den Personenkreis, den man weitergehend befragen muss, einzugrenzen.

Bei der Strafverfolgung ist es hilfreich, dass die Daten möglichst vieler Fälle gemeinsam gesammelt werden, damit sich aus dem Datenbestand Gemeinsamkeiten der Fälle ableiten lassen, die wiederum das Ableiten von Täterprofilen ermöglichen.

Im Falle der Aufklärung von Vorfällen im Umfeld der Informationssicherheit hat sich weder eine umfassende Lehre der Forensik gebildet, um anhand von Indizien die Abfolge von Angriffen nachzustellen, noch lässt sich eine ausreichende Grundgesamtheit an Daten über die Täter zusammentragen. Ersteres begründet sich dadurch, dass Unternehmen, die einem Angriff ausgesetzt waren, diesen selten lückenlos aufdecken und vor allem auch meist nicht aufdecken können. Die Rechte des Unternehmens sind häufig schon innerhalb der Unternehmensgrenzen eingeschränkt, um beispielsweise Protokolle über die Tätigkeit der Mitarbeiter zu führen. In vernetzten Systemen bewegt sich ein Mitarbeiter jedoch nicht mehr physikalisch und hinterlässt dadurch Spuren, sondern er führt seine Tätigkeiten unter Zuhilfenahme von Hardware und Software durch. Diese Hilfsmittel erzeugen von sich aus keine Verknüpfung zwischen der realen Person, die ihnen den Auftrag gab bestimmte Tätigkeiten auszuführen und sich selbst. Der zweite Aspekt begründet sich vor allem darin, dass die Strafverfolgung hoheitlich vom Staat durchgeführt wird, der somit alle Daten zentral sammeln kann. Wem sollte ein Unternehmen Daten über Vorfälle im eigenen Hause geben? Staatsorganen gegenüber tritt es häufig als Auftragnehmer auf, wobei in Verträgen die Informationssicherheit garantiert wird.

Andere Institutionen sind oftmals in nicht bekanntem Verhältnis mit Konkurrenzunternehmen, so dass hier verständlicherweise ein Vorbehalt besteht. Täterprofile lassen sich somit nicht einsetzen zur Aufklärung von Vorfällen im Bereich der Informationssicherheit.

Der Sinn von Täterprofilen bei der Verbrechensbekämpfung liegt in der Verhinderung von Straftaten, zumindest wird versucht sie dazu einzusetzen. Über deren Sinn lässt sich streiten, denn die Grenze zu pauschalisierenden Aussagen über bestimmte Bevölkerungsgruppen ist sehr schnell überschritten. Warnungen, die potentiellen Verbrechensopfern helfen sollen, können sehr schnell zu Hass gegen die Gruppen von potentiellen Tätern führen, und hierdurch diese Gruppen ihrerseits in ihren Persönlichkeitsrechten einschränken.

Trotz dieser Gratwanderung werden pauschale Aussagen über die Einstellung von Personen in bestimmten Positionen oder Tätigkeiten getroffen. Hierbei wird jedoch weniger eine Aussage über eine Bevölkerungsgruppe getroffen, sondern die Gesinnung, die ein Mitglied einer staatsfeindlichen Vereinigung haben muss. Ob diese Gesinnung tatsächlich für diese Einzelperson in der angestrebten Position oder bei der auszuführenden Tätigkeit zum Tragen kommt, ist unerheblich. Hierbei stellt die Maßnahme lediglich eine Schutzmaßnahme dar, die aufgrund der höheren Wahrscheinlichkeit des Missbrauches entgegengebrachten Vertrauens auch begründbar ist. Beispiele für ein solches Vorgehen findet man vorrangig im Rahmen des Staatsschutzes.

Im Sinne der Informationssicherheit hat man es mit derselben Problematik zu tun. Hierbei hat das Unternehmen jedoch ebenso wie bei der Aufklärung von Vorfällen keine gesicherten Daten über Täterprofile. Die Entscheidung gegen die Verwendung von bestimmten Personen an bestimmten Positionen oder bei der Ausführung bestimmter Tätigkeiten ist somit meist stark subjektiv. Man hat einfach ein schlechtes Gefühl dabei einen Mitarbeiter eines Konkurrenzunternehmens als Consultant an Schlüsselprojekten mitarbeiten zu lassen. Dieses Gefühl des Unwohlseins erstreckt sich meist jedoch nicht auf Mitarbeiter des eigenen Unternehmens, die mit einem nahezu unendlichen Vertrauensvorschuss ihre Arbeit beginnen. Wodurch ist dieses Vertrauen gerechtfertigt? Macht allein ein Arbeitsvertrag mit dem Unternehmen einen guten Menschen?

Das Misstrauen sollte trotzdem nicht auf die eigenen Mitarbeiter soweit ausgedehnt werden, dass eine Atmosphäre entsteht, in der niemand mehr arbeiten möchte. Es sollte aber klar geworden sein, dass ein gesundes Misstrauen auch gegenüber den eigenen Mitarbeitern angebracht ist. Heutige Unternehmens- und Arbeitsstrukturen führen zu einer immer schwächeren persönlichen Bindung der Mitarbeiter an das Unternehmen und parallel dazu zu einer verstärkten projektorientierten Kooperation mit Fachabteilungen auch von Konkurrenzunternehmen. Täterprofile für die Informationssicherheit sind somit nur sehr begrenzt einsetzbar.

3   Motivation

Die Ausbildung von Unbehagen beim Einsatz von Mitarbeitern eines Konkurrenzunternehmens hat primär damit zu tun, dass man diesen ein Motiv unterstellt dem eigenen Unternehmen mehr zu dienen als dem, in dem sie gerade tätig sind. Man wurde meist durch Zufall auf diesen Umstand hingewiesen oder aufmerksam.

Die Motivation, einem Unternehmen Schaden zufügen zu wollen, sich persönlichen Vorteil zu verschaffen oder einfach nur zu blockieren kann ganz unterschiedlich sein. Ganz unterschiedlich sind aber auch die Abwehrmaßnahmen gegen Angriffe, die mit gleicher Methodik, aber mit unterschiedlicher Motivation, durchgeführt werden. Eine somit die Methodik beleuchtende Sichtweise wird helfen zu verstehen, wie die potentiellen Täter aufgrund unterschiedlicher Motivation vorgehen und welche Abwehrmaßnahmen geeignet sind.

Die Wahrscheinlichkeit eines Angriffes Motivation ist für jedes Unternehmen oder sogar für jede Abteilung anders zu bewerten. Ohne Berücksichtigung der Motivation eines potentiellen Angreifers wird man die Gefährdung nur unzureichend erfassen. Als Schaden soll nicht nur der direkte Verlust von Finanzen verstanden werden, sondern auch entgangene Aufträge, Reputation, die Verlangsamung eines Entwicklungsprozesses oder die Vorteilsnahme eines Mitbewerbers.

Der Schaden, der dem Unternehmen zugefügt wird, lässt sich nur sehr begrenzt direkt messen und wird sehr oft auf Schätzungen angewiesen sein. Diese Schätzungen oder oftmals auch nur Einschätzungen basieren häufig auf der individuellen Bewertung von Einzelpersonen, die stark unterschiedlich ausfallen kann. Alle Versuche, objektive Verfahren zur Bewertung zu entwickeln sind entweder in einer Detailverliebtheit nicht mehr handhabbar geworden oder so global, dass man sie getrost als „Pi -mal-Daumen" Ansätze bezeichnen kann.

4   Technische Systeme

Jedes Unternehmen ist heutzutage abhängig von der Informationstechnik und ein steigender Anteil der Geschäftsprozesse sind nur mit Mitteln der Informationstechnik möglich. Gerade im Umfeld E-Commerce zeichnet sich ein Trend hin zu Geschäftsprozessen ab, die nicht durch traditionelle Methoden ersetzt werden könnten. Somit haben wir auf der einen Seite eine permanente Abhängigkeit von Systemen und auf der anderen Seite die stetige Einführung neuer Systeme, die Altes besser können oder gar komplett ersetzen.

Unternehmen sind häufig von Kernverfahren abhängig, mit denen sie ihre wesentlichen Geschäftsprozesse abgebildet haben. Diese Kernverfahren sind wesentlich schwieriger zu ersetzen, sobald sie einmal stabil laufen. Da hierbei auch häufig riesige Datenmengen bewegt werden, ist die Ablösung eines solchen Verfahrens auch eine Frage der Kosten für die Infrastruktur. Innovationen werden ständig schneller durch die Anwender gefordert und eingeführt, wobei die Systeme immer komplexer werden. Je kleiner die Kosten und je geringer der Aufwand für die Einführung neuer Technologien, desto eher wird es irgendwo im Unternehmen jemanden geben, der die neue Technologie ausprobieren und einsetzen will. Für den Fortschritt ist dies positiv. Wie sehr überschaut aber der Einsetzende die Schnittstellen zu unternehmensweit eingesetzten Verfahren? Wie sehr überschaut der Einsetzende die Gefährdung, die durch die Einführung dieser Technologie für das Gesamtunternehmen entstehen kann?

Diese Bedenken sind nicht in jedem Falle gerechtfertigt, denn neue Technologien werden in vielerlei Hinsicht auch den Bestand des Unternehmens sichern helfen. Kein Unternehmen kann sich technischem Fortschritt verschließen und neue Technologien unterstützen häufig sogar Funktionalitäten, die mit den eingeführten Verfahren gar nicht möglich wären. Die Einführung dieser Funktionalitäten bedingt einen Migrationspfad, der es oftmals notwendig macht, auf die neuen Funktionen, bis zur vollständigen Abschaltung der alten Verfahren, zu verzichten.

Es werden Entscheidungen notwendig, die naturgemäß nur für die Randbedingungen des Augenblicks der Entscheidung gültig sind. Die Dynamik, mit der sich auch diese Randbedingungen ändern, steigt auch ständig. Neben den bisher angesprochenen Problemen beim Umgang mit technischen Systemen ist ein typisch menschliches Verhalten zu beobachten. Wir können nur eine begrenzte Anzahl an Parametern beurteilen und kontrollieren. Dies führt dazu, dass wir versuchen die komplexe Welt auf ein Modell abzubilden, das für uns plausibel und real erscheint. Dabei vergessen wir jedoch sehr häufig, dass wir nur einen Teil des Gesamtsystems überschauen und somit das Modell nur unvollständig sein kann. Es ist Zufall, wenn die intransparenten Teile der Realität in unserem Modell aufgenommen wurden. Aufgrund dieses unvollständigen Modells bauen wir jedoch Hypothesen auf, die das dynamische Verhalten des Modells beschreiben sollen. Wir haben es somit mit vielen Fehlerquellen beim Umgang mit komplexen technischen Systemen zu tun.

Die Abwehr und die Minimierung von Risiken wird sich nicht bewerkstelligen lassen, wenn die Handelnden davon ausgehen, dass ihre Aktionen alleine dazu beitragen. Die Transparenz des Informationssystems ist eine Eigenschaft, die jedem Beteiligten - aktiv oder passiv - hilft kontrolliert zu handeln und behutsam vorzugehen. Verständnis über die Tätigkeit der Anderen erlaubt es Fehlverhalten zu erkennen und frühzeitig einzugreifen. Übermäßige Komplexität sollte nicht zu einer Vereinfachung des Modells, sondern zu einer Vereinfachung der Realität führen. Verständnis über die Zusammenhänge führt selbständig zu geeigneten Abwehrstrategien.

5 Informationen

Bis zur vorindustriellen Zeit, als unsere Gesellschaft größtenteils auf die Agrarwirtschaft ausgerichtet war, wurde Reichtum verbunden mit Landbesitz. Nach der industriellen Revolution wurde Wohlstand über den Besitz an den Produktionsmitteln, wie die Marxisten Fabriken und die entsprechenden Maschinen nannten, definiert. Jetzt, in der postindustriellen Gesellschaft bedeutet der Besitz von Wissen wahren Reichtum. Die Aussage „Wir leben in einer Informationsgesellschaft" gilt vor allem in der Zeit des Umbruchs zum 21. Jahrhundert. Sind Informationen für die Gesellschaft wichtig, so gilt das für Unternehmen um so mehr, denn der geschäftliche Erfolg heutiger Unternehmen hängt zunehmend von der Verfügbarkeit relevanter Informationen ab. Sie stellen die Basis dar für Geschäftsprozesse und Geschäftsentscheidungen. Bei der Abbildung von Geschäftsprozessen auf IT Infrastrukturen wird die Performance der zugrundeliegenden Netze und informationsverarbeitenden Systeme zunehmend unternehmenskritisch und entscheidend für den zukünftigen Geschäftserfolg. Eine neue Klasse von Consultingunternehmen beschäftigt sich mit dem Thema Infrastrukturarchitektur, um diese Anforderungen zu adressieren.

Die Korrektheit der Information ist weiterhin ein notwendiges Kriterium, um keine Fehlentscheidungen allein aufgrund mangelhafter Informationen zu fällen. Ganze Geschäftszweige beschäftigen sich ausschließlich mit der Informationsbeschaffung und -verteilung. Die geschäftsentscheidenden Informationen sind jedoch auch für Wettbewerber von Bedeutung. Unternehmen sind folglich darauf bedacht, möglichst viele Informationen zu erhalten, aber eigene Informationen nur kontrolliert und gezielt preiszugeben. Das Unternehmen befindet sich somit in der Zwickmühle, dass es gerne alles über die Randbedingungen seines wirtschaftlichen Schaffens wissen, aber diese Informationen und das eigene Know-How vertraulich halten möchte.

Beim Schutz von Informationen denkt man primär an den Schutz der Vertraulichkeit der Information. Dieses Kriterium ist mit Abstand am schwersten zu erfüllen, denn der Information ist ein Verlust der Vertraulichkeit nicht anzusehen - man hat keine Messgrößen, allenfalls ein paar Indikatoren. Wenn Informationen im Unternehmen zirkulieren, die eigentlich vertraulich gehalten werden sollten, Medien über Firmenentscheidungen berichten, bevor sie veröffentlicht wurden oder gar Konkurrenten in ihren Angeboten immer gerade so viel niedriger anbieten, wie es für den Zuschlag nötig ist, dann hält man damit entsprechende Indikatoren für einen Verlust der Vertraulichkeit in den Händen. Ursache und Art der Offenlegung bleiben dabei aber völlig verborgen. Auch kann man nicht davon ausgehen, dass man einen solchen Vertraulichkeitsverlust immer und vor allem schnell nach dem Vorfall mittels solcher Indikatoren bemerken wird. Dennoch ist es für Unternehmen wichtig, wenngleich nicht allgemein üblich, die Medien und das Verhalten der Konkurrenz nach solchen Indikatoren zu beobachten.

Wesentlich einfacher ist die Verfügbarkeit von Informationen zu gewährleisten oder zumindest der Dienste, welche die Informationen bereit stellen. Will man sich dann auch noch auf die Korrektheit der Informationen verlassen, so ist das entsprechende Kriterium die Integrität.

Diese drei Sicherheitskriterien - Verfügbarkeit, Integrität und Vertraulichkeit - lassen sich direkt den Informationen zuordnen. Man kann eine Verletzung dieser Sicherheitskriterien unabhängig von der Art und Weise der Speicherung oder Verarbeitung anhand von Merkmalen definieren. Diese Merkmale stellen somit ein Schutzprofil für diese Information dar, mit dem wir uns weiter unten befassen werden.

Diese Sicherheitskriterien müssen erweitert werden, wenn man bestimmte Hantierungsvorschriften für die Information fordert. Diese können beispielsweise die Art und Weise beinhalten, wie eine Unterschrift unter einem Vertrag beglaubigt werden muss, damit dieser rechtsgültig wird. Die Unterschrift wird somit verbindlich. Die Verbindlichkeit als Kriterium wird von uns immer dann verwendet, sobald wir uns mit dem Informationsfluss innerhalb von Geschäftsprozessen befassen. Ein Prozess ist dabei eine definierte und zielgerichtete Abfolge von Handlungen. Somit ist die korrekte Ausführung der Handlungen ein Qualitätsmerkmal für den Prozess. Die Verbindlichkeit der Tätigkeiten der Handelnden ist hier das entscheidende Sicherheitskriterium, welches vor allem im Umfeld E-Commerce/E-Business eine wesentliche Rolle spielt.

Bei den bisherigen Betrachtungen wurde außer acht gelassen, dass einzelne Informationen oder Prozesse ganz unterschiedlich hinsichtlich ihres Schutzbedarfes eingeschätzt werden. Dies liegt zum einen am Fehlen von objektiven Kriterien für die Ermittlung des Schutzbedarfes und zum Anderen an der unterschiedlichen Bewertung der „Wichtigkeit" der Informationen. Je nach Einbindung in den jeweiligen Geschäftsprozess wird derjenige, der zu beurteilen hat, ob die Information nun besonders zeitkritisch, korrekt oder vertraulich zu behandeln ist, aus seinem eigenen Erfahrungshintergrund zu anderen Ergebnissen kommen. Die Einordnung der Information in Schutzklassen, wird traditionell von verschiedenen Ansätzen im Bereich der Risikoanalyse vorgenommen.

Informationen sind häufig für sich alleine belanglos. Erst durch die Zusammenführung durch Aggregation und logische Schlüsse werden Teilinformationen wertvoll. Hier zeigt sich die Stärke von Management-Informations-Systemen, die genau dieses zum Ziel haben, aber auch die Gefahr, die entsteht, wenn unterschiedliche Informationen durch Angreifer zu einem Puzzle zusammengesetzt werden. Der Gelegenheitsangreifer oder ein neugieriger Mitarbeiter wird mittels eines Webbrowser leicht in die Lage versetzt im Intranet eines Unternehmens nach Informationen zu suchen, die zusammengesetzt ein umfassendes und detailliertes Bild ergeben. Bei weiterer Verwendung von externen Quellen lässt sich ein Angriff auf die Nervenstränge des Unternehmens leicht planen und durchführen. Hierbei besteht nahezu keine Gefahr des Entdecktwerdens.

Jedes Unternehmen bildet heutzutage seine Geschäftsprozesse auf einer IT Infrastruktur ab und viele Unternehmen sind gerade dabei den Schritt zum Electronic Business zu vollziehen. Das hierbei zugrundeliegende Modell sieht IT nicht mehr als unterstützend für Geschäftsprozesse an, sondern als deren elementaren Bestandteil. Es stellt sich die Frage, ob die Geschäftsprozesse überhaupt ablauffähig bleiben, wenn Teile des Informationssystems ausfallen. Somit gewinnt die Frage nach der Verfügbarkeit oder allgemein dem Schutz der IT Infrastruktur immer stärkere Bedeutung. Angriffe auf die kritischen Komponenten können über Gedeih und Verderb eines Unternehmens entscheiden.

Es stellt sich die Frage, ob allein die Kenntnis über die Struktur der IT Infrastruktur eine Bedrohung darstellt und ob diese Informationen schützenswert sind. Hierbei kann man schnell in die Diskussion einsteigen, ob Open Source Software besser ist oder warum es sinnvoll ist im Kriegsfall zu wissen, wo der Feind steht und welche Ausrüstung er hat. Beides hat seine Berechtigung und im Hinblick auf fehlerfreie Software ist es sicherlich sinnvoll viele Leute über den Source Code schauen zu lassen und im Hinblick auf eine Verteidigung ist es sicherlich sinnvoll, den Feind nicht über alle Schritte zu informieren.

Aus dieser Betrachtungsweise ergibt sich auch die Forderung, dass es sinnvoll ist, Informationssysteme einzusetzen, die möglichst fehlerfrei sind, beziehungsweise deren Komponenten möglichst fehlerfrei sind. Über die Verwendung dieser Komponenten im Zusammenspiel als IT Infrastruktur ist es dagegen sinnvoll dieses Know-How für sich zu behalten.

Potentielle Angreifer haben jedoch ein Interesse möglichst viel über die Infrastruktur zu erfahren, um potentielle Schwachstellen und Angriffspunkte zu finden, die für sie ein geringes Risiko des Entdecktwerdens oder die Möglichkeit einer möglichst breiten Öffentlichkeit bieten.

Bei Betriebsbesichtigungen von Produktionsbetrieben und Forschungseinrichtungen ist es eine altbekannte Tatsache, dass nicht die allerneueste Technologie gezeigt wird. Fachleute erkennen allein aus der Maschinenausstattung, welche Werkstücke bearbeitet werden können. Die Betriebsbesichtigung liefert somit Rückschlüsse auf das Potential und die Grenzen des Betriebes. Überträgt man dieses Wissen auf die Informationstechnologie, so wird schnell klar, dass allein aufgrund der Kenntnis über eingesetzte Softwareprodukte im Hause eine Einschätzung über die Möglichkeiten des Unternehmens getroffen werden kann. Die Möglichkeiten sind nicht nur in Analogie zum verarbeitenden Gewerbe hinsichtlich der Bearbeitbarkeit von Werkstücken zu sehen, sondern geht darüber wesentlich hinaus. Eine Einschätzung kann und wird sich hinsichtlich der potentiellen Angriffsziele, der Abwehrmechanismen, der Zukunftsausrichtung, der Abhängigkeit von bestimmten Herstellern usw. ausprägen. Aktuelle Trends gehen dazu über das eingesetzte Softwareportfolio eines Unternehmens auf wenige strategisch wichtige Produkte zu reduzieren. Dies bietet neben weiteren Vorteilen eine erheblich bessere Verhandlungsposition gegenüber dem Anbieter und reduzierte Wartungskosten für unterschiedliche Produkte. Auf der anderen Seite wird das Unternehmen allein dadurch angreifbar, dass potentielle Schwachstellen der eingesetzten Produkte flächendeckend zum Tragen kommen und somit ein Totalausfall der IT-Infrastruktur wahrscheinlicher wird. Vergleichbar mit der Agrarwirtschaft ist ein Schädlingsbefall, hier beispielsweise mit Computerviren, wesentlich einfacher einzudämmen, wenn keine Monokultur herrscht. Wir können und wollen hier keine Lanze für eine möglichst heterogene oder homogene Landschaft bei der eingesetzten Hard- und Software eines Unternehmens brechen. Eine Entscheidung wird sich nur für den Einzelfall treffen lassen.

Auf der Gegenseite benötigt auch ein potentieller Angreifer Informationen über aktuelle Angriffstools und Angriffsmethoden. Nur wenige der bekannt gewordenen Angriffe auf Unternehmensnetze gehen auf das Konto von Elitehackern, sondern es ist vermehrt der Typus des „Script-Kiddies" zu beobachten, der sich vorgefertigte Tools aus dem Internet besorgt und diese beim Angriff auf das Zielnetz einsetzt. Abhängig vom Erkenntnisstand des Angreifers werden diese Tools vorsichtig und mit Bedacht oder blind eingesetzt. Letzteres führt typischerweise zu einem

Entdecktwerden und ist somit meist nicht weiter tragisch. Wesentlich kritischer anzusehen ist es jedoch, wenn der Angreifer eine sorgfältige Recherche über die Tools, Methoden, Verfahren und IT-Infrastruktur des anzugreifenden Unternehmens durchgeführt hat. Dies erlaubt einen zielgerichteten Angriff, der meist nicht entdeckt wird.

6 Mythen

Bei heutiger Betrachtung der Stellung der Informationssicherheit im Unternehmen, kommt man schnell zu dem Schluss, dass Entscheider in vielfältiger Weise Mythen anhängen, die kontraproduktiv für die Sicherstellung der Geschäftsinteressen des Unternehmens sind. Zusammengestellt wurde eine solche Liste von Mythen 1998 durch „Economist Intelligence Unit Limited" und „Arthur Andersen". Im wesentlichen hängen Entscheider der Idee anheim, dass allein durch die Durchführung „einer" Aktion die Informationssicherheit wesentlich verbessert wird oder aber dass es gar nicht nötig sei, Informationssicherheit über das eingebaute Maß der eingesetzten Technologien hinaus voran zu treiben. Schaut man sich die heutige Herangehensweise an Informationssicherheit genauer an, so erkennt man, dass trotz eines theoretisch übergreifenden Ansatzes in der Praxis sehr schnell eine Fokussierung auf Details erfolgt. Wir haben es hier typischerweise mit dem Problem der Komplexität des Gesamtsystems zu tun, dass von den Handelnden in ihrem eigenen Modell heruntergebrochen wird auf einfacher zu verstehende Modelle. Informationssicherheit im Unternehmen findet heute noch sehr unkoordiniert statt und setzt an Punkten an, die alle für sich sinnvoll sind, aber alleine wirkungslos oder sogar kontraproduktiv sind. Somit sind die folgenden Mythen Beispiele für eine solche vereinfachende Modellbildung.

- Sicherheit dreht sich um den Schutz meiner Güter
- Sicherheit gehört nicht zur Unternehmensstrategie
- Technik wird das Sicherheitsproblem schon lösen
- Bei uns gibt es keine schützenswerten Informationen
- Der Feind ist draußen
- Firewalls sorgen für eine ausreichende Sicherheit
- Mein PC ist sicher, also bin ich sicher
- Im Internet kann nicht sicher kommuniziert werden
- Die eingebaute Sicherheit reicht aus
- Niemand wird Sicherheitsmaßnahmen tolerieren
- Sicherheitsprobleme hatten wir noch nie

7 PDC Modell

Ein altes Sprichwort besagt: „Vorbeugen ist besser als heilen." Diese Lebensweisheit lässt sich direkt auf die Belange der Informationstechnologie abbilden. Gegen Gefahren, die vorhergesehen wurden, kann man entsprechende Gegenmaßnahmen einleiten oder zumindest sich der Gefahr bewusst sein. In letzterem Fall ist es notwendig, ständig auf Warnsignale zu achten, die auf eine akute Gefahr oder einen Angriff schließen lassen. Ist es schließlich trotz aller Vorsichtsmaßnahmen oder aufgrund fehlender Beachtung der Gefährdung zu einem Vorfall gekommen, so bleibt nichts weiter übrig, als die Scherben aufzusammeln und hoffentlich den Neuaufbau unter erhöhten Sicherheitsvorkehrungen durchzuführen. Diesen Zyklus: Vorbeugen, Erkennen, Korrigieren kann man entsprechend der englischsprachigen Übersetzung als PDC-Modell bezeichnen: **Preventive, Detective, Corrective**.

Dieses Modell spiegelt auch eine Wertigkeit der Maßnahmen wider. Vorbeugende Maßnahmen sind nahezu immer kostengünstiger auf den Lebenszyklus gerechnet, als Korrigierende. So hat es sich gezeigt, dass ein Einbeziehen von Informationssicherheit in die Design-Phase der Softwareentwicklung und bei Betriebskonzepten erhebliche Vorteile hinsichtlich der Transparenz der Lösung und somit auch der späteren Handhabung bietet. Bewusst ausgeklammert wurde hier die Kostenersparnis aufgrund des Wegfalls von Korrekturen am Konzept oder der Lösung. Eine Lösung, die ohne Einbeziehung der Informationssicherheit in der Design-Phase entwickelt wurde, muss nicht zwangsläufig unsicher sein, die Wahrscheinlichkeit, dass sie es ist, steigt aber.

8 Sicherheit im Unternehmen

Verbindet man nun die bisher getroffenen Aussagen, so wird offenkundig, dass eine Einbeziehung des Betriebs und der laufenden Wartung sowie auch die potentielle Ablösung und Migration zu neuen Technologien für einen erfolgreichen Einsatz von Sicherheitskomponenten und -infrastrukturen im Unternehmen unabdingbar ist. Es ist somit sinnvoll auch eine Kombination der unterschiedlichen Ansätze zur Informationssicherheit anzustreben, die im folgenden kurz erläutert werden:

- **Grundschutz und Basissicherheit:** Hierbei wird für versucht, jede Komponente einer IT-Infrastruktur zu identifizieren, um dann ein getrenntes Sicherheitskonzept für diese zu erarbeiten.

- **Maßnahmenbasierte Sicherheit:** Entgegen der recht abstrakten Aufspaltung in Komponenten wird hierbei ein System als Ganzes betrachtet und Maßnahmen (Controls) definiert, die das System sicher gegenüber bekannten Angriffen machen. Die maßnahmenbasierte Sicherheit definiert somit Maßnahmen, die gegen unterschiedliche Schwachstellen und Gefährdungen wirken.

- **Gefährdungsbasierte Sicherheit:** Ein System kann oftmals auf sehr unterschiedliche Weise angegriffen werden. Die Gefährdung steigt, wenn nicht entsprechende Maßnahmen unternommen wurden. Die gefährdungsbasierte

Sicherheit listet dementsprechend zu jeder Schwachstelle eine mögliche Maßnahme auf.

- **Motivationsbasierte Sicherheit:** Da ein System auch aus den Anwendern und den Betreibern, Administratoren usw. besteht, versucht die motivationsbasierte Sicherheit das kreative Verhalten potentieller Angreifer nachzustellen und hierüber Einsichten in das Gesamtsystem zu gewinnen.

Sicherheit im Unternehmen beginnt primär mit der Daumenregel, dass einfache Dinge einfacher zu beherrschen sind. Je überschaubarer ein Teilsystem für die jeweiligen Administratoren bleibt, desto einfacher wird sich auch die Sicherheit für das Gesamtsystem realisieren lassen, das sich aus diesen Teilsystemen zusammensetzt. Schnittstellen und Überschaubarkeit, klares Design und intuitive Bedienbarkeit, Change Management und Kontrolle bilden auch in der Zukunft die Basis für Sicherheit im Unternehmen. Der Faktor Mensch in IT-Systemen ist und bleibt nicht zu unterschätzen.

Literatur

1. D. Dörner. Die Logik des Mißlingens - Strategisches Denken in komplexen Situationen. Rowohlt Verlag GmbH, 1998
2. AA/EIU MBRIA: Ten Myths about Information Technology Security - Managing Business Risks in the Information Age. The Economist Intelligence Unit Limited and Arthur Andersen, 1998
3. BSI IT Grundschutzhandbuch 1999 - Maßnahmenempfehlungen für den mittleren Schutzbedarf. Bundesamt für Sicherheit in der Informationstechnik, 1999
4. P. Cunningham, F. Fröschl. Electronic Business Revolution - Opportunities and Challenges in the 21st Century. Springer Verlag, 1999
5. S. Fischer, A. Steinacker, R. Bertram, R. Steinmetz, OpenSecurity, Springer Verlag, 1998
6. J. Voßbein, Integrierte Sicherheitskonzepte für Unternehmen. SecuMedia Verlag, 1999
7. S. McClure, J. Scambray, G. Kurtz. Hacking Exposed. Osborne/McGraw-Hill, 1999
8. L. McCarthy. Intranet Security - stories from the trenches. Sun Microsystems, 1998
9. Anonymous. Maximum Security, Sams Publishing, 1998
10. D. R. Zweck. Wie-werde-ich-Hacker - HOWTO. Http:// koeln.ccc.de/texte/hacker-werden.html, 1999

Teil II

Sicherheit in Medienströmen

Aspekte der Sicherheit multimedialer Daten und Anwendungen mittels Kryptographie und digitaler Wasserzeichentechniken

Jana Dittmann[1], Petra Wohlmacher[2]

[1] GMD-IPSI
D-64293 Darmstadt, Dolivostraße 15
`jana.dittmann@gmd.de`

[2] Universität Klagenfurt, Institute für Informatik – Systemsicherheit
A-9020 Klagenfurt, Villacher Straße 161
`petra.wohlmacher@uni-klu.ac.at`

Zusammenfassung. Der folgende Beitrag beschreibt die wichtigsten Sicherheitsanforderungen, die heutige Multimediasysteme und Multimediaanwendungen erfüllen müssen. Neben den Sicherheitsanforderungen, die an IT-Systeme im Allgemeinen gestellt werden, müssen für Multimediasysteme weitere Anforderung definiert werden, die sich durch die besondere Beschaffenheit und Komplexität der Mediendaten aber auch der Anwendungen ergeben. Zur Erfüllung der Anforderungen werden Sicherheitsmechanismen auf Basis der beiden kryptographischen Mechanismen Verschlüsselung und digitale Signatur und des steganographischen Mechanismus der digitalen Wasserzeichen diskutiert. Nach einer Einführung in ihre Grundlagen werden die Verfahrensparameter der digitalen Wasserzeichen beschrieben. Auf der Basis der in der Praxis und Literatur vorzufindenden Wasserzeichenverfahren wird ein Klassifikationsschema für Wasserzeichen vorgestellt, das es ermöglicht, eine Unterteilung der verschiedenen Verfahren nach Anwendungsgebiet und Verfahrensparameter vorzunehmen. Darüber hinaus werden Angriffe auf digitale Wasserzeichenverfahren klassifiziert und Qualitätsparameter für Wasserzeichen definiert.

1 Einführung

Durch die außerordentliche Leistungsfähigkeit heutiger IT-Systeme werden Anwendungen zunehmend multimedial gestaltet. Digitale Medien haben dadurch in den letzten Jahren ein gewaltiges Wachstum erfahren und sind dabei, die analogen Medien sukzessive abzulösen. Zu diesen digitalen Medien zählen Texte, Bilder, Video, Audio und 3D-Modelle, insbesondere aber auch deren Kombinationen.

Wie bei IT-Systemen im Allgemeinen so ist auch bei Multimediasystemen zu berücksichtigen, dass sie einer Reihe von Bedrohungen ausgesetzt sind, die ihre Zuverlässigkeit und Vertrauenswürdigkeit gefährden können. Aufgrund der Komplexität von Multimediadaten und ihrer Anwendungen ergeben sich jedoch auch Anforderungen an die Sicherheit, die über die bekannten, an IT-Systeme gestellten Sicherheitsanforderungen hinausgehen. Dies gilt insbesondere für monetäre und sicherheitsrelevante Multimediaanwendungen sowie für multimediale Anwendungen, in denen personenbezogene Daten verarbeitet werden.

Der Beitrag gliedert sich wie folgt. In Kapitel 2 werden zunächst Bedrohungen und Anforderungen an IT-Systeme im Allgemeinen und an Multimediasysteme im Speziellen sowie die sich daraus ableitenden Sicherheitsmaßnahmen und Sicherheitsmechanismen vorgestellt. In Kapitel 3 werden einführend kryptographische Mechanismen erklärt. Exemplarisch für kryptographische Sicherheitsmechanismen werden die Verschlüsselung und die digitale Signatur beschrieben. Es wird dargelegt, warum diese Mechanismen nicht in einfacher Weise für den Bereich Multimedia eingesetzt werden können. In Kapitel 4 werden die Grundlagen der digitalen Wasserzeichen beschrieben und die verschiedenen Arten an Wasserzeichen klassifiziert. Darüber hinaus wird aufgezeigt, welche Sicherheitsanforderungen von Wasserzeichen erfüllt werden können. Die Arbeit schließt mit einer Zusammenfassung und einem Ausblick.

2 Bedrohungen, Anforderungen und Mechanismen

Um die Vertrauenswürdigkeit von IT-Systemen im Allgemeinen messbar und damit vergleichbar zu machen, wurden in vielen Ländern Kataloge für Sicherheitskriterien erarbeitet [1], [2], [3], [4], [5]. Beispielhaft sei der europaweit geltende ITSEC-Kriterienkatalog [2] erwähnt, der Kriterien zur Evaluierung der Sicherheit von IT-Systemen beinhaltet. Er definiert Sicherheitskriterien in unterschiedlichen Stufen zu den folgenden drei grundsätzlichen Bedrohungen:

- Bedrohung der Vertraulichkeit (unbefugte Preisgabe von Informationen),
- Bedrohung der Integrität (unbefugte Veränderung von Daten),
- Bedrohung der Verfügbarkeit (unbefugte Vorenthaltung von Informationen oder Betriebsmitteln).

Aus diesen Bedrohungen leiten sich Anforderungen an die Sicherheit heutiger IT-Systeme ab, die mittels Sicherheitsmaßnahmen und Sicherheitsmechanismen erfüllt werden müssen. Im Wesentlichen werden dabei an die Systeme die folgenden Sicherheitsanforderungen gestellt, die mit den angegebenen kryptographischen Sicherheitsmechanismen erbracht werden können:

- Vertraulichkeit (Confidentiality): Informationen sollen nur den dazu berechtigten Parteien (dies können Personen oder auch Geräte sein) zur Verfügung stehen. Um die Informationen gegenüber Unbefugten geheim zu halten, können Verschlüsselungsverfahren eingesetzt werden.

- Integrität von Daten (Data Integrity): Es soll sichergestellt werden, dass Daten nicht unautorisiert geändert wurden. Unbefugte Änderungen an den Daten können mittels One-Way-Hashfunktionen, Message Authentication Codes und digitaler Signaturen erkannt werden.

- Verfügbarkeit (Availability): Informationen oder Betriebsmittel sollen bestimmten Parteien bei Bedarf zur Verfügung stehen. Um die unbefugte Vorenthaltung von Informationen oder Betriebsmitteln zu verhindern, können entsprechende Mechanismen beispielsweise redundante Systeme [6] eingesetzt werden, die jedoch nicht der Kryptographie zugeordnet werden.

- Authentizität (Authenticity): Sowohl Daten als auch Parteien, die miteinander kommunizieren, sollen auf ihre Echtheit hin geprüft werden können. Man unterscheidet dementsprechend zwischen der Authentizität des Datenursprungs (Data Origin Authenticity), die auch die Integrität der Daten beinhaltet, und der Authentizität der Parteien (Entity Authenticity). Um die Echtheit von Daten sicher zu stellen, können Message Authentication Codes und digitale Signaturen eingesetzt werden. Mittels Authentifizierungsverfahren (auch: Authentifizierungsprotokollen) kann nachgewiesen werden, dass die miteinander kommunizierenden Parteien die sind, für die sie sich ausgeben (Nachweis der Identität).
- Nichtabstreitbarkeit (Non-Repudiation): Mit Nichtabstreitbarkeitsmechanismen soll gegenüber Beteiligten und Unbeteiligten bewiesen werden, ob ein bestimmtes Ereignis eingetreten ist bzw. eine bestimmte Aktion ausgeführt wurde oder nicht. Das Ereignis oder die Aktion kann dabei das Erzeugen, das Übermitteln, die Entgegennahme oder das Vorlegen einer Nachricht sein. Non-Repudiation-Zertifikate, -Tokens und -Protokolle ermöglichen die Verbindlichkeit von Daten. Die verwendeten Mechanismen basieren auf Message Authentication Codes oder digitalen Signaturen in Verbindung mit den Diensten Notary Services, Timestamping Services und Evidence Recording.

Betrachtet man Multimediasysteme, so ist ihr Gesamtspektrum an Sicherheitsanforderungen mit den bereits genannten Anforderungen noch nicht abgedeckt. Bei der Verarbeitung von Mediendaten gewinnt der Schutz von Urheberrechten zusätzlich an Bedeutung. Da digitale Daten ohne Qualitätsverlust kopiert und mit digitaler Bildverarbeitung beliebig verändert werden können ohne Spuren zu hinterlassen, ist demnach die folgende weitere wichtige Bedrohung zu nennen:

- Bedrohung der Originalität (unbefugtes Erzeugen von Duplikaten).

Für digitale Mediendaten ergibt sich somit eine wichtige Sicherheitsanforderung:

- Die Gewährleistung von Authentizität der Daten im Sinne der Originalität: Es soll sichergestellt werden, dass die Daten unverändert und nicht in einer Kopie vorliegen. Die Identität des Besitzers oder Senders muss garantiert werden können, beispielsweise für die Durchsetzung von Urheberrechten. Hier können Wasserzeichenverfahren eingesetzt werden.

Darüber hinaus müssen auch die Aspekte der Veränderungen von Mediendaten berücksichtigt werden. Bei Multimediadatenformaten kann sich die Syntax (der Bitstrom) verändern, ohne dass dadurch die Semantik beeinflusst wird – sei es beispielsweise durch Übertragungsfehler, Kompression oder Skalierung. Hier ist es erforderlich, dass statt der Syntax der Daten vielmehr ihre Semantik gesichert wird. Die sich ergebende Bedrohung ist demnach gegen die Integrität gerichtet und führt zur Sicherheitsanforderung:

- Nachweis der Integrität der Daten im Sinne der Semantik: Um unerlaubte Manipulationen zu erkennen, können inhaltsbasierte Signaturen oder ebenfalls Wasserzeichenverfahren verwendet werden.

3 Kryptographische Mechanismen

Die wichtigsten kryptographischen Mechanismen werden mit Hilfe von Kryptosystemen realisiert. Kryptosysteme bestehen aus zwei Mengen an Funktionen, einer Menge an Schlüsseln, durch die diese Funktionen parametrisiert werden, und aus Mengen, auf denen diese Funktionen operieren. Man unterscheidet zwischen symmetrischen Kryptosystemen (oder Private-Key-Kryptosystemen) und asymmetrischen Kryptosystemen (oder Public-Key-Kryptosystemen).

Bei einem symmetrischen Kryptosystem besitzen die jeweils miteinander kommunizierenden Parteien den gleichen Schlüssel K. Dieser Schlüssel muss bei den rechtmäßigen Besitzern streng geheimgehalten werden. Er wird aufgrund dieser Anforderung geheimer Schlüssel genannt und stellt ein Geheimnis dar, das nur den miteinander kommunizierenden Parteien bekannt ist. Der Schlüsselraum, aus dem K gewählt wird, muss dabei so groß sein, dass es schwer ist, beispielsweise durch vollständige Suche auf den Schlüssel K schließen zu können.

Asymmetrische Kryptosysteme basieren auf Trapdoor-One-Way-Funktionen. Jede Partei besitzt ein Schlüsselpaar *(PK,SK)*, das aus einem geheimzuhaltenden Schlüssel *SK* (geheimer Schlüssel) besteht und dem zu diesem gehörenden Schlüssel *PK*, der veröffentlicht werden kann (öffentlicher Schlüssel). Der öffentliche Schlüssel *PK* jeder Partei kann beispielsweise in einem öffentlichen Schlüsselverzeichnis (Directory), ähnlich einem Telefonbuch, publiziert werden. Der geheime Schlüssel *SK* unterliegt strengster Geheimhaltung und repräsentiert ein Geheimnis, das nur sein rechtmäßiger Besitzer kennt. Das Schlüsselpaar *(PK,SK)* besitzt die Eigenschaft, dass es schwer ist, *SK* aus *PK* zu berechnen, mit Kenntnis der Trapdoor-Information jedoch leicht.

Die Kryptographie beruht neben der Annahme über die Berechenbarkeiten von Funktionen auf der Voraussetzung, dass Daten, die für kryptographische Mechanismen eingesetzt werden, authentisch sind (beispielsweise durch ihre Veröffentlichung) oder ihre Authentizität geprüft werden kann. Ein Datum oder eine Partei gilt dann als echt, wenn ein Prüfer einen Beweis akzeptiert, in dem ein Geheimnis verwendet wird, bei dem der Prüfer davon ausgeht, dass dieses Geheimnis nur dem rechtmäßigen Besitzer oder den rechtmäßigen Besitzern bekannt ist. Jeder andere, der das Geheimnis kennt, also auch ein Betrüger, kann das Geheimnis ebenfalls für einen entsprechenden Beweis einsetzen. Es ist Aufgabe der Sicherheitsstrategie (Security Policy) der jeweiligen Anwendung festzulegen, ob ein Prüfer einen Beweis akzeptieren kann. Die Sicherheitsstrategie muss definieren, wie hoch das Sicherheitsniveau der Anwendung zu setzen ist, beispielsweise: wie streng die Auflagen an die Sicherheit von Geheimnissen (wie Größe, Anzahl aber auch Aufbewahrungsort) sind und mit welchem Verfahren der Sicherheitsmechanismus realisiert wird, damit er als sicher im Sinne der Sicherheitsstrategie gilt. Hier müssen Kosten, die durch den Einsatz von Sicherheitsmechanismen entstehen, und Kosten, die durch Schäden ohne oder von in nur geringem Maße eingesetzten Sicherheitsmechanismen aufkommen, gegeneinander abgewogen werden.

Gegenstand der nachstehenden Ausführungen sind die beiden kryptographischen Sicherheitsmechanismen Verschlüsselung und digitale Signatur, die im Folgenden näher erläutert werden. Es wird dabei vorausgesetzt, dass alle Berechnungen in einer sicheren Umgebung durchgeführt und die Daten unverändert über den Kommunikationskanal gesendet werden. Darüber hinaus wird die Einsetzbarkeit der beiden Sicherheitsmechanismen für Mediendaten diskutiert.

3.1 Verschlüsselungsverfahren

Vertraulichkeit kann durch Verschlüsselungsverfahren erreicht werden. Diese Verfahren werden verwendet, um Informationen gegenüber unerwünschten Parteien geheim zu halten (Wahrung der Vertraulichkeit).

Bei diesen Verfahren werden Funktionen eingesetzt, die durch einen Schlüssel $K1$ aus dem Schlüsselraum parametrisiert sind (Verschlüsselungsfunktionen), und Funktionen, die durch einen Schlüssel $K2$ aus dem Schlüsselraum parametrisiert sind (Entschlüsselungsfunktionen). Die Funktionen besitzen die Eigenschaft, dass zu jedem Schlüssel $K1$ aus dem Schlüsselraum ein eindeutiger Schlüssel $K2$ aus dem Schlüsselraum existiert, derart, dass Verschlüsselungsfunktion und Entschlüsselungsfunktion invers zueinander sind. Die zu verschlüsselnden Daten werden mittels der durch $K1$ parametrisierten Verschlüsselungsfunktion transformiert. Aus dem so erzeugten Chiffrat können bei Kenntnis des Schlüssels $K2$ mittels der zur Verschlüsselungsfunktion inversen Entschlüsselungsfunktion die Daten zurückgewonnen werden.

Symmetrische und einige asymmetrische Kryptosysteme lassen sich als Verschlüsselungsverfahren verwenden. Darüber hinaus gibt es sogenannte Session-Key-Verfahren (oft auch hybride Kryptosysteme genannt), die beide Kryptosysteme einsetzen. Da das Session-Key-Verfahren zu einem der wichtigsten und verbreitetsten Verschlüsselungsverfahren gehört, wird es im Folgenden vorgestellt.

Bei einem Session-Key-Verfahren wird sowohl ein symmetrisches als auch ein asymmetrisches Kryptosystem als Verschlüsselungsverfahren eingesetzt (siehe Fig. 1. $x//y$ bezeichnet dabei die Konkatenation von x und y, $//$ symbolisiert den Kommunikationskanal).

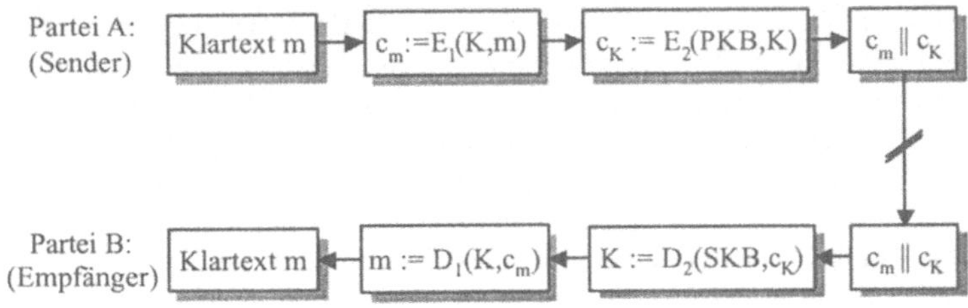

Fig. 1. Session-Key-Verfahren

Der Klartext m wird mit einem symmetrischen Kryptosystem verschlüsselt. Der geheime Schlüssel (Session Key K) für diese Verschlüsselung wird von Partei A vor Beginn einer jeden Kommunikation (Session) in Form einer Pseudozufallszahl erzeugt. Eine Pseudozufallszahl ist eine Zahl, die Element einer reproduzierbaren Zahlenfolge ist und mittels deterministischer Algorithmen ausgehend von einem echt zufällig gewählten Startwert berechnet wird. Diese Folge besitzt die Eigenschaft, dass es schwer ist, aus der Kenntnis einiger Zufallszahlen die als nächstes erzeugten Zufallszahlen vorherzusagen. Der so gebildete Session Key wird aus Sicherheitsgründen nur für eine einzige Sitzung verwendet.

Partei A (Sender) verschlüsselt nun mit der Verschlüsselungsfunktion, der durch den Schlüssel K parametrisierten Funktion E_1, den Klartext m. Für die sichere Übermittlung des geheimen Schlüssels K an Partei B (Empfänger) wird ein asymmetrisches Kryptosystem eingesetzt: Der Session Key K wird mit der Verschlüsselungsfunktion, der durch den öffentlichen Schlüssel PKB des Empfängers parametrisierten Funktion E_2, verschlüsselt (Schlüsselchiffrat c_K). Das Schlüsselchiffrat c_K wird dann zusammen mit dem verschlüsselten Klartext c_m an B übermittelt.

Partei B (Empfänger) gewinnt den Session Key K zurück, indem sie zunächst das Schlüsselchiffrat c_K entschlüsselt: basierend auf dem asymmetrischen Kryptosystem erhält sie mit Hilfe der Funktion D_2, die mit dem zum öffentlichen Schlüssel PKB gehörenden geheimen Schlüssel SKB parametrisiert ist, den Schlüssel K. Mit Hilfe von K berechnet B mit der Funktion D_1 des symmetrischen Kryptosystems aus den verschlüsselten Daten c_m den Klartext m.

Die Verschlüsselungsverfahren sind in der Praxis hauptsächlich auf herkömmliche Textdaten angewendet worden und haben dort sehr gute Ergebnisse hinsichtlich Sicherheit und Performance erzielen können. Das Session-Key-Verfahren ist insbesondere für die Verschlüsselung von großen Datenmengen geeignet, da die Performanceeigenschaften der beiden Kryptosysteme gewinnbringend genutzt werden können. Beispielsweise besitzt das bekannteste symmetrische Kryptosystem, der DES (Data Encryption Standard [7]), eine wesentlich bessere Performance als das bekannteste asymmetrische Kryptosystem, das RSA-Verfahren (benannt nach seinen Erfindern Rivest, Shamir, Adleman [8]): DES ist in Hardware ungefähr 1000 mal und in Software ungefähr 100 mal schneller als RSA [9]. Mediendaten, vor allem Video und Audio, unterscheiden sich jedoch aus folgenden Gründen von herkömmlichen Textdaten, so dass die Verschlüsselungsverfahren an das Medienmaterial angepasst werden müssen:

- Bei digitalem Video oder Audio fallen um Dimensionen größere Datenmengen an als bei Textdokumenten, so dass ein Schutz der Daten vor unberechtigtem Zugriff mit herkömmlichen Methoden der Kryptographie bei den gegenwärtigen Rechnerleistungen und Übertragungsraten der Netzwerke bei gleichzeitiger Echtzeitanforderung von verteilten Multimediaanwendungen nicht realisierbar ist.
- Die Verschlüsselung eines gesamten komprimierten Videos mit bekannten Verschlüsselungsalgorithmen bietet Angriffsmöglichkeiten, das Original ohne Kenntnis des Schlüssels zu berechnen, da nach der Kompression einige Resynchronisationsdaten im Video bzw. Audio eingebettet sind, die Rückschlüsse ermöglichen.
- Die Verschlüsselung nach der Kompression verursacht Probleme, wenn eine Umcodierung wie Wechsel der verfügbaren Bandbreite nötig wird, da der Transcoder mit dem geheimen Schlüssel versorgt werden muss.

In [10], [11], [12] und [13] werden abgestufte Sicherheitskonzepte vorgestellt, die hinsichtlich Effizienz und Sicherheitsniveau anpassbar sind und als partielle Verschlüsselungsmethoden für Video bezeichnet werden.

3.2 Digitale Signatur

Mit digitalen Signaturen kann neben der Integrität der Daten auch die Authentizität (Echtheit) des Datenursprungs geprüft werden. Bei diesen Verfahren handelt es sich um einen Detektionsmechanismus. Die gesicherten Daten liegen unverändert im Klartext vor.

Die Idee und der Begriff der digitalen Signatur erscheinen zum ersten Mal als „digital signature" bei Diffie und Hellman [14]. Sie schlagen vor: Die digitale Signatur einer Partei A zu ihren Daten m soll ein Wert sein, der von m und von einer zusätzlichen, geheimen Information abhängt, die nur A bekannt ist. Jeder Benutzer des digitalen Signaturverfahrens kann die Echtheit der von A erstellten Signatur überprüfen (Verifikation), indem er eine weitere, bekannt gegebene, also öffentliche Information von A benutzt. Es muss gesichert werden, dass diese Information tatsächlich zu A gehört. Da nur A im Besitz der geheimen Information ist, kann nur sie mit der Signierfunktion S diese digitale Signatur zu den Daten m erstellen. Somit besitzt die digitale Signatur auch Beweiskraft gegenüber Dritten.

Als digitale Signaturverfahren eignen sich asymmetrische Kryptosysteme, da sie Trapdoor-One-Way-Funktionen verwenden. Es gibt auch auf symmetrischen Kryptosystemen basierende Signaturverfahren. Da diese jedoch nicht sehr anwendungsfreundlich sind, werden sie hier nicht betrachtet.

Bei digitalen Signaturverfahren darf das zu signierende Dokument m eine bestimmte Größe, die durch den Zahlenraum des jeweiligen digitalen Signaturverfahrens bestimmt wird, nicht überschreiten. Die durch Schlüssel parametrisierten Funktionen der digitalen Signaturverfahren operieren beispielsweise auf den endlichen Zahlenräumen $\mathbb{Z}_n$? $\mathbb{Z}_n$ mit $n = p \cdot q$ oder $GF(p)$? $GF(p)$ mit p und q prim. Um trotzdem zu Daten, die außerhalb der Zahlenräume liegen (im Beispiel $m \overline{=} n$ oder $m \overline{=} p$) digitale Signaturen erstellen und verifizieren zu können, sind zwei Möglichkeiten denkbar: Bei der ersten Möglichkeit werden die Daten m in Blöcke $m_1,...,m_k$ mit beispielsweise $m_i < n$ aufgeteilt und jeder Block einzeln signiert. Bei der zweiten, in der Praxis üblichen Methode wird eine Kopie von m mittels einer Hashfunktion auf einen Wert $H(m) < n$ reduziert, der dann signiert wird. Die Signatur wird damit nicht aus den Daten selbst, sondern aus dem Hashwert der Daten berechnet. Diese Methode erhöht sowohl die Performance als auch die Sicherheit, beispielsweise kann die Reihenfolge der signierten Daten nicht mehr unbemerkt verändert werden.

Um die Authentizität von Daten mit Hilfe von digitalen Signaturverfahren zu sichern, geht man in der Praxis wie folgt vor (siehe Fig. 2). Die Beschreibung beschränkt sich hierbei auf die einfachste Ausführung eines digitalen Signaturverfahrens (beispielsweise RSA [8]).

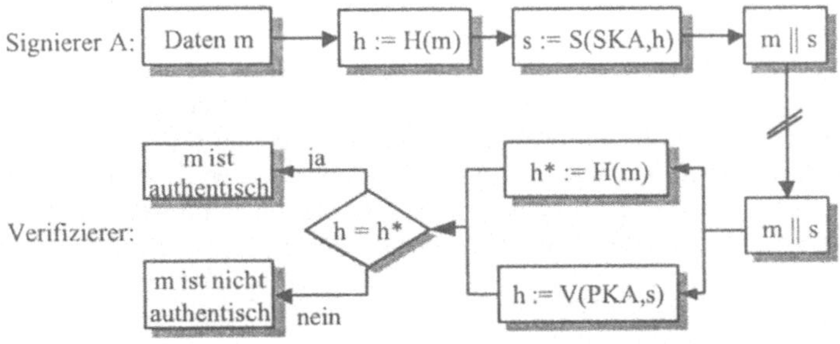

Signierer A will seine Daten m unter Verwendung einer Hashfunktion H digital signiert an einen Verifizierer übermitteln. A bildet zu m mit Hilfe der Hashfunktion H den Hashwert $h := H(m)$. Anschließend berechnet A mit der Signierfunktion S, die durch einen nur ihm bekannten Wert, seinem geheimen Schlüssel SKA, parametrisiert ist, den Wert $s := S(SKA,h)$. A sendet seine Daten m mit der dazugehörigen digitalen Signatur s an den Verifizierer. Das Konkatenat $m//s$ wird dabei als signierte Nachricht bezeichnet.

Der Verifizierer benötigt zur Prüfung der digitalen Signatur s den öffentlichen Schlüssel PKA von A, die von A benutzte Hashfunktion H und die Verifikationsfunktion V. Er bildet zunächst einen Hashwert $h* := H(m)$. Mit Hilfe von V, parametrisiert durch den öffentlichen Schlüssel PKA, entscheidet er nun, ob die Signatur zu m korrekt und m damit unverändert ist oder nicht: Er berechnet aus der Signatur s den Hashwert $h := V(PKA,s)$ und prüft, ob $h = h*$ gilt. Bei Gleichheit gilt die Signatur von A als korrekt und die Daten m als unverändert. Da nur A im Besitz des geheimen Schlüssels SKA ist, kann nur er eine korrekte Signatur s zu m bilden. Ist $h \ne h*$, so gilt die Signatur als falsch und die Daten als nicht authentisch. Dies kann beispielsweise durch die Veränderung der Daten m oder der Signatur s zwischen dem Zeitpunkt des Signierens und Verifizierens verursacht worden sein. Es kann aber auch der öffentliche Schlüssel falsch sein, beispielsweise dadurch, dass er nicht dem Signierer gehört.

Neben diesen relativ einfachen Möglichkeiten zur Berechnung und Prüfung der Signatur (Signature With Appendix [15]) gibt es weitere, komplexere Methoden, die die Signaturbildung selbst betreffen (wie Signature Given Message Recovery oder Signature Given Limited Message Recovery [16]).

Im Vergleich zu herkömmlichen Textdaten ergeben sich in der Praxis beim Versand von Audio- und Videodaten jedoch auch hier Probleme. Tritt bei der Datenübertragung ein Bitfehler auf, der sich bis in die Anwendungsebene zieht und sind Mechanismen für den Integritätsschutz verwendet worden, wird dem Empfänger eine Schutzverletzung angezeigt. Es ist für ihn nicht erkenntlich, ob dies durch eine fehlerhafte Übertragung oder durch einen Angriff hervorgerufen worden ist. Bei multimedialen Daten ist ein Mechanismus für Integrität wenig sinnvoll, wenn ein Prüfergebnis erstellt wird, welches von der gesamten Datenmenge abhängig ist. Wurde das gesamte Datenmaterial beispielsweise signiert, gilt auch das gesamte Material als verfälscht, obwohl nur partielle Fehler auftraten. Angepasste Verfahren zur Authentizitätsprüfung werden zum Beispiel von [17] und [18] als inhaltsbasierte Signaturen angesprochen. Bei Mediendatenformaten sollte nicht lediglich der Bitstrom als Eingabe für die kryptographische Authentifizierung und den Integritätsnachweis verwendet werden, da sich die Syntax, der Bitstrom, bei Multimediadatenformaten verändern kann, ohne die Semantik zu beeinflussen. Beispielsweise würde nach Kompression oder Skalierung eine Integritätsverletzung angezeigt werden, obwohl die Semantik der Daten unverändert ist.

Neben digitalen Signaturen bieten digitale Wasserzeichenverfahren interessante Lösungsmöglichkeiten für diese Problematik. Sie versuchen, die Authentizität (den Urheber und die Herkunft des Datenmaterials) oder Integrität nachzuweisen, indem Informationen direkt in das Datenmaterial eingefügt werden. Die eingebrachte Information soll dabei für das menschliche Auge oder Gehör nicht wahrnehmbar sein. Sie wird so mit dem Datenmaterial verwoben, dass ein einfaches Entfernen weitgehend unmöglich ist, ohne das Datenmaterial selbst zu beschädigen. Im folgenden Kapitel werden Grundlagen sowie Verfahrensparameter von digitalen Wasserzeichen diskutiert und eine Klassifizierung der Verfahren vorgenommen.

4 Grundlagen digitaler Wasserzeichen

Mit digitale Wasserzeichen können die Authentizität (den Urheber und die Herkunft des Datenmaterials) oder Integrität nachgewiesen werden, indem Informationen direkt in das Datenmaterial eingefügt werden.

4.1 Definition und Terminologie

Unter einem digitalen Wasserzeichen versteht man ein transparentes, nicht wahrnehmbares Muster, welches in das Datenmaterial (Bild, Video, Audio, 3D-Modell) mit einem Einbettungsalgorithmus unter Verwendung eines geheimen Schlüssels eingebracht wird.

Jeder Wasserzeichenalgorithmus besteht in Analogie zur Steganographie aus:
- einem Einbettungsprozess E: Watermark Embedding und
- einem Abfrageprozess/Ausleseprozess R: Watermark Retrieval.

Der *Einbettungsprozess E* fügt die Wasserzeicheninformation W (Watermark Message) in das Datenmaterial C (Cover/Carrier oder auch Original) ein, zum Beispiel in ein Bild, und es entsteht das Datenmaterial mit einem Wasserzeichen C_W (Watermarked Cover/Carrier). Man spricht auch davon, dass eine Markierung aufgebracht wird. Da steganographische Verfahren und somit auch Wasserzeichenverfahren symmetrisch sind, muss ein Sicherheitsparameter K benutzt werden, damit das Wasserzeichen nicht von Angreifern manipuliert oder gelöscht werden kann. Das Verfahren selbst langfristig geheim zu halten, erweist sich als schwierig. Deshalb wird ein geheimer Schlüssel K benutzt, von dem das Wasserzeichen abhängt:

$$C_W = E(C,\ W,\ K). \tag{1}$$

In der Praxis benötigen die Verfahren meist weitere zusätzliche Parameter wie Wasserzeichenstärke oder Initialisierungswerte. Da bisherige Verfahren auf steganographischen Verfahren aufbauen, die symmetrisch arbeiten, kann nur unter Nutzung des gleichen Verfahrens und des passenden Schlüssels der *Abfrageprozess R* die Informationen aus dem Datenmaterial wieder auslesen:

$$W = R(C_W,\ K). \tag{2}$$

Der Abfrageprozess R bekommt das Watermarked Cover C_W sowie den geheimen Schlüssel übergeben und gibt die Wasserzeicheninformation W aus. Da Wasserzeichen aus dem Datenmaterial nicht entfernbar sein sollen, kann mit dem Abfrageprozess R auch bei Kenntnis des Schlüssels K das Original C nicht wieder hergestellt werden. Die Wasserzeicheninformation kann lediglich ausgelesen, auf das Original kann jedoch nicht geschlossen werden. Abhängig vom konkreten Wasserzeichenverfahren werden meist statistische Analysen wie Korrelations- oder Hypothesentests im Abfrageprozess R durchgeführt, die feststellen, ob die Information, die durch E eingebracht wurde, im Datenmaterial C vorhanden ist. R nutzt dabei die Regeln von E, wo und wie das Wasserzeichen eingebracht wurde. Manche Verfahren benötigen neben dem Prüfmaterial das Original, so dass ein dritter Parameter C hinzukommen kann.

Das eingebrachte Muster repräsentiert die eingebrachte Information. Typischerweise kann das Muster folgende Informationen darstellen:

- Präsentwasserzeichen: Identifizierung des Urhebers über ein Schlüssel abhängiges Muster, d.h. der Nachweis der Urheberschaft wird über das Vorhandensein des Wasserzeichenmusters angezeigt und somit der Urheber identifiziert (an dieser Stelle können zum Beispiel bei Bildwasserzeichen auch urheberspezifische Bilder eingebracht werden).
- Codierung von Informationen, meist binär codiert, im Allgemeinen von:
  - Urheberdaten, zur Kennzeichnung der Urheberrechte,
  - Kundendaten, zur Kennzeichnung legaler und zur Verfolgung illegaler Kopien, oder
  - jeder Art von beschreibenden Daten (Metadaten).

Da es sich, wie bereits erwähnt, um öffentlich bekannte Wasserzeichenverfahren handelt, wird bei textuellen Wasserzeichen der einzubringende Bitstrom vor dem Einbetten in das Cover meist mit dem geheimen Schlüssel verschlüsselt, um etwaige Angriffe auf das Wasserzeichen zu erschweren.

4.2 Verfahrensgrundlagen

Prinzipiell basieren Wasserzeichenverfahren auf den beiden steganographischen Vorgehensweisen der substitutionalen und der konstruktiven Steganographie. Verfahren auf Basis von konstruktiver Steganographie sind geeigneter, um Robustheit und Sicherheit zu erreichen, da das Wasserzeichen die Originaldaten lediglich leicht abändert und modelliert, ohne komplette Ersetzungen zu erzwingen. Für beide Anwendungsfälle existieren bisher Verfahren, die auf zwei generellen Techniken beruhen, um die Wasserzeicheninformation einzubringen:

- man modifiziert direkt im Datenmaterial, beispielsweise im Bildbereich (spatial domain) auf den Farb- und Helligkeitskomponenten, weshalb man auch von Bildraumverfahren spricht, oder
- man führt Transformationscodierungen durch, beispielsweise eine DCT (Discrete Cosine Transform), FFT (Fast Fourier Transform) oder DWT (Discret Wavelet Transform), und bringt die Information in die transformierten Komponenten des Datenmaterials ein, wobei danach wieder zurücktransformiert wird. Diese Verfahren werden als Frequenzraumverfahren bezeichnet.

Die Wasserzeicheninformation wird, wie bereits erwähnt, meist in ein Zufalls-Rauschsignal (pseudo-noise signal) transformiert, welches signal-adaptiv oder nicht-signal-adaptiv ist, je nachdem, wie der Wahrnehmungsaspekt berücksichtigt wird.

Das Zufalls-Rauschsignal ist meist entweder binär, Gauss oder uniform verteilt. Im Allgemeinen wird vor der Einbettung des Wasserzeichens analysiert, welche Eigenschaften das Datenmaterial aufweist, um die Informationen transparent einbringen zu können. Hier werden psychovisuelle und psychoakustische Modelle herangezogen.

Im Falle substitutionaler Steganographie wird analysiert, welche Komponenten im Datenmaterial vorhanden sind. Anschließend werden in geeignet ausgewählten Positionen die Ursprungsdaten mit der transformierten Wasserzeicheninformation ersetzt. Sollen statt eines spezifischen Rauschmusters, das den Urheber eindeutig identifiziert, mehrere Informationsbits eingebracht werden, wird die Wasserzeichennachricht meist zuerst mit dem Schlüssel verschlüsselt, um analytische und statistische Angriffe auszuschließen. Unter Beachtung der psychovisuellen und der psychoakustischen Perspektive, d.h. der Maskierung und Verdeckungseffekte, werden die selektierten Rauschkomponenten durch die verschlüsselte Wasserzeicheninformation direkt ersetzt oder manipuliert. Die Markierungspositionen werden meist pseudozufällig über den benutzten Schlüssel bestimmt. Da Rauschkomponenten bei der Kompression abgeschnitten werden können, muss man, um Robustheit gegenüber Kompression zu erlangen, das Wasserzeichen in solchen Rauschkomponenten einfügen, die gerade nicht mehr von der Kompression eliminiert werden, aber gleichzeitig auch nicht wahrgenommen werden können. Es erfolgt eine Abwägung, wieweit man in nicht-hörbaren oder nicht-sichtbaren Bereichen markiert. Eine Annäherung an den wahrnehmbaren Bereich unter Beachtung von Sichtbarkeits- bzw. Hörbarkeitseigenschaften erfolgt hierbei zur Optimierung der Robustheit gegenüber Kompression. Messverfahren zur Beurteilung der visuellen oder psychoakustischen Qualität sind nicht Schwerpunkt unserer Diskussionen.

Konstruktive Steganographie dagegen modifiziert das Original. Es treten im Allgemeinen weniger Probleme bei Kompression auf. An bestimmten Teilbereichen des Datenmaterials, den Markierungspunkten, werden Modifikationen vorgenommen, die die Semantik des Originals nicht zerstören dürfen. Eingebracht wird die mit dem Schlüssel verschlüsselte Wasserzeicheninformation. Um das Wasserzeichen auszulesen, muss die erzeugte Veränderung gemessen werden. Dazu wird die Schlüsselinformation benutzt und es müssen die gleichen Markierungspunkte wieder gefunden werden.

Heutige Wasserzeichenverfahren bieten im Allgemeinen zwei Alternativen: wird das Original im Abfrageprozess verwendet, erfolgt zuerst eine Subtraktion des Originals vom zu überprüfenden Datenmaterial, und anschließend wird der Abfrageprozess gestartet. Wird das Original nicht verwendet, erfolgt sofort der Abfrageprozess. Wurde ein spezifisches Rauschmuster eingebracht und stimmt das ausgelesene Muster mit dem eingebrachten überein, kann der Urheber nachgewiesen werden. Wurde statt dessen ein binärer Text eingebracht, wird, falls ein fehlerkorrigierender Code verwendet wurde, zuerst die Fehlerkorrektur vorgenommen. Anschließend erfolgt die Entschlüsselung mit dem geheimen Schlüssel und die Wasserzeicheninformation wird ausgegeben. Das Identifikationsproblem des Urhebers und Copyright-Infrastukturen sind nicht Schwerpunkt unserer Diskussion, bilden aber neben der technischen Sicherheit der Wasserzeichenverfahren eine wesentliche Voraussetzung für die Anwendbarkeit.

4.3 Verfahrensparameter

Jede Wasserzeichentechnik hat bestimmte Eigenschaften, welche von der Applikation abhängig sind. Als wichtigste Eigenschaften eines Wasserzeichenverfahrens betrachten wir:

- **Robustheit:** Die eingebrachte Wasserzeicheninformation W (Watermark Message) ist robust, wenn die Information zuverlässig aus dem Datenmaterial ausgelesen werden kann, auch wenn das Datenmaterial modifiziert (aber nicht vollständig zerstört) wurde. Robustheit bezeichnet somit die Widerstandsfähigkeit der in ein Datenmaterial eingebrachten Wasserzeicheninformation gegenüber zufälligen Veränderungen des Datenmaterials oder Medienverarbeitungen.
- **Nicht-Detektierbarkeit:** Diese Eigenschaft wird vor allem bei sicherer, verdeckter Kommunikation (secure cover communication), dem geheimen versteckten Kommunizieren zweier oder mehrerer Parteien, verlangt.
- **Nicht-Wahrnehmbarkeit:** Diese Eigenschaft bezieht sich auf die Eigenschaften des menschlichen Wahrnehmungssystems. Es wird die Fragestellung betrachtet, ob das eingebrachte Muster akustisch oder optisch wahrnehmbare Veränderungen erzeugt. Die eingebrachte Information W ist nicht wahrnehmbar und somit transparent, wenn ein durchschnittliches Seh- bzw. Hörvermögen nicht zwischen markiertem Datenmaterial und Original unterscheiden kann.
- **Security:** Der Wasserzeichenalgorithmus wird als sicher (secure) eingestuft, wenn die eingebrachte Information nicht zerstört, aufgespürt oder gefälscht werden kann, wobei der Angreifer volle Kenntnis des Wasserzeichenverfahrens hat, ihm mindestens ein markiertes Datenmaterial vorliegt, ihm jedoch der geheime Schlüssel unbekannt ist. Die Eigenschaft Security beschreibt im Gegensatz zur Robustheit die Sicherheit gegen gezielte (nicht-blinde) Angriffe auf das Wasserzeichen selbst. Beispielsweise darf es nicht möglich werden, Fälschungen anzufertigen.
- **Komplexität:** Die Komplexität beschreibt den Aufwand, der erbracht werden muss, die Wasserzeicheninformation einzubringen und wieder auszulesen. Bedeutend ist dieser Parameter bei Echtzeitansprüchen. Der Parameter beschreibt außerdem, ob zum Auslesen der Markierung im Abfrageprozess das Originalbild verwendet werden muss oder nicht.
- **Kapazität:** Dieser Parameter misst, wie viel Informationen in das Original eingebracht werden können und wie viel Wasserzeichen parallel im Datenmaterial zugelassen bzw. möglich sind.
- **Geheime/öffentliche Verifikation:** Dieser Parameter sagt aus, ob nur der Urheber oder eine dedizierte Personengruppe das Wasserzeichen aufdecken können (geheim) oder ob die Verifikation öffentlich erfolgen kann bzw. soll. Da digitale Wasserzeichen auf steganographischen Verfahren beruhen und diese symmetrisch arbeiten, ist es sehr schwer, ein sicheres öffentliches Wasserzeichen zu konstruieren.

Die aufgeführten Parameter an Wasserzeichenverfahren konkurrieren miteinander und können meist nicht zur selben Zeit optimiert werden.

4.4 Klassifizierung der Wasserzeichen

In der Literatur finden wir sehr unterschiedliche Ansätze für Wasserzeichentechniken. Um sie vergleichen zu können, schlagen wir als erstes Klassifikationsmerkmal das Anwendungsgebiet, d.h. eine Unterscheidung nach der Art der eingebrachten Information, vor. Innerhalb dieses Klassifikationsmerkmals werden wir die Verfahren in zweiter Ebene nach den optimierten Verfahrensparametern unterteilen.

Klassifikationsmerkmal erste Ebene: Anwendungsgebiet. Für die Vielzahl existierender Wasserzeichenverfahren identifizieren wir folgende Anwendungsgebiete:

- **Verfahren zur Urheberidentifizierung (Authentifizierung):** *Robust Authentication Watermark*
  Autoren, Urheber, Produzenten etc. fügen in das Datenmaterial eine eindeutige Markierung ein, um die Urheberschaft oder das Copyright zu sichern. Der Urheber verwahrt das Original und verbreitet das markierte Datenmaterial mit dem Urheber- oder Copyright-Vermerk.

- **Verfahren zur Kundenidentifizierung (Authentifizierung):** *Fingerprint Watermark*
  Wird das Datenmaterial an unterschiedliche Personen ausgeliefert, will man häufig ein kundenspezifisches Merkmal in das Datenmaterial integrieren, um einerseits legale Kunden zu identifizieren und andererseits illegale Kopien zum Verursacher zurück verfolgen zu können (traitor tracing). Es werden sogenannten Fingerabdrücke, eindeutige Kundenidentifizierungen, in das Datenmaterial eingefügt.

- **Verfahren zur Annotation des Datenmaterials:** *Caption Watermark, Annotation Watermark*
  Mit dieser Markierung können Beschreibungen zum Datenmaterial, wie Szenen- und Verwendungsbeschreibungen, aber auch Lizenzhinweise in das Datenmaterial selbst eingebracht werden.

- **Verfahren zur Durchsetzung des Kopierschutzes oder Übertragungskontrolle:** *Copy Control Watermark, Broadcast Watermark*
  Diese Markierung dient dazu, dass eine Applikation entscheiden kann, ob das Datenmaterial angeschaut und/oder kopiert werden darf.

- **Verfahren zum Nachweis der Unversehrtheit (Integritätsnachweis):** *Integrity Watermark, Verification Watermark*
  Als Wasserzeichen können Informationen in das Bild eingebracht werden, die erlauben festzustellen, ob das Datenmaterial manipuliert worden ist oder ob bestimmte Zusatzinformationen zum Datenmaterial korrekt sind. Wichtig ist, dass die Wasserzeicheninformation die Semantik des Datenmaterials widerspiegelt. Diese Art von Wasserzeichen werden auch als unsichtbar-zerbrechliche Wasserzeichen bezeichnet. Bei einem Verification Watermark können auch Umstände oder weitere Eigenschaften des Datenmaterials als Wasserzeichen integriert werden, die später verifiziert werden sollen.

Klassifikationsmerkmal zweite Ebene: Verfahrensparameter. Die Klassifikation in erster Ebene unterteilen wir in einer zweiten Ebene nach den Verfahrensparametern. Aus den in der Literatur vorgefundenen Verfahrensparameter definieren wir die für uns Wichtigsten:

1. Nach dem Wahrnehmungsaspekt (Sichtbarkeit/Hörbarkeit bzw. Transparenz):
   - wahrnehmbare Wasserzeichen,
   - nicht-wahrnehmbare Wasserzeichen, adaptive Wasserzeichen, die sich an der Wahrnehmung des Menschen orientieren und entsprechend an das Datenmaterial angepasste Wasserzeichen aufbringen.
2. Nach der Robustheit:
   - Robust Watermarking,
   - Fragile Watermark.
3. Nach der Verifizierbarkeit der Markierung:
   - geheim, nur dem Markierer oder einer bestimmten Gruppe von Personen bekannt (Private Watermarking, manchmal auch als symmetrisches Wasserzeichen bezeichnet);
   - öffentlich (Public Watermarking, manchmal auch als asymmetrisches Wasserzeichen bezeichnet).
4. Nach der Verwendung des Originals beim Abfrageprozess:
   - blinde Verfahren (Oblivious Watermarking) benötigen im Abfrageprozess kein Original: $W = R(C_W, K)$.
   - nicht-blinde Verfahren (Non-oblivious Watermarking) benötigen das Original: $W = R(C, C_W, K)$. Sie werden in der Literatur teilweise auch als private Verfahren bezeichnet, da bei Verwendung des Originals Geheimhaltung gefordert ist. Um die Verwechslung mit der Art und Weise der Verifizierbarkeit zu vermeiden, wird von dieser Terminologie Abstand genommen und der Begriff nicht-blind benutzt.
   - Abhängigkeit vom Original hinsichtlich Eindeutigkeit bei Mehrfachmarkierung.
5. Nach der Kapazität:
   - Einbringen von Mustern,
   - Einbringen von Text,
   - Schutz einzelner oder kombinierter Komponenten, z.B. einzelner Video-Frames oder einer Folge von Frames im Video, kombinierter Schutz z.B. von Audio und Video.
6. Nach Datenformaten:
   - unterstützte Medien, Medienformate;
   - Unterstützung von kombinierten Medien.
7. Nach Komplexität:
   - Echtzeit-Fähigkeit beim Einbetten bzw. Auslesen,
   - Einbettung in Orts- und/oder Frequenzraum.

Attacken. In der Literatur werden eine Reihe von Angriffen auf Wasserzeichenverfahren beschrieben. Die folgende Klassifizierung der Angriffe nehmen wir vor [19]:
- Angriffe auf die Robustheit
- Angriffe auf die Eindeutigkeit des Urhebers

- Angriffe auf das Wasserzeichen selbst
- Angriffe auf die Übertragbarkeit des Wasserzeichens auf andere Dokumente
- Angriffe auf unterschiedliche Kopien

Gleichzeitig besteht eine starke Wechselwirkung zwischen Robustheit zur Urheberidentifizierung und Manipulationserkennung, so dass es schwierig wird, neben Authentizität gleichzeitig Integrität nachzuweisen.

Wichtige Qualitätsparameter für Wasserzeichen. Basierend auf den aufgestellten Verfahrensattributen schlagen wir Qualitätsparameter für die unterschiedlichen Wasserzeichenarten der ersten Ebenenklassifizierung nach dem Anwendungsgebiet vor (siehe Tabelle).

Die Qualitätsparameter können zur Bewertung der unterschiedlichen Verfahren verwendet werden und schaffen somit eine einheitliche Bewertungsgrundlage. Die Tests von [20] zeigen, dass folgende Qualitätsanforderungen bisher nicht optimal erfüllt werden können:

- Robustheit gegen kombinierte lineare und nicht-lineare Transformationen.
- Anpassungen an die Wahrnehmung des Menschen bei gleichzeitiger Robustheitsgarantie.
- Hohe Kapazität, um eine größere Folge von Bits einzubringen, Schutz einzelner Medien bzw. Medienkombinationen.
- Berücksichtigung der Koalitionsattacke bei digitalen Fingerabdrücken zur kundenspezifischen Kennzeichnung des Datenmaterials.
- Entwurf von zerbrechlichen Wasserzeichen, die bei Inhaltsänderungen eine Integritätsverletzung anzeigen und bei zugelassenen Modifikationen Unversehrtheit ausweisen.
- Komplexitätsreduktion, Optimierung der Laufzeiteffizienz und Robustheit, ohne im Abfrageprozess das Original zu verwenden (besonders wichtig bei Video und Audio).

Tabelle: Wasserzeichenverfahren und ihre Qualitätsparameter

Wasserzeichenart	Qualitätsparameter
Verfahren zur Urheberidentifizierung	Wahrnehmbarkeit: an die Wahrnehmung des Menschen angepasstes Wasserzeichen
	Robustheit: hohe Robustheit gegen Kompression und geometrische Transformationen sowie erweiterter Medienverarbeitungen (Mosaikattacke, StirMark ist Referenztest)
	Kapazität: an die Robustheit angepasst
	Komplexität: je nach Anforderung
	Security: Problem Invertierbarkeit und Zeitstempel, Fälschungssicherheit, Fehlererkennungen müssen gering sein

Verfahren zur Kundenidentifizierung	Wie (1)
	Security: zusätzlich Sicherheit gegen Koalitionsangriffe
Verfahren zur Annotation des Datenmaterials	Wahrnehmbarkeit: an die Wahrnehmung des Menschen angepasstes Wasserzeichen
	Robustheit: gegen Kompression und leichte geometrische Transformationen
	Kapazität: hohe Kapazität gefordert
	Komplexität: geringe Komplexität nötig
	Security: Security kann geringer sein
Verfahren zur Durchsetzung des Kopierschutzes	Wie (1)
	Security: zusätzlich Blackbox-Sicherheit, öffentlich über Blackboxlösung verifizierbar
	Komplexität: geringe Komplexität nötig
Verfahren zum Nachweis der Unversehrtheit	Wahrnehmbarkeit: an die Wahrnehmung des Menschen angepasstes Wasserzeichen
	Robustheit: Robustheit solange semantische Integrität nicht verletzt wird
	Kapazität: meist hohe Kapazität gewünscht
	Komplexität: je nach Anforderung
	Security: hohe Security zur Manipulationserkennung bei Mehrfachmarkierung

5 Zusammenfassung und Ausblick

Viele der heute existierenden Verfahren sind sehr anwendungsspezifisch und haben uneinheitliche Verfahrensparameter sowie teilweise geringe Sicherheitsniveaus hinsichtlich Robustheit und Security. Die Entwicklung und Analyse von verbesserten Verfahren zum Schutz von Multimediadaten wie inhaltsbasierte Signaturen oder Wasserzeichenverfahren stellen deshalb zur Zeit ein herausforderndes Forschungsfeld dar, welches interdisziplinäres Wissen und Techniken aus der Kommunikationstheorie, Signalverarbeitung, Kryptologie und Steganographie erfordert. Eine große Herausforderung stellen die Vielfalt an möglichen Medienoperationen dar, die von den Wasserzeichen gemeistert werden müssen. Um jedoch neben den wesentlichen Aspekten Robustheit und Security auch Beweisbarkeit zu erreichen, müssen zusätzlich Aspekte wie Copyright-Infrastrukturen, Probleme der eindeutigen Urheberidentifizierung sowie einheitliche Wasserzeichenprotokolle und Qualitätsbewertungen mit betrachtet werden [19]. Ein sehr wesentlicher Punkt ist auch die Analyse öffentlich verifizierbarer Wasserzeichenverfahren. Ob und in welcher Weise Multimediasysteme Sicherheitsanforderungen erfüllen, wird letztendlich die Akzeptanz und Verbreitung von Multimedia stark beeinflussen.

Literatur

1. Department of Defense: Department of Defense Trusted Computer System Evaluation Criteria (Orange Book). DOD 5200.28-STD, Dec 1985.
2. Information Technology Security Evaluation Criteria (ITSEC): Provisional Harmonised Criteria. Version 1.2, Jun 1991.
3. National Computer Security Center: Trusted Network Interpretation of the Trusted Computer System Evaluation Criteria (Red Book). NCSC-TG-005, Version 1, Jul 1987.
4. National Computer Security Center: Trusted Database Management System Interpretation of the Trusted Computer System Evaluation Criteria. NCSC-TG-021, Version 1, Apr 1991.
5. NATO: NATO Trusted Computer System Evaluation Criteria (Blue Book). NATO AC/35-D/1027, 1987.
6. A.S. Tanenbaum: Verteilte Betriebssysteme. München: Prentice Hall, 1995.
7. National Bureau of Standards: Data Encryption Standard (DES). FIPS PUB 46-1, Jan 1988.
8. R.L. Rivest, A. Shamir, L.A. Adleman: A Method for Obtaining Digital Signatures and Public-Key Cryptosystems. In: Communications of the ACM, Vol. 21, Nr. 2, Feb 1978, S. 120-126.
9. B. Schneier: Applied Cryptography. John Wiley & Sons, Inc. 1996, S. 469.
10. T. Kunkelmann: Sicherheit für Videodaten. Vieweg-Verlag, ISBN 3-528-05680-0, 1998.
11. C. Griwodz: Video Protection by Partial Content Corruption. In: Multimedia and Security Workshop at the Sixth ACM International Multimedia Conference, September 12-16, 1998, Bristol, England; Workshop notes published by GMD – Forschungszentrum Informationstechnik GmbH, GMD Report 41, 1998, S. 37-39.
12. J. Dittmann, A. Steinmetz: A Technical Approach to the Transparent Encryption of MPEG-2 Video. In: Katsikas, Sokratis (Ed.): Communications and Multimedia Security, Vol. 3, Chapman & Hall, 1997, S. 215-226.
13. L. Qiao, K. Nahrstedt: A new Algorithm for MPEG Video Encryption. In: Proc. of 1st International Conference on Image Science, Systems and Technology, Las Vegas, NV, 1997.
14. W. Diffie, M.E. Hellman: New Directions in Cryptography. IEEE Transactions on Information Theory, Vol. 22, Nr. 6, 11/1976, S. 644-654.
15. ISO/IEC 9796:1991 Information Technology – Security Techniques – Digital Signature Scheme giving Message Recovery.
16. ISO/IEC 14888:1998 Information Technology – Security Techniques – Digital Signatures with Appendix.
17. C.Y. Lin, S.F. Chang: Generating Robust Digital Signature for Image/Video Authentication. In: Multimedia and Security Workshop at the Sixth ACM International Multimedia Conference, September 12-16, 1998, Bristol, England; Workshop notes published by GMD – Forschungszentrum Informationstechnik GmbH, GMD Report 41, 1998, S. 49-54.
18. J. Dittmann, A. Steinmetz, R. Steinmetz: Content-based Digital Signature for Motion Pictures Authentication and Content-Fragile Watermarking. In: Proc. of IEEE Multimedia Systems, Multimedia Computing and Systems, June 7-11, 1999, Florence, Italy, Vol. 1, 1999, S. 574-579.
19. J. Dittmann: Digitale Wasserzeichen. Springer-Verlag, ISBN 3-540-66661-3, 2000.
20. F. Petitcolas, R. Anderson: Evaluation of Copyright Marking Systems. In: Proc. of IEEE Multimedia Systems, Multimedia Computing and Systems, June 7-11, 1999, Florence, Italy, Vol. 1, 1999, S. 574-579.

Asymmetric Watermarking Schemes

Joachim J. Eggers[1], Jonathan K. Su[1], and Bernd Girod[2]

[1] Telecommunications Laboratory, University of Erlangen-Nuremberg
Cauerstr. 7/NT, 91058 Erlangen, Germany
{eggers,su}@LNT.de
[2] Information Systems Laboratory, Stanford University
Stanford, CA 94305-9510, USA
girod@ee.stanford.edu

Abstract. Unauthorized copying and distribution of digital data is a severe problem in protecting intellectual property rights. The embedding of digital watermarks into multimedia content has been proposed to tackle this problem, and many different schemes have been presented in the last years. However, almost all of them are symmetric, meaning the key used for watermark embedding must be available at the watermark detector. This leads to a security problem if the detectors are implemented in consumer devices that are spread all over the world. Therefore, the development of asymmetric schemes becomes important. In such a scheme the detector only needs to know a public key, which does not give enough information to make watermark removal possible. In this paper, we review recent proposals for asymmetric watermarking and analyze their performance.

1 Introduction

The digital representation of audio signals, images, and video has become popular due to the ease of transmitting digital data and copying without loss of quality. However, the problem arises that unauthorized copying and distribution of digital data is simplified, too. For this reason, researcher have started looking for techniques that allow copy control of digital multimedia data and enable copyright enforcement. It was realized that common cryptographic means are not sufficient since the data is without any protection as soon it is used, e.g., decrypted and displayed in the case of image or video data. A potential aid in solving this problem is digital watermarking. Digital watermarking is the imperceptible embedding of information into multimedia data, where the information remains detectable as long the quality of the content itself is not rendered useless. It is commonly assumed that digital watermarking is only one of several measures that have to be combined to build a good copy protection mechanism [8].

One particular problem with state-of-the-art watermarking schemes is that they are symmetric. The keys necessary for watermark embedding and detection are identical. Thus, the watermark detector knows all critical parameter of the watermarking scheme that also allow efficient removal of the embedded watermark. We will discuss such methods in more detail in Section 3. Using watermark technology for copy protection, the watermark detector needs to be implemented in many cheap consumer devices all over the world. A symmetric watermarking scheme presents a security risk, since the detector has to know the required private key. However, cheap tamper-proof devices are hardly produceable [8], and thus, pirates can obtain the private key from such devices and use them to outwit the copy protection mechanism. For this reason, we would like to develop a watermarking scheme where detection of the watermark is possible with a public key that does not give enough information to impair the embedded watermark. Such a scheme is called asymmetric. The intention of this paper is to give an overview of proposals for such a mechanism and discuss their pros and cons.

First, we will explain our notation and describe a general point of view on watermarking schemes in Section 2. For a better understanding of the differences between symmetric and asymmetric schemes, both methods are described. In Section 3, we will discuss two symmetric watermarking schemes and possible attacks if the private key can be accessed by an attacker. Several proposals of asymmetric watermarking schemes are discussed in Section 4. Finally, an assessment of the state-of-the-art is given, and future research directions are proposed.

2 Digital Watermarking: A Communications Problem

We view digital watermarking as a communications problem, where the watermark information $b \in \mathcal{B}$, with $\mathcal{B}$ denoting the finite set of all possible watermark messages, is transmitted over an hostile channel. The host signal $\underline{x}$ serves as the carrier for the watermark information. In this paper, we adopt vector notation for signals, that is $\underline{x} = [x[0], x[1], \ldots, x[N-1]]^T$ with $x[i]$ being the ith signal sample. We do not focus on a specific data type. $\underline{x}$ can denote audio, image or video data, or any transform domain representation of such multimedia data. In practice, watermarking schemes have to be optimized for the specific features of different host signals. Here, our intention is to compare basic concepts without considering details that are strongly dependent on the specific multimedia data.

Any modification of the host signal $\underline{x}$ does affect its quality, thus an assessment of watermarking schemes is not possible without defining a quality measurement. Good quality measurements are again strongly dependent on the data at hand. However, as a rough approximation, the *mean squared error* (MSE) between the original host signal and any modified signal can be used as a quality measurement.

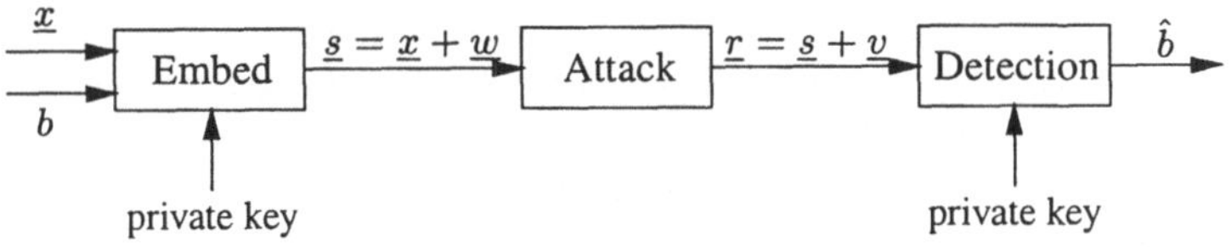

Fig. 1. General blind symmetric watermarking scheme.

Fig. 1 depicts a general blind symmetric watermarking scheme. The term "blind" indicates that the host signal $\underline{x}$ is not known at the watermark detector. The watermark information b is embedded into the host signal $\underline{x}$ dependent on a private key. All modifications introduced by the embedding process are denoted by the watermark signal $\underline{w}$, so that the public signal $\underline{s}$ can be expressed as $\underline{s} = \underline{x} + \underline{w}$. The distortion introduced by the embedding of the watermark is given by $D_E = \mathrm{E}\left\{(s - x)^2\right\} = \mathrm{E}\left\{w^2\right\}$. Here, $\mathrm{E}\{\cdot\}$ denotes expectation.

The public signal $\underline{s}$ is subject to a variety of different *attacks*. We use the term *attack* for any signal processing that, intentionally or not, reduces the reliability of watermark detection. The modifications introduced by the attack(s) can be summarized by the additive, but not necessarily independent, signal $\underline{v}$. Of course, an attack is useless if the attacked signal $\underline{r} = \underline{s} + \underline{v}$ has such poor quality that its value is lost. Thus, the quality of the attacked signal must be sufficiently good. Many watermarking schemes can be successfully attacked by desynchronizing the embedded watermark relative to the watermark signal the detector is looking for. We do not consider desynchronization attacks formally, but point out where synchronization is a particularly difficult problem. Assuming synchronization, the quality of the attacked signal $\underline{r}$ is measured relative to the original host signal $\underline{x}$. We measure the distortion of an attacked signal by $D_A = \mathrm{E}\left\{(r - x)^2\right\}$.

Finally, the detector computes an estimate $\hat{b}$ of the transmitted watermark information b, depending on the private key and the received signal $\underline{r}$. The probability $\mathrm{Pr}(\hat{b} \neq b)$ of false detection should be as small as possible.

The constraints on the qualities D_E and D_A are strongly dependent on the given data and the application in mind. However, it is reasonable to assume that the allowable D_A is at least at the order of D_E, and in many cases even much larger. We use the ratio $D_{A,\mathrm{min}}/D_E$ as a robustness criteria, with $D_{A,\mathrm{min}}$ being the minimal distortion for a successful attack. Chen and Wornell [2] introduced the term "distortion penalty" for $D_{A,\mathrm{min}}/D_E$.

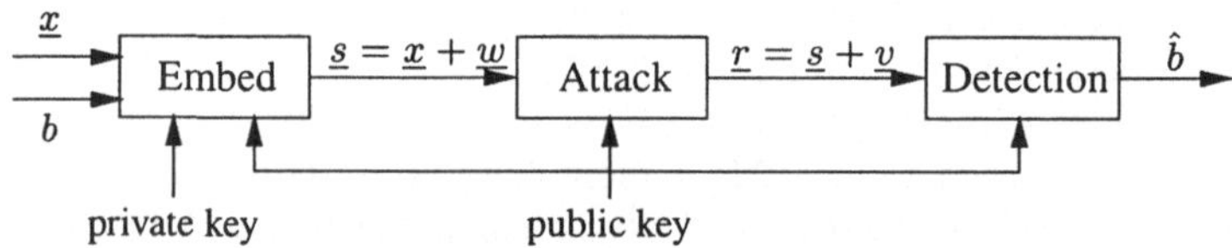

Fig. 2. General asymmetric watermarking scheme.

Fig. 2 depicts a general asymmetric watermarking scheme. With aid of a private and a public key, the watermark is embedded into the host signal $\underline{x}$. The significant difference to the symmetric scheme depicted in Fig. 1 is that all entities, embedding, attack and detection, have access to the public key necessary for watermark detection. Obviously, an attacker can try to use the knowledge of the public key to destroy the embedded watermark information.

3 Symmetric Watermarking and Public Detection

In this section, two techniques for blind symmetric watermarking will be briefly reviewed and their security risks in combination with public detectors will be discussed.

3.1 Spread-Spectrum Watermarking

Spread-spectrum watermarking is one of the first methods used for blind symmetric watermarking (e.g., [3, 11]) and is still the most popular one. Many modifications are possible, depending on the characteristics of the host signal and the application in mind. Here, it is sufficient to focus on the basic approach, which can be described as follows:

1. A random signal $\underline{z}$ is defined. For instance, the samples $z[i]$ can be drawn independently and equiprobably from the binary alphabet $\{-1, +1\}$. $\underline{z}$ serves as the private key of the watermarking scheme. Watermark embedding is implemented by simple addition of the watermark signal $\underline{w} = b\alpha\underline{z}$. The scale factor α determines the power of the watermark signal and must be chosen such that the watermark is imperceptible, but sufficient reliably detectable. The factor $b \in \mathcal{B}$ depends on the watermark information to be transmitted. For instance, unipolar transmission is obtained for $\mathcal{B} = \{0, 1\}$, and for bipolar transmission $\mathcal{B} = \{-1, +1\}$.

2. For detection, the correlation between the received signal $\underline{r} = \underline{x} + \underline{w} + \underline{v}$ and the private-key signal $\underline{z}$ is measured. Spread-spectrum watermarking relies on the assumption that the key signal $\underline{z}$ is statistically independent from the host signal $\underline{x}$ and the distortion $\underline{v}$, which leads to $\mathrm{E}\{zr\} = \mathrm{E}\{z(x+v)\} + b\alpha\mathrm{E}\{z^2\} = 0 + b\alpha\mathrm{E}\{z^2\}$. For finite-length signals, the correlation can be measured only with a certain level of accuracy. The estimated watermark information $\hat{b}$ can be obtained from a hypothesis test on the measured correlation $c = (1/N) \sum_{i=0}^{N-1} z[i]r[i]$. Here, the power of the interfering signals $\underline{x}$ and $\underline{v}$ becomes important and the detection performance increases with the signal length N and embedding strength α. For $\mathcal{B} = \{-1, +1\}$, the estimated watermark information can be obtained easily from the sign of the measured correlation: $\hat{b} = \mathrm{sign}(c)$.

Without knowing $\underline{z}$, it is difficult to attack the embedded watermark. However, knowing the private key, the watermark can be removed easily. First, the watermark information b is detected and the watermark signal $\underline{w} = b\alpha\underline{z}$ is reconstructed. In the most simple case, when the attacker has the purely watermarked public signal $\underline{s}$ without any further distortion, he can subtract $\underline{w}$ to obtain the non-distorted host signal $\underline{x}$. Having an already distorted public signal $\underline{r} = \underline{s} + \underline{v}$, the attacker maximizes the signal quality and minimized the ability of watermark detection by cancelling the signal components that are correlated with $\underline{w}$. This can be achieved by $\underline{r} - (\underline{w}^T\underline{r}/\,||\underline{w}||^2)\underline{w}$. Thus, keeping the key $\underline{z}$ private is crucial to the security of spread-spectrum watermarking.

3.2 Quantization Index Modulation (QIM)

Chen and Wornell [1, 2] proposed a blind watermarking technique where the host signal $\underline{x}$ is quantized differently depending on the watermark information to be embedded. The general scheme is called *quantization index modulation* (QIM).

A quantizer can be uniquely described by a set of reconstruction points $\mathcal{Q}$ in an L-dimensional space and a rule for assigning a length-L input signal to one of the points defined in $\mathcal{Q}$. Here, we will always use the minimum-distance rule for selecting the appropriate points and characterize different quantizers solely by their reconstruction points $\mathcal{Q}$.

The basic principle of QIM can be described as follows:

1. A set of different quantizers $\{\mathcal{Q}_0, \mathcal{Q}_1, \mathcal{Q}_2, \ldots, \mathcal{Q}_{B-1}\}$ is defined. The index set $\mathcal{B}=\{0, 1, 2, \ldots, B-1\}$ denotes the B considered watermark messages.
2. For embedding the watermark information $b \in \mathcal{B}$, the host signal $\underline{x}$ is quantized using the quantizer $\mathcal{Q}_b$ to obtain the public signal $\underline{s}$. Thus, the expected embedding distortion D_E is equal to the introduced quantization noise.
3. The watermark detector quantizes the received signal $\underline{r}$ by the union of all quantizers $\{\mathcal{Q}_0, \mathcal{Q}_1, \mathcal{Q}_2, \ldots, \mathcal{Q}_{B-1}\}$. The detector determines the index of the quantizer containing the reconstruction point closest to the received signal. This index corresponds to the received watermark information $\hat{b}$.

QIM does not suffer from host signal interference like blind spread spectrum watermarking does. Thus, QIM offers high watermark rates when the distortion introduced by attacks is small. Since quantization always includes a loss of detail ("many-to-one mapping"), it is not possible to reconstruct the host signal $\underline{x}$ perfectly from a given public signal $\underline{s}$, even if the watermark information b and the watermarking scheme is completely known. Nevertheless, QIM must be considered a symmetric watermarking technique, since encoder and decoder have to have the same knowledge; in particular the involved quantizer sets must be known.

Chen and Wornell argued in [2] that QIM could be used as a public-key watermarking scheme, since successful removal of the watermark information is not possible without introducing additional distortion. Although this is true in theory, we have found that the distortion introduced by successful attacks is smaller than the embedding distortion and therefore might be acceptable in many circumstances. Here, we will discuss two example QIM schemes. First, binary dither modulation using a shifted uniform scalar quantizer [1, 2], and second, dithered hexagonal lattice quantization.

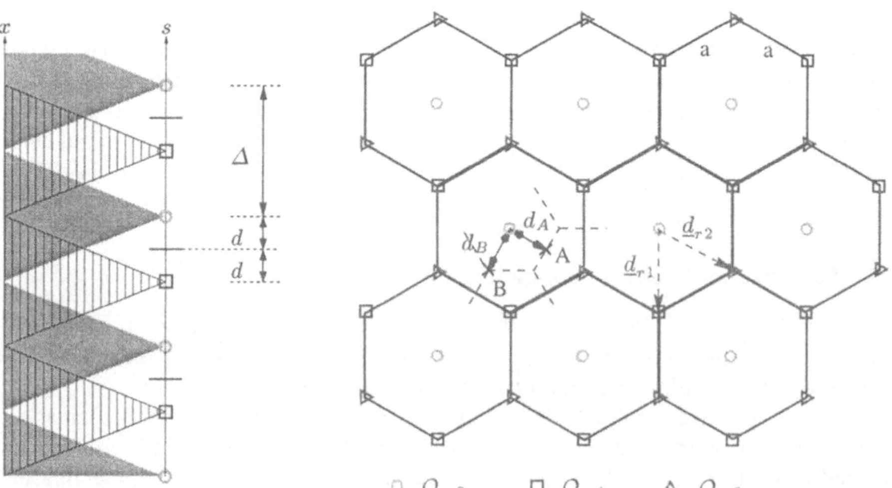

Fig. 3. Example QIM schemes based on dithered uniform scalar quantization (left) and dithered hexagonal lattice quantization (right)

For binary dither modulation, the mapping of the range of host signal values x onto a public signal value s is depicted in the left diagram in Fig. 3. The set $\mathcal{Q}_0$ (circles) is defined by an uniform scalar quantizer with step size Δ. The set $\mathcal{Q}_1$ (squares) is another uniform scalar quantizer, however, with an offset of $\Delta/2$. Switching between both quantizers can be considered dithered quantization. Since decoding the watermark is based on the closest distance rule, a detection error can occur after modifying the public signal sample s by at least $\pm d$.

If the detection process is publicly known, an attacker can perturb the public signal $\underline{s}$ in such a way that the attacked signal $\underline{r}$ exactly lies on the decision boundary between different quantizer points. For binary dither modulation these points are depicted by the short lines in Fig. 3 (left). After such an attack, the decoder can only randomly guess whether the received signal sample was originally quantized by $\mathcal{Q}_0$ or $\mathcal{Q}_1$. Thus, the watermark information is completely lost. Note that no channel coding can help to recover information from the such attacked signal.

Of course, Chen and Wornell's statement that QIM can never be attacked without introducing additional distortion still holds. However, the distortion penalty for the described attack and binary dither modulation is only $D_{A,\mathtt{min}}/D_E = 1.75 \equiv 2.43$ dB.

We also investigated a two-dimensional QIM scheme using hexagonal lattice quantization. Fig. 3 (right) depicts the considered quantizer $\mathcal{Q}_0$, $\mathcal{Q}_1$ and $\mathcal{Q}_2$. We depicted also the decision boundaries for $\mathcal{Q}_0$. They form a hexagonal lattice. The quantizer $\mathcal{Q}_1$ and $\mathcal{Q}_2$ are obtained from $\mathcal{Q}_0$ by dithering with the dither vectors $\underline{d}_{r1}$ and $\underline{d}_{r2}$. Making the sets $\mathcal{Q}_0$, $\mathcal{Q}_1$ and $\mathcal{Q}_2$ public again enables the attack of putting the public signal samples $\underline{s}$ on the decision boundary between the three possible quantizers. Two special versions of this attack are considered. First, a point in the middle of two quantizers $\mathcal{Q}_i$ and $\mathcal{Q}_j$, with $i \neq j$, is chosen . We marked such a point in Fig. 3 (right) by "A". Another option is to choose a point in the middle of all three quantizers. An example point is marked in Fig. 3 (right) by "B". Attack A gives a smaller attack distortion since the distance $d_A < d_B$. On the other hand, some watermark information remains since the detector can exclude one of the three possible quantizers. The watermark information is completely erased in case of attack B. For the attack "A", a distortion penalty of $D_{A,\mathtt{min}}/D_E = 1.6 \equiv 2.04$ dB results, whereas for the attack "B" a distortion penalty of $D_{A,\mathtt{min}}/D_E = 1.8 \equiv 2.55$ dB is achieved. These values are very similar to the distortion penalty found for binary dither modulation.

We conclude that for the investigated QIM schemes, public-key watermarking is possible, but the distortion penalty for successfull attacks is too low for many practical applications.

4 Properties of Proposed Asymmetric Watermarking Schemes

In the last section it was illustrated that some symmetric watermarking schemes are no longer robust when the private key for watermark detection is made public. In this section we review proposals for asymmetric watermarking and discuss their robustness against attacks.

4.1 Spread Spectrum Watermarking with Partly Known Key

Hartung and Girod [10] discussed a public-key watermarking approach that is a simple modification of spread-spectrum watermarking. Recall from Section 3.1 that the private key z must be known for spread-spectrum watermark detection. However, if long watermark signals can be obtained, it is possible to detect a spread-spectrum watermark even if some samples of z are modified. Based on this idea, every recipient of the watermarked data gets a different "public key" z_k, where only a subset of the samples of z_k match those in z. The rest of z_k is chosen randomly. Using this approach, client k cannot modify the part of the watermark detected by z_j (with $j \neq k$) and client j cannot modify the part of the watermark detected by z_k.

However, it was mentioned already in [10] that recipient k, knowing the public key sequence z_k can easily make detection based on this public key impossible. For this, the correlation between z_k and the received signal r must be removed, which can be achieved by $r - (z_k^T r / ||z_k||^2) z_k$. Using this attack, the quality of the attacked signal might be even better than that of the watermarked signal.

It is obvious that such a public watermarking scheme cannot solve the copy-protection problem described in Section 1. Thus, the term "public watermark" is misleading. Instead, the scheme has applications in multiple watermarking of one document, where several spread-spectrum watermarks are combined in an elegant way.

4.2 Asymmetric Watermarking based on One-Way Signal Processing

Furon and Duhamel [7] concluded from comparisons to public-key cryptosystems that a one-way signal-processing function is needed to build an asymmetric watermarking scheme. They identified the power density spectrum (PDS) of a signal as a candidate of such an one-way function. The PDS of a signal describes the signal to some extent, but in general does not allow perfect reconstruction due to the loss of the signal phase. Furon and Duhamel implemented and tested their approach for image and audio signals [7–9]. We briefly describe the basic principle of the proposed scheme. After that an effective attack is discussed.

First, the host signal is randomly permuted. For brevity, we denote the permuted host signal by x and its power by P_x. The main purpose of the permutation is to break statistical dependencies between adjacent signal samples so that x has a flat PDS. As in spread-spectrum watermarking, an independent watermark signal w is added to the permuted host signal to obtain the permuted public signal $s = x + w$. However, in this scheme, the watermark signal is colored noise, which can be obtained by filtering a white noise signal z of power P_z. Let $H(\Omega)$ denote the frequency response of the selected filter. The PDS of the watermark signal is given by $\Phi_{ww}(\Omega) = P_z |H(\Omega)|^2$. Since the watermark signal w is independent from the host signal x, the PDS of the public signal s is straightforwardly derived as $\Phi_{ss}(\Omega) = P_x + P_z |H(\Omega)|^2$.

The public detection process is based on the specific shape of the PDS of the public signal s. Furon and Duhamel describe an hypothesis test that, given a permuted received signal r, allows one to decide whether its PDS is flat or resembles the shape of $\Phi_{ss}(\Omega)$. Obviously, permutation of the host signal is necessary, since the hypothesis test is designed on the assumption of a flat PDS of x.

Note that the watermark sequence $\underline{w}$ need not to be known for watermark detection. The shape of $\Phi_{ss}(\Omega)$ is the public key that allows watermark detection. In general, it is impossible to find $\underline{w}$ from $\Phi_{ss}(\Omega)$. Thus, the described scheme was thought to be secure against malicious attacks.

However, there is a way of making public watermark detection impossible without knowing $\underline{w}$. One simply has to filter the permuted public signal $\underline{s}$ so that its PDS is whitened. In personal communications, Teddy Furon pointed out that such filtering has to be implemented carefully, since phase modifications of the public signal can have a perceivable effect on the signal quality. One way of implementing the attack is to compute the Fourier spectrum of the public signal, modify only its absolute values and use the inversely transformed data as the attacked public signal $\underline{r}$. This attack is successful without decreasing the signal quality since mainly watermark components are filtered out.

4.3 Legendre Watermarking

Van Schyndel et al. [12] proposed an asymmetric watermarking scheme based on a length-N Legendre sequence $\underline{a}$. Legendre sequences have a simple relationship to their DFT, namely $\mathbf{G}_{\mathcal{DFT}}\underline{a} = \underline{A} = A_1\,\underline{a}^\star$, where $\mathbf{G}_{\mathcal{DFT}}$ is the DFT matrix, the scalar A_1 can be complex, and $\underline{a}^\star$ denotes the conjugate Legendre sequence. Large letters, e.g. $\underline{A}$, denote frequency-domain values. The Fourier invariance of the Legendre sequence is a property that does not hold for general sequences. Therefore, van Schyndel et al. proposed to use the Legendre sequence as a watermark $\underline{w} = \underline{a}$, so that the public signal is $\underline{s} = \underline{x} + \underline{a}$. The watermark is detected in the received signal $\underline{r} = \underline{x} + \underline{v} + \underline{a}$ by correlating $\underline{r}$ with its conjugate Fourier transform $(\mathbf{G}_{\mathcal{DFT}}\underline{r})^\star = \underline{R}^\star = (\underline{X} + \underline{V})^\star + A_1^\star\underline{a}$. A large correlation value $c = \underline{r}^H\mathbf{G}_{\mathcal{DFT}}\underline{r}/N$ indicates the existence of the embedded Legendre watermark. Here, $\underline{r}^H$ denotes the conjugate transpose of $\underline{r}$. The detection works reliably if $(\underline{x} + \underline{v})^T(\underline{X} + \underline{V})^\star \approx 0$ is fulfilled.

The embedded Legendre sequence $\underline{a}$ need not to be known explicitly for the described detection process. Thus, the watermarking scheme can be used as a public-key scheme, where the embedded Legendre sequence $\underline{a}$ serves as the private key and the sequence length N is the public key. One shortcoming is that only $N - 2$ different, non-degenerate Legendre sequences of length N exist. Therefore, an attacker might be able to determine the embedded Legendre sequence by exhaustive search. Another disadvantage is that Legendre sequences exist only for prime length N. There are also malicious attacks against the Legendre watermarking scheme [5]. Those will be discussed in the next subsection.

4.4 Eigenvector Watermarking

The key idea of the Legendre watermaking scheme is that the DFT maps a Legendre sequence back to itself, except for conjugation and a scale factor. We looked at modifications of this approach and proposed an asymmetric watermarking scheme using eigenvectors of linear transforms [6].

The eigenvector watermarking scheme is based on a $N \times N$ transform matrix $\mathbf{G}$ and a watermark vector $\underline{w}$ with the property $\mathbf{G}\underline{w} = \lambda_0\underline{w}$, thus $\underline{w}$ is an eigenvector of

G, and λ_0 the corresponding eigenvalue. The watermark sequence $\underline{w}$ must be so small that $\underline{x}$ and $\underline{s}$ are perceptually equal.

For watermark detection, the correlation $c = \underline{r}^H \mathbf{G}\underline{r}/N$ between the received signal $\underline{r}$ and its transformed signal $\mathbf{G}\underline{r}$ is measured. A large correlation value c indicates that the received signal $\underline{r}$ contains an eigenvector of $\mathbf{G}$. The described watermarking scheme is asymmetric, since the embedded watermark signal $\underline{w}$ is not needed in the detection process. The matrix $\mathbf{G}$ serves as the public key.

An analysis of the properties of Legendre watermarking and eigenvector watermarking can be found in [6]. Due to space constraints, we can only summarize the major results:

- Legendre watermarking and eigenvector watermarking suffer significantly from host-signal interference. Compared to symmetric spread-spectrum watermarking, the watermark signal length N has to be increased dramatically, in particular when small watermark-to-document ratios (WDRs) are desired.
- Legendre watermarks are not secure against exhaustive search for the embedded sequence. Eigenvector watermarks can be much more secure, if the eigenvector belongs to an eigenvalue of $\mathbf{G}$ with a large geometric multiplicity. However, attacks like the sensitivity attack described by Cox and Linnartz in [4] might be successful if good objective quality measurements without reference to the original signal are known.
- Instead of removing an embedded watermark, an attacker can try to confuse the public watermark detector by adding another signal $\underline{z}$ with the property $\mathbf{G}\underline{z} = -\beta\lambda_0\underline{z}$, where $\beta > 0$. The additional distortion of a successful confusion attack depends on the eigenvalues of $\mathbf{G}$. The largest distortion penalty of $D_{A,\min}/D_E = 3 \equiv 4.771$ dB was found for $\mathbf{G}$ being a certain permutation matrix. The confusion attack can also be used with minor modification against the Legendre watermarking scheme. In this case the distortion penalty is $D_{A,\min}/D_E = 2 \equiv 3$ dB.
- Anybody can embed a watermark $\underline{w}$ that is publicly detectable by $\mathbf{G}$. Thus, eigenvector watermarking is only usefull for certain applications. One application might be copy control. A signal is not copied if it contains an eigenvector watermark. No pirate would intentionally embed such a watermark.

Teddy Furon has found an effective attack against the eigenvector watermarking scheme. The public signal $\underline{s}$ is projected onto the subspace defined by all eigenvectors of $\mathbf{G}$ belonging to the eigenvalue λ_0. This projection $\underline{p}$ is scaled by a factor ν and subtracted from $\underline{s}$ to obtain the attacked signal $\underline{r} = \underline{s} - \nu\underline{p}$. The factor ν can be found analytically or simply by trial-and-error until the public detector no longer works. The distortion introduced by this attack is acceptable. Depending on the WDR, it is even possible to obtain a signal $\underline{r}$ having a higher quality than $\underline{s}$.

5 Conclusions

We presented attacks for two symmetric watermarking schemes combined with public detectors. Spread-spectrum watermarks can be easily removed by simultaneously improving the signal quality. QIM watermarks can be destroyed only by decreasing the average signal quality; however, the distortion penalty for a successful attack is small, about 2-2.5 dB.

We reviewed some proposals for asymmetric watermarking schemes and discussed their pros and cons. It was found that none of the schemes is sufficiently robust against malicious attacks.

For future research, it seems appropriate to develop a stronger theoretical foundation of asymmetric watermarking so that fundamental limits can be found. It is still not clear whether asymmetric watermarking might ever lead to secure public watermark detection. However, the topic is highly relevant since multimedia content providers already complain about huge financial losses due to illegal copying of the digital data.

6 Acknowledgement

We thank Teddy Furon for the frequent email discussion concerning the topic of asymmetric watermarking schemes.

References

1. B. Chen and G. W. Wornell. Digital watermarking and information embedding using dither modulation. In *Proc. of IEEE Workshop on Multimedia Signal Processing* , Redondo Beach, CA, USA, December 1998.
2. B. Chen and G. W. Wornell. Dither modulation: a new approach to digital watermarking and information embedding. In *Proc. of SPIE Vol. 3657: Security and Watermarking of Multimedia Contents*, San Jose, January 1999.
3. I. Cox, J. Kilian, T. Leighton, and T. Shamoon. Secure spread spectrum watermarking for multimedia. *IEEE Transactions on Image Processing*, 6(12):1673–1687, 1997.
4. I.J. Cox and J.-P. Linnartz. Some general methods for tampering with watermarks. *IEEE Journal on Selected Areas in Communications*, 16:587–593, May 1998.
5. J. J. Eggers and B. Girod. Robustness of Public Key Watermarking Schemes. In V^3D^2 *Watermarking Workshop*, Erlangen, Germany, October 1999.
6. J. J. Eggers, J. K. Su, and B. Girod. Public Key Watermarking by Eigenvectors of Linear Transforms. In *Proc. of European Signal Processing Conf.*, Tampere, Finland, April 2000. To appear.
7. T. Furon and P. Duhamel. An Asymmetric Public Detection Watermarking Technique. In *Workshop on Information Hiding*, Dresden, Germany, October 1999.
8. T. Furon and P. Duhamel. Copy Protection of Distributed Contents: An Application of Watermarking Technique. In *Workshop COST 254: Friendly Exchange through the net*, Bordeaux, France, March 2000.
9. T. Furon, N. Moreau, and P. Duhamel. Audio Public Key Watermarking Technique. In *Proc. of the IEEE Intl. Conf. on Speech and Signal Processing 2000* , Istanbul, Turkey, June 2000. To appear.
10. F. Hartung and B. Girod. Fast Public-Key Watermarking of Compressed Video. In *Proc. of the IEEE Intl. Conf. on Image Processing 1997* , Santa Barbara, CA, USA, October 1997.
11. F. Hartung and B. Girod. Watermarking of uncompressed and compressed video. *Signal Processing*, 66(3):283–301, May 1998.
12. R. G. van Schyndel, A. Z. Tirkel, and I. D. Svalbe. Key independent watermark detection. In *Proc. of the IEEE Intl. Conf. on Multimedia Computing and Systems*, volume 1, Florence, Italy, June 1999.

Handschriftliche Authentifikation für digitale Wasserzeichenverfahren

Claus Vielhauer[1,2]

1 Platanista GmbH
D-64289 Darmstadt, Pankratiusstrasse 7
claus.vielhauer@platanista.com

2 Technische Universität Darmstadt – Industrielle Prozess- und Systemkommunikation (KOM)
D-64283 Darmstadt, Merckstrasse 25
claus.vielhauer@KOM.tu-darmstadt.de

Abstract. In diesem Beitrag befassen wir uns mit Möglichkeiten der biometrischen Authentifizierung für digitale Wasserzeichenverfahren. Es wird untersucht, wie biometrische Merkmale anhand von handschriftlichen Signalen zur vereinfachten Authentifizierung der Urheber oder Lizenznehmer herangezogen werden können. Digitale Wasserzeichenverfahren benötigen Schlüssel zum Einbetten der Informationen in das Multimediadokument bzw. zum Auslesen aus diesem. Zur Schlüsselgenerierung können grundsätzlich biometrische Verfahren, wie beispielsweise Fingerabdruck-, Iris-, Handflächen- oder Gesichterkennung oder Verifikationsverfahren, die auf Schrift- oder Stimmerkennung basieren, eingesetzt werden. Aufgrund der impliziten Willenserklärung, aber auch der breiten Benutzerakzeptanz stellt die Eingabe handschriftlicher Dokumente, wie z.B. die Unterschrift auf Digitizer-Tabletts oder mobilen Displays, ein bevorzugtes Verfahren dar. Im Beitrag werden handschriftliche Charakteristiken vorgestellt und klassifiziert. Anhand der Charakteristiken werden Referenzmodelle vorgestellt, die zur Authentifikation herangezogen werden können. Basierend auf diesen biometrischen Referenzen werden drei Ansätze zum Einsatz handschriftlicher Authentifikation bei digitalen Wasserzeichenverfahren dargestellt, wobei sich zwei Verfahren mit der Generierung von Schlüsseldaten aus handschriftlichen Eingaben befassen und ein drittes die Möglichkeit erörtert, biometrische Referenzdaten als elektronische Signatur in Multimediadokumente einzubetten. Der Aspekt der Kombination biometrischer Verfahren und Wasserzeichentechniken ist neu und eröffnet noch viel Forschungsspielraum. Unser Beitrag wird die Grundlagen, Probleme und Lösungsmöglichkeiten diskutieren. Unsere weiteren Arbeiten, zur Erhebung und Auswertung von Daten im Feldversuch, zur Bestimmung von biometrischen Kenngrößen, sowie zur Untersuchung zur Anwendung auf mobilen Displays bleiben hier unberücksichtigt.

1. Motivation

Grundsätzlich werden zum Einbetten und Auslesen von digitalen Wasserzeichen in Mediendaten Schlüssel benötigt. Bisher kommen dabei vor allem symmetrische Schlüssel in Frage [3]. Diese geheimen Schlüssel verbleiben beim Einbringer (Urheber) der Wasserzeicheninformation. Da die Verwaltung dieser Schlüssel aufwendig und nicht sehr anwenderfreundlich ist, werden neue Ansätze zur Schlüsselverwahrung oder Generierung gesucht. So bieten z.B. Chipkarten die Möglichkeit, einen oder mehrere komplexe Schlüssel, abgesichert mit einer PIN-basierten Verschlüsselung, abgespeichert mit sich zu führen.

Noch anwenderfreundlicher erscheinen Ansätze, die biometrische Merkmale verwenden. Hier kann der Schlüssel oder die PIN nicht mehr vergessen werden, da das Individuum selbst Träger des Merkmals ist und Schlüsselwerte direkt oder indirekt aus den biometrischen Eigenschaften abgeleitet werden können.

Neben biometrischen Verfahren wie Fingerabdruck-, Iris-, Gesicht- und Handflächenerkennung, die jedoch keine explizite Willenserklärung beinhalten, existieren Möglichkeiten, physiologische Eigenschaften wie Stimme und Handschrift mit einer aktiven Willenserklärung zu kombinieren. Hierzu kommen bei handschriftlicher Eingabe z.B. Passphrase oder Unterschrift in Frage.

Der neue Ansatz, biometrische Eigenschaften handschriftlicher Eingaben im Rahmen von Wasserzeichenverfahren einzusetzen, basiert auf der Überlegung, daß solcherlei Eingaben, insbesondere in der Form von Unterschriften, bereits im Alltag als Nachweis der Authentizität eingesetzt werden. Im künstlerischen Umfeld erscheint das Signieren eines Werkes als sehr intuitiv, demzufolge kann eine erhöhte Akzeptanz gegenüber anderer biometrischer Verfahren erwartet werden.

Die zunehmende Verbreitung von mobilen Computern mit der Möglichkeit zur Stift-basierten Eingabe auf dem Display eröffnet weiterhin das Potential, ohne spezielle Eingabegeräte digitale handschriftliche Dokumente mobil zu erfassen und ggf. sogar auf Hand-Held Computern auszuwerten

In den folgenden Kapiteln befassen wir uns zunächst in Kapitel 2 mit den Grundlagen handschriftlicher Merkmale, den physikalischen Kenngrößen, sowie der Frage, wie sich diese Kenngrößen mathematisch darstellen lassen. In Kapitel 3 werden unsere Ansätze der Nutzung von handschriftlichen Eingaben diskutiert, d.h. die Frage erörtert, welche Semantik sich für handschriftliche Eingaben zur Authentifizierung grundsätzlich eignet. Basierend auf diesen Grundlagen werden in Kapitel 4 biometrische Charakteristiken als Referenzgrößen vorgestellt. Neben der Präsentation, wie solche Referenzmodelle mathematisch aufgebaut werden, ist hier der Speicherbedarf solcher Referenzgrößen relevant. Unsere Vorschläge, wie die zuvor entwickelten Referenzmodelle handschriftlicher Merkmale beim Einbetten und Auslesen von Informationen in Wasserzeichen eingesetzt werden können, werden in Kapitel 5 diskutiert. Im abschließenden Kapitel 6 werden offene Forschungsfelder dargestellt und ein Ausblick auf vielversprechende Ansätze vorgenommen.

2. Handschriftliche Merkmale

Mit der zunehmenden Verfügbarkeit und dem Einsatz von Stift-basierten Eingabegeräten (z.B. Digitizer Tablets, drucksensitive LCD Displays) ergeben sich aus der Analyse handschriftlicher Eingaben neue wissenschaftliche Herausforderungen. Es finden sich bereits zahlreiche Ansätze zur Analyse handschriftlicher Eingaben hinsichtlich Schrifterkennung und Unterschriftverifikation. Dabei wird nach [6] zwischen zwei Arten der Erfassung handschriftlicher Daten unterschieden: die Offline- und Online-Erfassung.

Die Offline-Erfassung beschreibt die Repräsentation einer optisch gescannten handschriftlichen Probe und kann in Pixel- oder Vektorform dargestellt werden.

Bei der Online-Erfassung werden zu den örtlichen Koordinaten zusätzlich Informationen über die Stiftbewegung aufgezeichnet. Diese Informationen beinhalten zum einen zeitliche Zusammenhänge des Schreibvorgangs (die Dynamik) und zum anderen Größen des Schriftverlaufs orthogonal zur Schreibunterlage (Druckinformationen, Stiftauf- und absetzpunkte, Aufsetzwinkel des Stiftes).

Generell erscheinen Online-Schriftproben aufgrund des erhöhten Informationsgehalts gegenüber der Offline-Variante geeigneter für die Handschriftanalyse. In der weiteren Betrachtung werden aus diesem Grund und zum Zweck der Authentifizierung lediglich Online-erfaßte Schriften betrachtet.

Handschriftliche Eingaben wie Texte oder Zahlenfolgen zeigen eine Reihe von Charakteristiken auf, die zur personenunabhängigen Zeichen- und Umrisserkennung, als Indikator für individuelle Schriftstile (und somit als Kandidat für biometrische Merkmale) oder aber auch für beides interessant erscheinen. Digitale stiftbasierte Eingabegeräte liefern Signale, die wir im Folgenden als Kenngrößen zum Einsatz in digitalen Wasserzeichen betrachten [7,9]. Wir betrachten folgende Signale:

Physikalische Meßsignale
- x- und y-Schreibsignal $x(t)$ und $y(t)$
- Schreibdruck $p(t)$
- Stiftwinkel $\varphi(t)$

Abgeleitete Signale
- x- und y-Geschwindigkeitssignal $v_x(t) = x'(t)$ und $v_y(t) = y'(t)$
- x- und y-Beschleunigungssignal $a_x(t) = x''(t)$ und $a_y(t) = y''(t)$
- Schreibdruckänderung $p'(t)$
- Stiftwinkeländerung $\varphi'(t)$

Beschreibungen einer Vielzahl statistische Parameter der Eingabe finden sich in der Literatur [1]. Auszugsweise seinen hier genannt:

- Anzahl und Verhältnis Auf- und Absetzpunkte $N_{PenDown}$, N_{PenUp} und $N_{PenDown}$ / N_{PenUp}
- Kumulierte Auf- und Absetzzeiten, sowie derer Verhältnis $T_{PenDown}$, T_{PenUp} und $T_{PenDown}$ / T_{PenUp}

- Mittelwert μ, Standardabweichung σ und Varianz DX der physikalischen und abgeleiteten Signale über einen oder mehrere Zeitintervalle des Schriftverlaufs
- Anzahl und Verhältnis lokaler Minima und Maxima, beispielsweise für das y-Schreibsignal N_{yMin}, N_{yMax} und N_{yMin} / N_{yMax}

Weiterhin unterscheidet man zwischen globalen Parametern, die über die gesamte Eingabedauer bestimmt werden und lokalen, zu deren Bestimmung die Eingabe anhand von Merkmalen in mehrere Sequenzen zerlegt wird. Für jede Sequenz werden dann separat die Parameter errechnet.

2.1 x- und y-Schreibsignal

Im Weg-Zeit Diagramm wird die vom Stift zurückgelegte Strecke in x und y Richtung über den Zeitverlauf der Schrifteingabe dargestellt. Man legt den Koordinatenursprung bei einer solchen Darstellung in die linke obere Ecke des Eingabefeldes und zeichnet die Horizontalbewegung entlang der x- Achse als Funktion $x_{(t)}$ und die Vertikalbewegung entlang der y-Achse als $y_{(t)}$ auf. Es ergibt sich bei Schrifteingabe in lateinischer Schrift für $x_{(t)}$ ein Graph, der einer stetig steigenden Funktion gleicht. $y_{(t)}$ nähert den Verlauf einer Schwingung unterschiedlicher Amplitude, Frequenz und variierender Nulllinie an. Aufgrund des Schriftverlaufs von links nach rechts in der lateinischen Sprache erscheint das $y_{(t)}$ Diagramm ein gegenüber dem $x_{(t)}$ Diagramm erhöhten Informationsgehalt auf zuweisen.

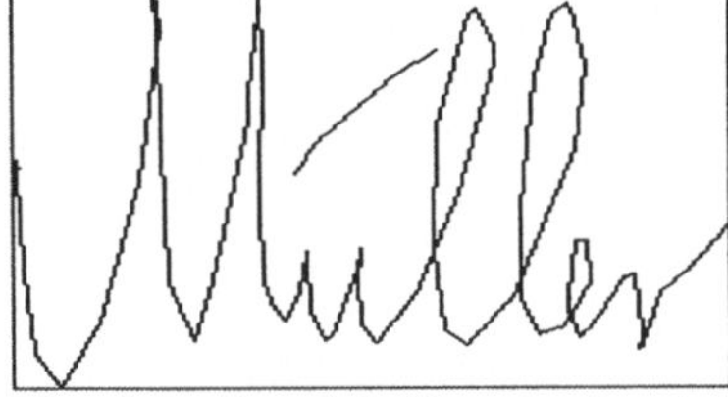

Fig. 1 Online-Schriftprobe in x/y Darstellung

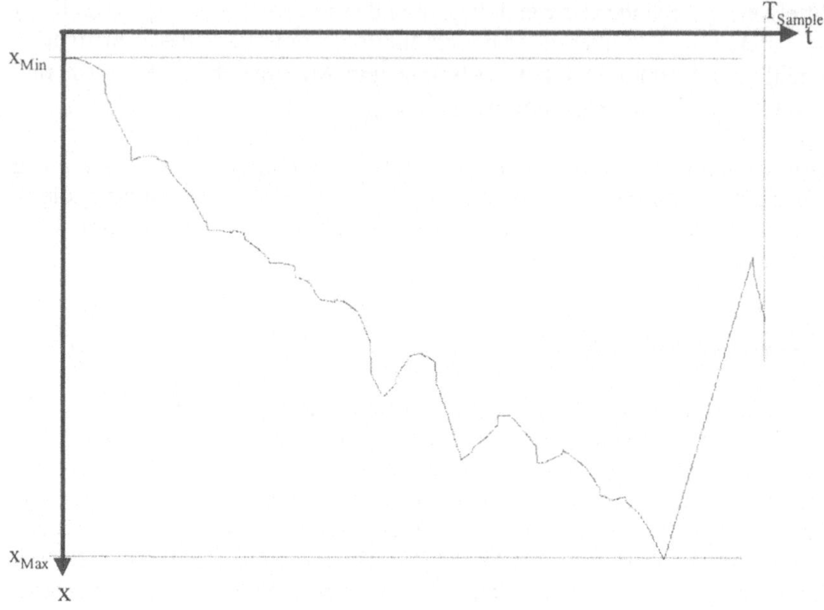

Fig. 2. Online-Schriftprobe in $x_{(t)}$ Darstellung

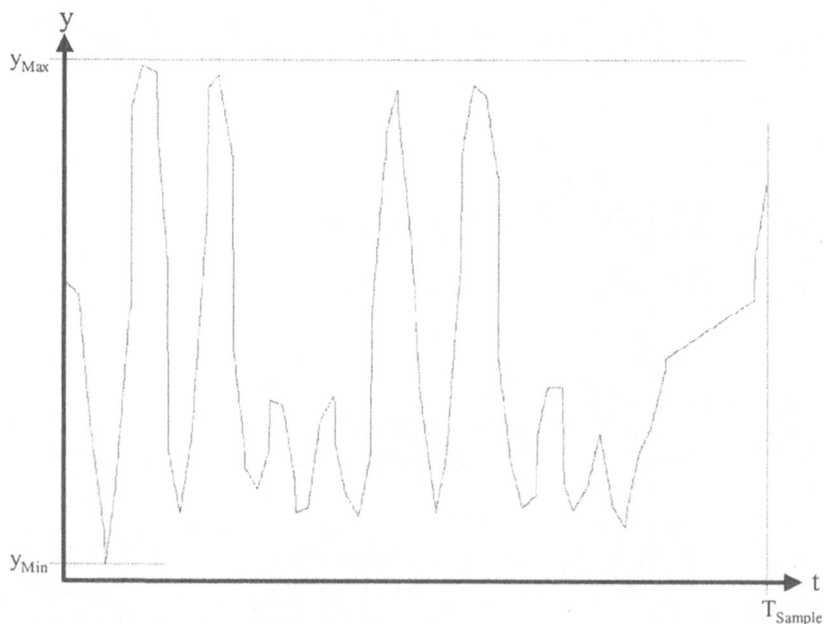

Fig. 3. Online-Schriftprobe in $y_{(t)}$ Darstellung

Möglichkeiten zur Authentifizierung bestehen in der Definition von Toleranz-intervallen basierend auf einer oder mehrerer Schriftproben, sowie von zugehörigen Schwellwerten. Zur Authentifizierung werden anhand der Toleranzintervalle und der vorliegenden Schriftgröße Kennwerte errechnet.

Ansätze, die z.B. die mittlere quadratische Abweichung von den Außenbegrenzenden der Toleranzintervalle oder gewichtete Abweichungen einer gemittelten Kennlinie heranziehen, werden derzeit im Rahmen von Feldversuchen von uns untersucht.

2.2   Schreibdrucksignal

Einige Verifikationsverfahren verwenden, zusätzlich zu den Schreibsignalen und den darauf basierenden abgeleiteten Signalen Geschwindigkeit und Beschleunigung, die Funktion des Druckverlaufs als Signal. Diese werden entweder an der Stiftspitze [2,11] oder von vier Druckaufnehmern an jedem der Ecken des rechteckigen Schriftaufnehmers erfaßt [5]. Die zugrunde liegenden Verfahren sind jedoch nicht veröffentlich.

Aufgrund unseres Bestrebens, Verifikationsverfahren für digitale Wasserzeichen mittels handelsüblicher Eingabegeräte auf plattformunabhängige Weise zu realisieren, berücksichtigen wir nur Pen-Down- und Pen-Up-Charakteristik, die als Schwellwertinformation binär die Auf- bzw. Absetzpunkte des Stiftes im Schreibstrom definiert. Hierbei definieren wir das binäre Stiftsignal wie folgt

$$p_{PenDown}(t) = \begin{array}{ll} 0, \text{ wenn Schreibstift zum Zeitpunkt t abgesetzt,} \\ 1, \text{ wenn Schreibstift zum Zeitpunkt t aufgesetzt} \end{array} \qquad (1)$$

2.3   Stiftwinkelsignal

Neben Digitalisierungstabletts, die Signale zu Schreibkoordinaten und Druck liefern, werden Schreibstiftprototypen beschrieben, die zusätzlich Informationen über den Stiftneigungswinkel aufnehmen [9]. Diese Signale werden entweder über Kraft- und/oder Beschleunigungssensoren erfaßt. Da solche Systeme noch nicht als Produkte existieren, wird der Stiftwinkel bei unseren Untersuchungen nicht weiter berücksichtigt.

2.4   Abgeleitete Signale

Die abgeleiteten Geschwindigkeit- und Beschleunigungssignale der physikalischen Meßgrößen bieten weitere Charakteristiken handschriftlicher Eingaben. So ist z.B. ein Stroke definiert als das Schreibsignal im Intervall zwischen zwei Nulldurchgängen der Schreibgeschwindigkeitssignale $v_x(t)$ und $v_y(t)$ [10]. Dies entspricht der Betrachtung der Schreibsignale $x(t)$ und $y(t)$ zwischen ihren jeweiligen lokalen Minima und Maxima. Die vollständige handschriftliche Eingabe kann somit segmentiert werden in eine Abfolge von Strokes, eine Möglichkeit der Merkmalsextraktion.

Weitere Charakteristiken finden sich in der Schreibbeschleunigung $a_x(t)$ und $a_y(t)$. Hier bieten Intervalle zwischen Minima und Maxima Segmentierung in Intervalle zwischen maximaler Geschwindigkeitsänderung und somit ein starkes Merkmal der Schreibdynamik.

3 Semantikklassen zur Nutzung von handschriftlichen Dokumenten als biometrische Identikatoren

Mit der generellen Feststellung, daß handschriftliche Eingaben aufgrund der Einzigartigkeit der menschlichen Physiologie und Sensorik als biometrische Merkmale angesehen werden können [9], stellt sich uns die Frage, welche Klasse von Semantik einer solche Eingabe zur Authentifizierung geeignet sind. Da es sich hierbei um vertrauenswürdige Daten des täglichen Gebrauchs handelt, muß der zu schreibende Inhalt für Anwender zum einen leicht zu merken, zum anderen mühelos in Form von Handschrift zu reproduzieren sein, ohne sehr starke Streuungen der biometrisch relevanten Eigenschaften zu produzieren.

Zwei Ad-Hoc Domänen erscheinen uns sinnvoll: Unterschrift (Signatur) und PIN-Codes. Während die erste sicherlich bezüglich Benutzerakzeptanz und Reproduzierbarkeit interessant erscheint, scheinen PIN-Codes aufgrund der Beschränktheit des verwendeten Alphabets, aber auch aufgrund der kurzen Zeichenfolge, relativ wenig biometrische Kapazität zu besitzen. Wir wählen deshalb für unsere Untersuchungen neben der Unterschrift auch Pass-Phrases (kurze Sequenz von typischerweise 3-5 alphanumerischer, einzelner Worte), die eine gegenüber PINs erhöhte Kapazität aufweisen, sowie einfache grafische Symbole, zusammengesetzt aus geometrischen Grundfiguren (z.B. Folge von Kreis, Quadrat und Rechteck). Diese Sequenz von Symbolen nennen wir Sketche.

3.1 Unterschrift als Träger der biometrischen Information

Die Unterschrift ist das handschriftliche Merkmal, das seit Jahrhunderten als Garant für Authentizität steht. Aufgrund der ständigen Anwendung ist dieses Merkmal individuell leicht zu wiederholen, bei geringer Streuung der biometrischen Kenngrößen.

Insbesondere die Dynamik einer elektronischen Unterschrift scheint eine starke personenbezogene Ausprägung zu haben. Es ist leicht, eine Unterschrift bei vorliegender Referenz graphisch zu fälschen, sie jedoch mit identischer Dynamik (Schwung) nachzuzeichnen und gleichzeitig die graphische Ähnlichkeit zu erzielen, erscheint sehr kompliziert und erfordert genaue Kenntnis über den Schreibstil des Urhebers.

3.2 Passphrase als Träger der biometrischen Information

Eine Passphrase bietet dem Anwender den Vorteil, daß er sich, ohne seine Identität offenzulegen, authentifizieren kann. Ferner ermöglicht die Passphrase die freie Wahl des textuellen Inhalts der Eingabe, sowie dessen spätere Änderung. Im Vergleich zu Passwörtern oder PINs ist i.d.R. der größere Informationsgehalt vorteilhaft, der sich aus längerer Eingabedauer und aus dem größeren Alphabet ergibt, was bei der Authentifizierung eine höhere Fehlersicherheit bedeutet. Aus Gründen der Praktikabilität und Laufzeitbeschränkung der Verifikationsalgorithmen ist jedoch eine Beschränkung auf 3-5 Worte notwendig.

3.3 Sketch als Träger der biometrischen Information

Auch bei Sketches gilt die Wahlfreiheit seitens des Benutzers. Hier muß allerdings noch untersucht werden, welche Art von Symbolen biometrische Eigenschaften beinhalten. Sehr einfache graphische Symbole wie z.B. Punkte oder Linien werden keine oder wenige individuelle Ausprägungen aufweisen, während eine komplexe Folge solcher Symbole durchaus Potential für biometrische Attribute besitzen (z.B. Zeichnen eines Gegenstandes wie „Haus").

Generell ist es bei dem Einsatz von Sketches Sequenzkontinuität erforderlich, d.h. es den Benutzern bewußt ist, daß es auf die Gestik der Schriftprobe ankommt, nicht das Aussehen. Dies bedeutet, ein Symbol (z.B. „Haus") muß immer in der gleichen Sequenz von primitiven Elementen (z.B. Linien) gezeichnet werden, ansonsten wird die Authentifizierung unmöglich. Andererseits ergibt sich dadurch ein deutlich sichereres biometrisches Merkmal, als es eine reine „Tinte- und Papier" Aufzeichnung bieten kann. Abbildung 4 zeigt exemplarisch zwei unterschiedliche Sequenzen beim Zeichnen des Sketches „Haus".

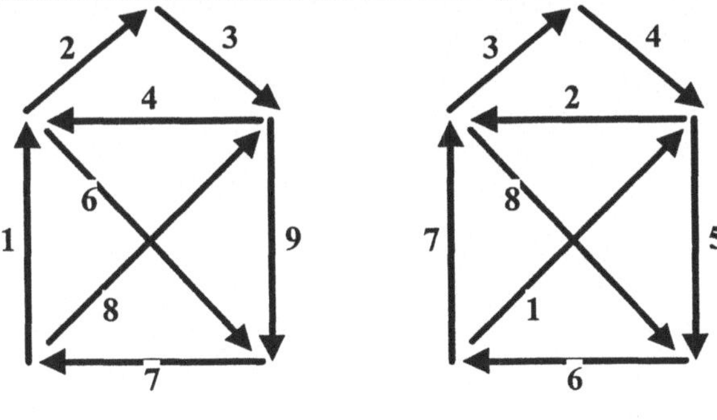

Fig. 4. Sequenzkontinuität am Beispiel zweier Sketche des Symbols „Haus"

4   Biometrische Charakteristika als Referenzgrößen

Im folgenden betrachten wir, auf welche Art die biometrischen Eigenschaften von handschriftlichen Eingaben als Referenzgrößen bestimmt werden können. Man wird hier mehrere Eingaben mit identischer Semantik zur Generierung einer Referenzmenge herziehen, die dann bei dem Authentifizierungsvorgang mit der vorliegenden, zu verifizierenden Eingabe verglichen wird. Diese biometrischen Kenngrößen können in folgende Kategorien klassifiziert werden:

- Referenzsignalverläufe, die sich aus einer oder mehrerer diskreter Funktionen ergeben
- Parameter, die sich als statistische, skalare Werte aus den Referenzsignalverläufen der handschriftlichen Eingabe errechnen und in einem Parametervektor darstellen lassen
- Strukturelle Ausprägung, wie z.B. Strokes [9]
- Zeit-Frequenzanalyse [9]
- Merkmalbasierte Segmentierung bei Betrachtung von Referenzsignalen im Zeitfenster jedes Segmentes, z.B. mit Methoden der Dynamischen Programmierung [12]

Exemplarisch wird in Abbildung 5 der Signalverlauf eines y(t)-Vertrauensintervalls als Referenzgröße mit Pen-Down / Pen-Up Parametern als Resultat von 3 Referenzeingaben während des Enrollments dargestellt.

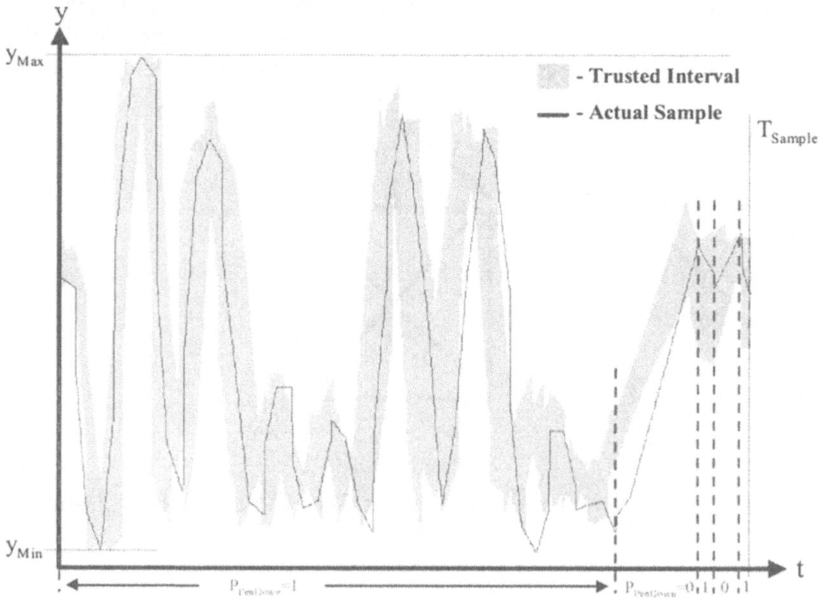

Fig. 5. Handschriftliche Eingabe mit Y(t)- Vertrauensintervall und Pen-Up / Pen-Down Timing

Der Verifikationsprozeß basiert in parameterbasierten Verfahren auf personenspezifischer, gewichteter Merkmalsbewertung, während beim Einsatz von Referenzsignalverläufen das Maß der Ähnlichkeit der Schriftprobe gegenüber den gespeicherten Referenzsignalen gefragt ist. Hierzu bieten sich Verfahren wie Bestimmung von Kreuzkorrelationen [9] oder die Bildung von Vertrauensintervallen und anschließender Betrachtung der Abweichung hiervon an.

Unabhängig von dem gewählten Verifikationsverfahren stellt sich die Frage der zur Speicherung von Referenzen benötigten Kapazität. Dies stellt beim Einsatz in digitalen Wasserzeichen aufgrund des begrenzten Speicherplatzes ein relevantes Attribut dar und wird für beide Kategorien diskutiert.

4.1 Biometrische Kennlinien und –felder

Biometrische Kennlinien sind diskrete Signale über das gesamte Zeitintervall T_{Sample} der Eingabe, wie sie in Kapitel 2 - Handschriftliche Merkmale vorgestellt wurden. Dabei wird aus einer Menge von Referenzkennlinien entweder eine „besonders typische" bestimmt, oder durch Vorverarbeitung (Wertbereichnormierung, Zeitnormierung, Frequenzfilterung) und anschließende Mittelwertbildung eine Referenzkennlinie als Signalverlauf errechnet.

Beim Authentifizierungsvorgang wird die vorliegende Schriftprobe ebenfalls zunächst vorverarbeitet und dann mit der Referenzkennlinie verglichen. Als Vergleichskriterium können z.B. Korrelation, Abstand, Standardabweichung oder gewichtete Differenzen zwischen Referenz- und Prüffunktion herangezogen werden. Entsprechende Verfahren werden im Feldversuch von uns untersucht.

Kennfelder ergeben sich aus derjenigen Fläche im Koordinatensystem, die durch zwei oder mehr Signalfunktionen begrenzt wird. Es ergeben sich Kennfelder, wie in Abbildung 5 dargestellt, die dann beim Authentifizierungsvorgang gewichtet oder ungewichtet der Schriftprobe gegenübergestellt werden. Eine einfache Realisierung eines Kennfeldes ist beispielsweise die Minimum / Maximum Strategie, die für jeden diskreten Zeitpunkt jeweils über alle Referenzfunktionen den kleinsten und größten Funktionswert bestimmt und diese Werte zur Begrenzung des Kennfeldes heranzieht. Hier sind auch weitere statistische Funktionen, wie z.B. Anwendung einer Normalverteilung anwendbar.

Die benötigte Kapazität zur Speicherung von Referenzsignalen ergibt sich aus der Samplingrate des Eingabegeräts, der zeitlichen Dauer der handschriftlichen Eingabe, sowie der Auflösung des Eingabegeräts.

Unsere Untersuchungen werden mit Tablets angestellt, die heutzutage als preiswerte Massenware erhältlich ist, seitens der Auflösungen aber eher das untere Ende des derzeit technisch Machbaren darstellen. Es ist unser Bestreben zu zeigen, daß handschriftliche Authentifizierung mit einfachen Komponenten und hardwareunabhängig realisierbar ist. Aufgrund der Auflösungen des von uns eingesetzten Acecad-III errechnen sich typische Kapazitäten wie folgt:

Sampling Rate des Digitizers:	28 Hz
Typische Dauer einer Eingabe (Unterschrift):	3 bis 5 Sekunden
Normalisierte Auflösung der Y-Koordinaten:	500 Pixel

Table 1. Auflösung und Eingabedauer auf Acecad-III

Somit ergeben sich z.B. für $y_{(t)}$ Signale Größenordnungen von 756 bis 1260 Bit für Eingaben von 3 bis 5 Sekunden. Für $x_{(t)}$ Kennlinien ist, je nach Breiten / Höhenverhältnis des eingegebenen Schriftstücks, mit dem etwa 2 bis 5-fachen der Kapazität zu rechnen.

Diese Kapazitäten können jedoch durch verlustfreie und/oder verlustbehaftete Kompression noch reduziert werden. Möglichkeiten bestehen z.B. in der Reduktion der Samplingrate. So ergaben Untersuchungen, daß Frequenzen von $F_G > 10$ Hz als Rauschen betrachtet werden können [8]. Somit sollten sich bereits mit niedrigen Samplingrate praktikable Ergebnisse erzielen lassen.

4.2 Biometrische statistische Parameter

Als ideal zur Verwendung biometrischer Charakteristiken in Wasserzeichenverfahren sehen wir einfache geometrische Kenngrößen, die sich als skalare Funktion über eine oder mehrere Referenzfunktionen errechnen. Größen wie Anzahl der Strokes, Anzahl Ab- und Aufsetzpunkte des Stifts oder die Charakteristik des binären Schreibsignals $p_{PenDown}(t)$ können erwartungsgemäß in Kapazitäten von wenigen Bits gespeichert werden und somit, wie in Kapitel 5.3 - Einbettung der Charakteristik handschriftlicher Eingaben als Wasserzeichen beschrieben, auch direkt als Wasserzeicheninformation gespeichert werden. Inwieweit solche Parameter – als Merkmalsvektoren über verschiedene Kenngrößen – als sichere Authentifizierungsmerkmale geeignet sind, muß sich im Rahmen von Feldversuchen zeigen.

Bereits vorliegende Arbeiten zeigen, daß rein parameterbasierte Verfahren mit statistischer Analyse False-Rejection-Rates (FFR) von etwa 12,8% und False-Acception-Rates von etwa 13,7% realisiert wurden, während Zeit-Frequenz-Analyseverfahren zu FFR $\approx$ 4,3% und FAR $\approx$ 0,44% führen [9].

Zu erwartende Kapazitäten am Beispiel von Samples mit $T_{Sample} \leq 5$ sec, bei einer Samplingrate von r_{Sample}=30Hz und einer y-Quantisierung von 500 Pixeln:

Parameter / Signal	Größenordnung	Benötigte Kapazität
Anzahl Strokes N_{Stroke}	20 – 100	≤ 7 Bit
Anzahl Absetzpunkte N_{PenUp}	5 – 20	≤ 5 Bit
Binäres Schreibdrucksignal $p_{PenDown}(t)$	≤ 150 Bit	≤ 50 Bit, LL-kodiert
x-Schreibsignal $x_{(t)}$	≤ 150 Samples á 9Bit	≤ 1350 Bit

Table 2. Exemplarische Kapazitätsanforderung verschiedener Referenzen

Offensichtlich ist, daß aufgrund der geringen verfügbaren Kapazitäten bei der Verwendung zur Einbettung in das Wasserzeichen parameterbasierte Vektoren oder Signale mit geringer Quantisierung (z.B. das binäre Schreibdrucksignal) zur

Referenzbildung herangezogen werden müssen. Die Vektorbildung vergrößert den Merkmalsraum und bietet damit eine detailliertere biometrische Referenz.

5 Einbetten und Auslesen von Informationen durch digitale Wasserzeichen mit Hilfe von Handschriftlichen Merkmalen

Im folgenden stellen wir drei Ansätze vor, wie handschriftliche Eingaben bei der Einbettung von Informationen in ein Multimediadokument durch Wasserzeichentechniken genutzt werden können.

Zwei der Ansätze befassen sich mit der Thematik, wie aus handschriftlichen Eingaben Schlüssel (Stego-Keys) abgeleitet werden können, während der dritte sich damit befaßt, wie die handschriftliche Eingabe selbst als Wasserzeicheninformation eingebracht werden kann.

5.1 Generierung des Schlüssels aus der handschriftlichen Eingabe

Unter Generierung des Schlüssels aus der handschriftlichen Eingabe verstehen wir das direkte Generieren von Schlüsseln aus der handschriftlichen Eingabe, ohne Zuhilfenahme einer Referenzgröße. Aufgrund der zu erwartenden Streuung der aufgenommenen Eingabe kommen für die direkte Ableitung eines Schlüssels nur skalare Parameter in Frage, wie sie in Kapitel 4 - Biometrische Charakteristika als Referenzgrößen beschrieben werden. Kann mit vertretbarer Sicherheit gewährleistet werden, daß derartige Parametervektoren für identische Personen und Eingabe-semantik geringen Streuungen unterliegen und mit ebenfalls vertretbarer Wahrschein-lichkeit ausgeschlossen werden kann, daß Parametervektoren anderer Personen in Konflikt geraten, d.h. zu ähnlichen Kennzahlen führen, erscheint diese Anwendung sinnvoll.

Im Rahmen unserer Feldversuche werden wir solche deterministischen Parameter identifizieren, wobei eine Kombination von personenunabhängigen und individuellen Größen als Schlüsselbasis angedacht ist. Personenunabhängige Merkmale wie z.B. Strokes sollen dabei verhindern, daß zufällig Eingaben mit vollständig unterschiedlicher Semantik zu identischen Schlüsseln führen können, während die individuellen Merkmale die biometrische Einzigartigkeit in den Schlüssel einbringen sollen. Hier liegen die größten Erwartungen in Größen wie Pen-Up / Pen-Down Charakteristik oder Anzahl der Absetzpunkte, welche – in den Einzelkriterien mit einer bestimmten Gewichtung versehen – als zusammengesetztes Merkmal eine hohe Sicherheitsrate aufweisen soll. Man spricht in diesem Fall auch von dem Fingerprint einer handschriftlichen Eingabe.

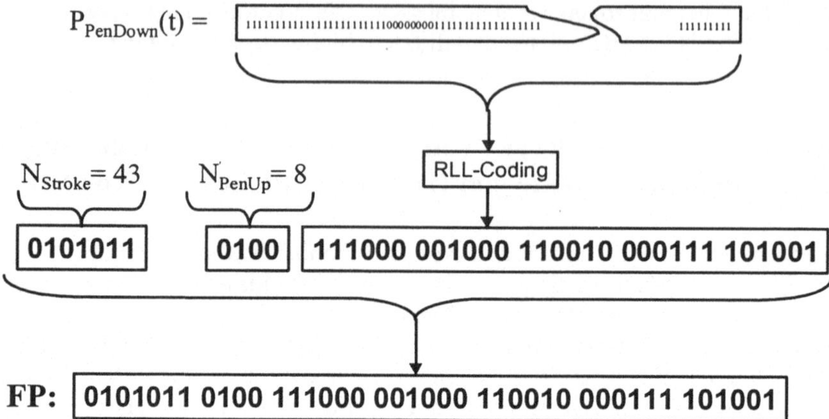

Fig. 6. Exemplarisch zusammengesetzter Fingerprint einer handschriftlichen Eingabe aus den Attributen N_{Stroke}, N_{PenUp} und $P_{PenDown}(t)$

Eine Problematik dieser Vorgehensweise liegt in der Tatsache, daß für alle digitalen Wasserzeichenprozesse immer derselbe Schlüssel verwendet wird. Fridrich [4] zeigt, daß in solchen Fällen Koalitionsattacken eingesetzt werden können, um in den Besitz des Schlüssels zu kommen. Aus diesem Grund empfiehlt sich die Einbeziehung dokumentabhängiger Parameter (z.B. Merkmale oder visuelle Hashwerte über das Multimediadokument).

Ein weiterer Problempunkt ist die Tatsache, daß bei Unverfügbarkeit des Urhebers des Fingerprints die Extraktion der User-Daten aus dem Wasserzeichen nicht möglich ist, falls der Schlüssel nicht bei einer vertrauenswürdigen Instanz hinterlegt wird. Hier sind entsprechende Infrastrukturen gefordert.

5.2 Nutzung der handschriftlichen Eingabe zur Schlüsselfreigabe aus einem Zertifizierungssystem

Die Nutzung der handschriftlichen Eingabe zur Schlüsselfreigabe aus einem Zertifizierungssystem basiert auf dem Ansatz, die handschriftliche Eingabe als Authentifikationsmittel gegenüber einem Serversystem einzusetzen, welches die Stego-Schlüssel verwaltet. Ein solches Serversystem kann auch als vertrauenswürdige Zertifizierungsinstanz angesehen werden.

Die Initialisierung einer solchen Schlüsselabfrage kann entweder aufgefordert oder unaufgefordert erfolgen.

Bei der unaufgeforderten Variante wird die ad-hoc Eingabe des Nutzers dem Zertifizierungssystem zugeführt, welches nach dem Authentifizierungsprozeß im Erfolgsfall mit der Ausgabe eines Schlüssels, mit Mißerfolgsfall mit der Ausgabe eines Fehlercodes reagiert.

Vorteilhaft bei der aufgeforderten Vorgehensweise ist die Möglichkeit, den Nutzer zur Eingabe einer bestimmten Semantikklasse (z.B. Unterschrift oder Passphrase) aufzufordern, wobei mehrere Referenzen pro Klasse je Benutzer gespeichert werden können. Beide Verfahren erlauben ferner mehrstufige Authentifizierungsschritte:

1. Aufforderung: „Bitte geben Sie Ihre Unterschrift ein" – Verifizierung

2. Falls Zweifel an der Authentizität besteht, kann weitere Aufforderung erfolgen „Bitte geben Sie Ihre Passphrase ein"

Weiterhin bietet die Verwaltung der Schlüssel auf einem Server die Möglichkeit, bestimmte Nutzer zu sperren, z.B. wenn zu viele Fehlversuche als nicht authentisch eingestuft wurden.

Wird aus dem Dokument, welches das Wasserzeichen enthält, noch zusätzlich eine inhaltsbezogenes Merkmal (z.B. Hash-Wert) mitgeliefert, kann eine solches Zertifizierungssystem auch dokumentabhängige Schlüssel liefern.

Nachteilhaft in diesem Szenario ist die Tatsache, daß zur Bestimmung eines Schlüssels zum Auslesen der Wasserzeicheninformation stets eine Online Verbindung zum Zertifizierungssystem bestehen muß, und diese Verbindung über sichere Kanäle erfolgen muß.

5.3 Einbettung der Charakteristik handschriftlicher Eingaben als Wasserzeichen

Die Einbettung der Charakteristik handschriftlicher Eingaben als Wasserzeichen beschreibt das Verfahren, handschriftliche Charakteristiken nicht zur Schlüsselgenerierung einzusetzen, sondern die Charakteristik selber als Referenz in das Dokument einzubetten. Hierzu kann ein Standardschlüssel definiert werden, über den aus allen Dokumenten beispielsweise eines Verlages die Charakteristik der handschriftlichen Unterschrift des Urhebers extrahiert werden kann. Als Alternative zum Standardschlüssel kann eine Hash-Funktion, basierend auf dem Inhalt des Dokuments, als Ausleseschlüssel herangezogen werden. Nach Auslesen dieser Charakteristik kann dann mit den in Kapitel 4 - Biometrische Charakteristika als Referenzgrößen diskutierten Verfahren im Zweifelsfall verifiziert werden.

Diese Anwendung ähnelt dem klassischen Wasserzeichenverfahren, bei denen in Form von Steganographie eine verdeckte Signatur beispielsweise in Gemälde eingebracht werden.

Problematisch bei dieser Anwendung erscheint der relativ hohe Speicherbedarf der handschriftlichen Charakteristiken von etwa 756 bis 1260 Bit (siehe Kapitel 4 - Biometrische Charakteristika als Referenzgrößen). Derzeitige Wasserzeichen- verfahren auf digitale Bilder erlauben Kapazitäten in der Größenordnung von bis zu etwa 100 Bit [3], so gilt es auch hier, Kompressionsverfahren für Kennlinien und Kennfelder zu entwickeln, die eine Einbettung als Wasserzeichen erlauben und gleichzeitig sichere Rückschlüsse auf die Biometrie des Urhebers erlauben.

6 Offene Forschungsfelder und Ausblick

In diesem Beitrag haben wir Ansätze der Kombination von handschriftlichen Verifikationsverfahren mit Wasserzeichen aufgezeigt.

Sowohl die Problematik der Verifizierung und Authentifizierung von Personen anhand biometrischer Eigenschaften handschriftlicher Dokumente, sowie die Anwendung solcher Verfahren auf digitale Wasserzeichen, sind neue Forschungsgebiete. Da Kenntnisse über die Eignung bestimmter Charakteristiken nur empirisch gewonnen werden können, steht zunächst eine weitere Datenerhebung im Rahmen eines Feldversuchs mit den Semantikklassen „Unterschrift", „Passphrase", „Sketches" sowie vordefinierten Schlüsselwörtern mit 20-40 Probanten an.

Basierend auf der Datenerhebung wird die statistische Auswertung des Feldversuchs hinsichtlich personenabhängiger signalbasierter Merkmale wie Weg-Zeit Diagramm und Beschleunigungs-Zeit Diagramm, sowie die Untersuchung kombinierter personenabhängiger und unabhängiger statistischer Parameter als biometrische Referenzgrößen folgen. Hinsichtlich der Anwendung auf digitalen Wasserzeichen steht hierbei vor allem der Aspekt der Speicherplatzminimierung im Vordergrund.

Großes Interesse besteht insbesondere im Bereich der biometrischen Parameter, da für solche biometrischen Hashwerte neben dem Einsatz in digitalen Wasserzeichenverfahren noch eine Vielzahl von weiteren Anwendungen denkbar sind. Die gewonnenen Erkenntnisse werden dann zur Entwicklung eines Verifikationssystems im Kontext der digitalen Wasserzeichen angewendet.

Weiterhin ist eine Analyse, inwieweit die vorgestellten Ansätze auch auf Kleinstcomputern mit Stift-basierten Eingabedisplays realisierbar ist, geplant.

Literatur

[1] Crane & Ostrem (1983). *Automatic signature verification using a three-axis-force-sensitive pen.* IEEE Transaction on Systems, Man and Cybernetics, 13, 329-337

[2] Cybersign (2000). http://www.cybersign.com

[3] Dittmann (2000). *Digitale Wasserzeichen.* Springer Verlag, ISBN 3 –540 –66661 – 3

[4] Fridrich (2000). *Visual Hash for Oblivious Watermarking.* SPIE Photonic West Electronic Imaging 2000, Security and Watermarking of Multimedia Contents, http://www.ssie.binghamton.edu/fridrich/resume.html

[5] HESY (2000). http://www.hesy.de

[6] Teulings et. al. (1989). *An online handwriting-recognition system based on unreliable moduled.* 4th International Graphonomics Society Conference, Trondheim

[7] Plamondon & Lorette (1987). Automatic signature verification and writer identification – the state of the art. In: Pattern Recognition,22,2:107-131

[8] Pladmondon (1992). *A multi-level signature verification system.* In: S. Impedovo and J.C. Simon (eds.) : *From Pixels to Features III*, Elsevier Science Publishers

[9] Schmidt (1999). On-line Unterschriftenanalyse zur Benutzerverifikation. Dissertation, Shaker Verlag, Aachen

[10] Schomaker (1991). *Simulation and Recognition of Handwriting Movements.* Dissertation, NCI, Nijmeegs Instituut voor Cognitie-onderzoek en Informatietechnologie, Nijmegen, Niederlande

[11] WACOM (2000). http://www.wacom.com

[12] Wirtz (1995). *Stroke-Based Time Warping for Signature Verificatoin.* International Conference on Document Analysis and Recognition, 1, 179-182

Digitale Wasserzeichen für unkomprimierte und komprimierte Audiodaten

Christian Neubauer

Fraunhofer Institut für Integrierte Schaltungen
Am Weichselgarten 3, D-91058 Erlangen
`neu@iis.fhg.de`

Zusammenfassung Digitale Wasserzeichen sind eine Methode, Zusatzdaten – für den Menschen nicht wahrnehmbar – in Multimediadaten einzubetten. Im Bereich der Audiowasserzeichen arbeiten die meisten Systeme mit nichtkomprimierten Daten als Eingangssignal. Einige wenige Verfahren jedoch sind in der Lage, Wasserzeichen direkt in bereits komprimiertes Audiomaterial einzubetten. In diesem Beitrag werden nach einem kurzen Überblick über verschiedene Wasserzeichenmethoden zwei Verfahren vorgestellt, die – zueinander kompatibel – Wasserzeichen in unkomprimierte und komprimierte Audiosignale einbetten können. Die Funktionsweise der Verfahren, der derzeitige Stand der Entwicklung sowie die Leistung der Verfahren werden dargestellt.

1 Einführung

Das Einbringen nicht-wahrnehmbarer Information – sog. Wasserzeichen – in beliebige Daten[1, 2], wird seit längerem im Bereich der Bild- und Videoverarbeitung erfolgreich angewendet [3]. Im Gegensatz dazu ist die Einbettung von Wasserzeichen in Audiosignale ein recht neues Gebiet, das durch die Methoden aus dem Bereich der Bildverarbeitung stark beeinflußt wird. Arbeiten von Boney, Gruhl und anderen [4, 5, 6] zeigen die prinzipielle Möglichkeit, Wasserzeichen in Audiodaten einzufügen.

Dieser Beitrag beschäftigt sich mit Verfahren zur Einbettung von Wasserzeichen in Audiosignale. Nach einer kurzen Einführung werden zunächst in Abschnitt 2 generelle Anforderungen an Wasserzeichen vorgestellt und ein kurzer Überblick über bestehende Verfahren im Bereich der Audiowasserzeichen gegeben. Die Abschnitte 3 und 4 stellen Verfahren vor, die es erlauben, Wasserzeichen in unkomprimierte und komprimierte Audiosignale so einzubetten, daß sie mit dem gleichen Extraktor (Abschnitt 5) extrahierbar[1] sind. Eine Diskussion der Leistungsfähigkeit der Verfahren in Bezug auf Audioqualität, Robustheit, Übertragungsqualität und Rechenaufwand schließt den Beitrag ab.

---

[1] Es hat sich zur Vermeidung von Begriffsverwechselungen als günstig erwiesen, die von der Audiokodierung bereits belegten Begriffe *En/Dekoder bzw. en/dekodieren* nicht für Wasserzeichenbelange zu verwenden. In diesem Beitrag werden stattdessen die Begriffe *Einbetter/Extraktor* im Zusammenhang mit Wasserzeichen verwendet und *En/Dekoder*, wenn von Audiokodierung die Rede ist.

2 Überblick

2.1 Anforderungen an Audiowasserzeichen

Nachfolgend wird ein kurzer Überblick über wichtige Eigenschaften von Audiowasserzeichen gegeben:

- **Unhörbarkeit** der Wasserzeichen wird häufig als die wichtigste Eigenschaft betrachtet und sollte daher in jedem Fall gewährleistet werden.
- **Robustheit** bezeichnet die Eigenschaft von Wasserzeichen gegen absichtliche oder unabsichtliche Signalmodifikationen resistent zu sein. Dies heißt, daß ein Wasserzeichen nur bei gleichzeitigem starkem Qualitätsverlust des Trägersignals entfernbar sein darf.
- **Datenrate** hängt stark vom verwendeten Wasserzeichenprinzip ab. Die Rate reicht von wenigen bit/s bei Spreizbandsystemen bis in den Bereich kbits/s bei nicht-robusten Verfahren.
- **Arbeitsbereich** drückt aus, ob das Verfahren unkomprimierte (PCM) oder komprimierte (Bitstrom) Audiodaten verarbeitet. Daher leiten sich auch die Bezeichnungen *PCM Wasserzeichen* und *Bitstrom Wasserzeichen* ab.
- **Interoperabilität** bezeichnet die Tatsache, daß PCM- und Bitstrom Wasserzeichen mit dem gleichen Extraktor extrahierbar sind. Diese Eigenschaft ist sehr wichtig, da bei einem vorliegenden Signal nicht entschieden werden kann, ob die Einbettung des Wasserzeichens im unkomprimierten oder im komprimierten Bereich stattgefunden hat.
- **Komplexität** bezieht sich auf den Rechenaufwand, den eine Implementierung des Verfahrens benötigt.
- **Blinde Extraktion** bezeichnet die Tatsache, daß das Wasserzeichen ohne Verwendung des Originalsignals extrahierbar ist – wie ist heute bei den meisten Verfahren üblich.

Die meisten der oben genannten Forderungen sind bereits durch das Systemdesign bzw. verfahrensinhärente Eigenschaften festgelegt. Die Forderungen nach *Unhörbarkeit*, *Robustheit* und *Datenrate* hingegen können nicht unabhängig voneinander eingestellt werden. Bild 1 veranschaulicht diesen Sachverhalt. Der Arbeitspunkt des Systems muß abhängig von der Anwendung eingestellt werden, d.h. für erhöhte Robustheit, wie sie z.B. in Sicherheitsanwendungen benötigt wird, kann der Arbeitspunkt auf Kosten der Rate in Richtung Robustheit verschoben werden und umgekehrt.

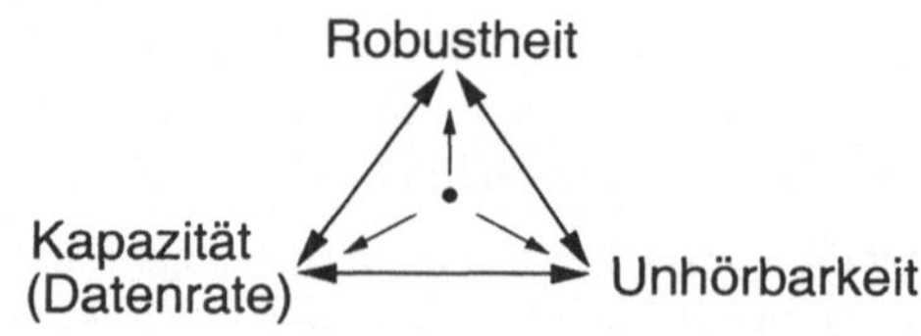

Abbildung 1. Tradeoff zwischen Robustheit, Datenrate und Unhörbarkeit.

2.2 Audiowasserzeichen - Verfahren

Echo Hiding Eine der ersten Arbeiten auf dem Gebiet schlägt vor, Wasserzeichen durch Addition exponentiell abklingender Echos einzubringen [6]. Dabei erfolgt die Kodierung der binären Daten über die Echoverzögerung. Das heißt, eine logische "1" wird z.B. durch 3 ms Echoverzögerung, eine logische "0" durch 5 ms Verzögerung dargestellt. Das Verfahren beruht auf dem psychoakustischen Effekt der Nachverdeckung, der besagt, daß kurz nach dem Verklingen eines Signals ein anderes (energieärmeres) Signal nicht wahrgenommen wird. Das Verfahren wurde jüngst erneut aufgegriffen [7] und verbessert. Die Detektion erfolgt mittels Cepstralanalyse.

Peak Modifikation In [8] wird ein Verfahren beschrieben, das direkte Modifikationen des Zeitsignals vornimmt. Dabei werden blockweise Spitzen im Signal gesucht und so skaliert, daß deren Höhe einen Schwellwert über- oder unterschreitet. Spitzen, die den Threshold über- bzw. unterschreiten stellen eine logische "1" bzw. "0"dar. Das Verfahren vermeidet dadurch Interferenz mit dem Trägersignal, kann aber nicht die Unhörbarkeit der Wasserzeichen garantieren.

Schmalbandsystem Ein weiteres System [9] verwendet aus dem hörbaren Spektrum nur einen schmalen Bereich (z.B. 3 kHz$\pm$500 Hz), um darin mittels Bandfiltern Signalenergien zu modifizieren. Das Verfahren fällt aufgrund seiner einfachen Angreifbarkeit weniger unter den Begriff Wasserzeichen als unter "Zusatzdatenübertragung". Es wird vor allem im Bereich der Rundfunkforschung angewendet, um z.B. Senderreichweiten oder Zuhörerzahlen zu ermitteln.

Breitbandsysteme Schließlich existiert noch die große Klasse der breitbandigen Wasserzeichensysteme. Darin sind Multicarrier und Spreizbandsysteme [3, 4, 10, 11] einzuordnen, die ein breitbandiges Rauschsignal mit geringer Energiedichte zu den Trägerdaten addieren. Das Rauschsignal wird durch Multiplikation des Datensignals mit einer sog. Spreizsequenz erzeugt. Die Detektion erfolgt durch Korrelation des wasserzeichenbehafteten Signals mit der (im Empfänger bekannten) Spreizsequenz. Dabei kann die Spreizsequenz, die im Wasserzeicheneinbetter verwendet wurde, als eine Art Schlüssel betrachtet werden, da der Extraktor ohne Wissen um die Sequenz keine Korrelation und damit keine Detektion durchführen kann. Die Spreizbandverfahren haben den großen Vorteil, daß durch die relativ geringe Energiedichte des Wasserzeichensignals die Unhörbarkeit des Wasserzeichens bei gleichzeitiger hoher Robustheit erreicht werden kann. Naturgemäß können diese Verfahren keine großen Datenraten realisieren, übliche Werte liegen im Bereich weniger bit/s bis zu einigen hundert bit/s.

3 PCM Wasserzeichen Einbetter

Die Aufgabe eines PCM Wasserzeichen Einbetters ist es, in unkomprimierte Audiodaten Wasserzeichendaten einzubringen. Prinzipiell können alle in Abschnitt 2.2 vorgestellten Verfahren angewendet werden. Das hier vorgestellte

Verfahren fällt jedoch aufgrund der gewünschten hohen Robustheit und der Unhörbarkeitsforderung in die Klasse der Spreizbandsysteme. Der Einbetter ist in Abb. 2 gezeigt und kombiniert die Vorteile der Spreizbandmodulation mit denen eines Maskierungsmodells, das Eigenschaften des menschlichen Gehörs abbildet und somit die Unhörbarkeit des Wasserzeichens garantieren kann.

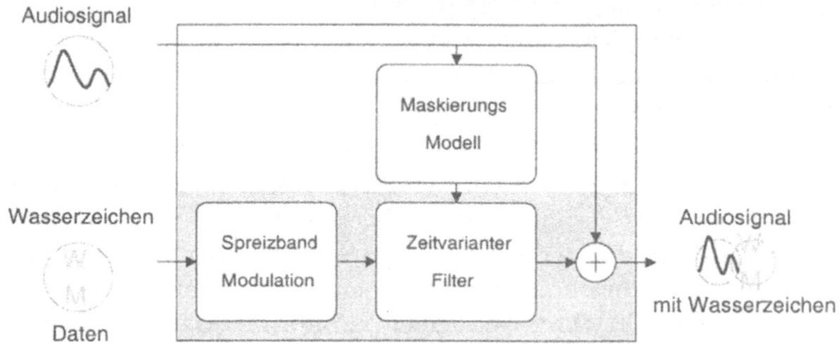

Abbildung 2. Blockdiagramm des PCM Wasserzeichen Einbetters.

Spreizbandmodulation Spreizbandsysteme werden unter anderem durch ihr *Process Gain* G_p gekennzeichnet. Das Process Gain wird dazu verwendet, um das schlechte Signal-Rauschverhältnis am Extraktoreingang zu verbessern. Andererseits gilt bei gegebener Bandbreite: Je größer das Process Gain, desto kleiner die Datenrate. Ein Process Gain von $G_p = 10\log_{10}(2048) = 33.1$ dB hat sich als guter Kompromiß zwischen Datenrate und Robustheit (Signal-Rausch-Verhältnis) herausgestellt. Die erreichte Datenrate beträgt damit ca. 11.6 bit/s. Die Übertragung findet im Basisband statt, d.h. eine zusätzliche Modulation des gespreizten Signals auf eine Trägerfrequenz findet nicht statt.

Als Wasserzeichen wurden in der vorgestellten Implementierung folgende Datenframes implementiert: Stringübertragung, Bitfehlermeßdaten und die Spezifikation von SDMI[2].

Maskierungsmodell Das hier verwendete Modell basiert auf dem Modell, das im Audio Codec ISO/MPEG-2 Advanced Audio Coding (AAC) [12, 13] verwendet wird. Es arbeitet blockweise und unterteilt das hörbare Spektrum in Teilbänder. Für jedes Teilband wird eine sog. Maskierungsschwelle errechnet, die die Energie eines Rauschsignals angibt, das im jeweiligen Band gerade nicht hörbar ist, weil es vom Audiosignal maskiert wird. Die Maskierungsschwelle wird anschließend vom zeitvarianten Filter verwendet, um das Datensignal spektral so anzupassen, daß es vom Audiosignal maskiert wird.

---

[2] SDMI: Secure Digital Music Initiative, s. auch http://www.sdmi.org

Zeitvarianter Filter Die spektrale Formung erfolgt frequenzbandweise durch Gewichtung mit einem für jedes Band spezifischen Faktor. Nach der Gewichtung ist die spektrale Energieverteilung des Datensignals so eingestellt, daß bei Addition zum Musiksignal das Datensignal vom Musiksignal gerade maskiert wird. Dies sichert die Unhörbarkeit des Datensignals für das menschliche Ohr.

4 Bitstrom Wasserzeichen Einbetter

Die Aufgabe des Bitstrom Wasserzeichen Einbetters ist es, Wasserzeichen direkt in ein komprimiertes Audiosignal (Bitstrom) so einzubetten, daß nach dessen Dekodierung das Wasserzeichen extrahiert werden kann. Dabei ist zu beachten, daß jede Implementierung auf die speziellen Gegebenheiten des Audioenkoders, dessen Bitströme verarbeitet werden sollen, zugeschnitten ist. Das nachfolgend vorgestellte Verfahren verarbeitet Bitströme des MPEG-2 AAC Verfahrens [12, 13]. Das Blockdiagramm des Bitstrom Wasserzeichen Einbetters ist in Abb. 3 dargestellt. Grundsätzlich könnte die Aufgabe durch Hintereinanderschaltung von Audiodekoder, PCM Wasserzeichen Einbetter und Audioenkoder erfüllt werden. Es ist jedoch aus Gründen der Audioqualität und der Komplexität weitaus günstiger nur Teile der Komponenten Audiodekoder, PCM Wasserzeichen System und Audioenkoder zu verwenden.

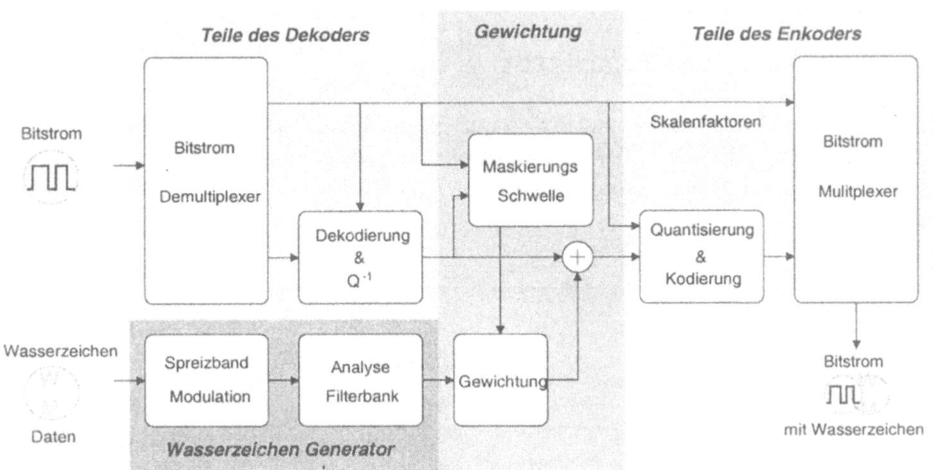

Abbildung 3. Blockdiagramm des Bitstrom Wasserzeichen Einbetters.

Teile des Audiodekoders Der Eingangsbitstrom wird im Bitstromdemultiplexer zerlegt und anschließend die Entropiekodierung sowie die Quantisierung der Spektrallinien aufgehoben. Dadurch ergibt sich eine spektrale Repräsentation des Eingangssignals. Für die spektrale Gewichtung müssen die Maskierungsthresholds (s. Abschnitt 3) des Audiosignals zur Verfügung stehen. In der derzeitigen Implementierung werden diese daher vom vorausgehenden Audioenkoder in den Bitstrom geschrieben. Weitere Alternativen zur Schätzung der Maskierungsschwelle sind in [14] dargestellt.

Spreizbandmodulation/Analyse Filterbank/Gewichtung Der Modulator des Bitstrom Wasserzeichen Einbetters entspricht exakt dem in Abschnitt 3 vorgestellten. Aufgrund dieser Wahl ist die Repräsentation des Wasserzeichensignals identisch zu der des PCM Wasserzeichen Einbetters, was die Verwendung des gleichen Extraktors für beide Systeme erlaubt. Die Analyse Filterbank erzeugt eine spektrale Darstellung des Wasserzeichensignals, das anschließend unter Verwendung der Maskierungsschwelle im Gewichtungsblock spektral geformt wird.

Teile des Audioenkoders Schließlich wird das resultierende Summensignal aus gewichtetem Wasserzeichensignal und Audiosignal erneut in eine Bitstromrepräsentierung umgewandelt. Dazu muß das Spektrum neu quantisiert, entropiekodiert und in einen Bitstroms gemultiplext werden. Zur Quantisierung werden die Skalenfaktoren des Eingangsbitstromes erneut verwendet. Dieses Verfahren vermeidet aufgrund der Anwendung der gleichen Quantisierungsintervalle sog. Tandemkodierungseffekte[3].

5 Wasserzeichen Extraktor

Der Extraktor basiert im wesentlichen auf einem Spreizband Empfänger [15]. An seinem Ausgang wird eine Bitfehlerratenmessung vorgenommen, um die Qualität der Wasserzeichenübertragung zu messen. Das Blockdiagramm ist in Abb. 4 zu sehen.

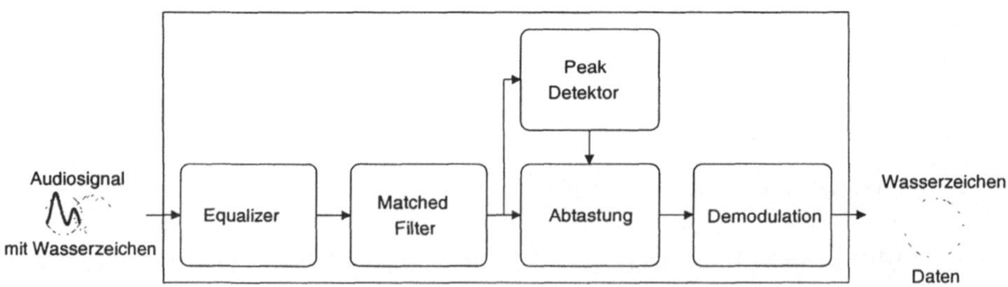

Abbildung 4. Blockdiagramm des Extraktors.

Das Musiksignal kann in Bezug auf die Wasserzeichendekodierung als Störsignal aufgefaßt werden, das mit dem Datensignal interferiert und somit die De-

---

[3] Störungsakkumulation durch wiederholte Kodierung/Dekodierung

kodierung stört. Der zentrale Bestandteil des Extraktors ist daher das *Matched Filter*, das einen SNR-Gewinn um G_p an seinem Ausgang bringt. Hinter dem Matched Filter werden schmale Impulse beobachtet, deren Vorzeichen die übertragene Information darstellt. Diese Impulse entstehen im Abstand der Symboldauer. Der Abstand der Impulse enthält Timinginformation, die im Extraktor für die Synchronisation auf das Datensignal verwendet wird. Wenn der exakte Abtastzeitpunkt bekannt ist, kann das Signal abgetastet und demoduliert werden.

6 System Performance

In diesem Abschnitt werden die Ergebnisse einer Implementierung von PCM und Bitstrom Wasserzeichen Einbetter vorgestellt. Dies beinhaltet die erreichte Audioqualität, Verfahrenskomplexität, Robustheit und Dekodierbarkeit der Wasserzeichen.

6.1 Audioqualität

Die Audioqualität wurde mit Hilfe von Hörtests bestimmt. Die ausgewählten Teststücke sind aus der Audiokodierung als kritisch bekannt[4] und wurden auch für die Wasserzeichen Hörtests als Testmaterial verwendet. Das Testmaterial enthält Sprache (es01-es03), Orchesterstücke (sc01-sc02), Popmusik (sc03), und Einzelinstrumente (si01-si03,sm01-sm03). Abb. 5 zeigt die Ergebnisse des Hörtests für PCM Wasserzeichen (linke Balken), Bitstrom Wasserzeichen (rechte Balken) und – als Referenz – die Qualität der Bitströme, die für das Bitstrom Wasserzeichen System als Eingangssignale verwendet wurden (mittlere Balken).

Man erkennt, daß die Störungen durch das PCM Wasserzeichensystem minimal sind. Lediglich bei Sprachstücken ergeben sich noch signifikante Artefakte. Außerdem ist zu bemerken, daß die Qualität mit Ausnahme der Sprachstücke in allen Fällen besser ist als die Qualität des MPEG-2 AAC[5] Referenz Coders, dem das Attribut "EBU broadcast quality" zugeschrieben wird.

Das Bitstrom Wasserzeichen System schneidet etwas schlechter als das PCM Wasserzeichensystem, aber ebenfalls sehr gut ab. Diese Tendenz läßt sich u.a. darauf zurückführen, daß der Audioenkoder selbst bereits Störungen in das Signal einbringt und die Qualität der wasserzeichenbehafteten Signale niemals besser als die Audioenkoders werden kann. In jedem Fall bewegen sich die Ergebnisse beider Systeme im Bereich sehr guter Audioqualität.

6.2 Robustheit

Für das vorgestellte PCM Wasserzeichen Verfahren wurde die Robustheit gegenüber Angriffen getestet. Es zeigt sich Robustheit gegenüber Filterung, Audiokodierung, Digital-Analog Umsetzung, Addition von Echos, Equalization und

---

[4] Die Stücke wurden zur Evaluierung der MPEG-4 Audiokoder verwendet.
[5] Es wurde das low complexity profile verwendet.

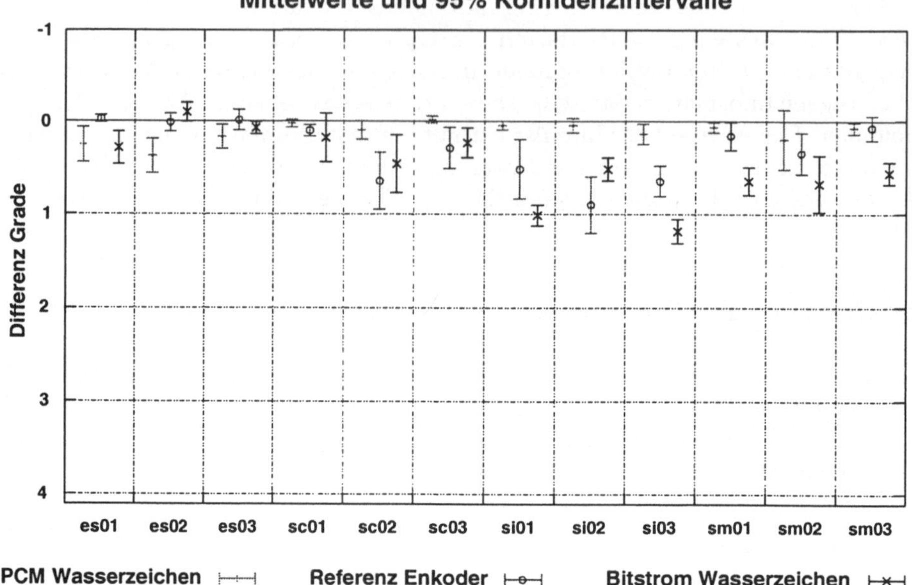

Abbildung 5. Ergebnisse des Hörtests für PCM Wasserzeichen, Referenz Audioenkoder und Bitstrom Wasserzeichen.

Resampling. Bei der Allpaßfilterung wird die Extraktion aufgrund der Phasenänderungen durch den Allpaß unmöglich. Bei Zeitachsenmodifikationen bestehen ebenfalls Probleme mit der Extraktion, da aufgrund der langen Korrelatoren nicht mehr das gesamte Process Gain zur Verfügung steht.

6.3 Komplexität

Abb. 6 veranschaulicht die Komplexität beider Wasserzeichen Verfahren. Die y-Achse ist auf die Dauer des Teststückes normalisiert, d.h. Werte kleiner 1 bezeichnen eine Programmausführung schneller als Echtzeit. Die Ergebnisse wurden auf einem PII@400Mhz mit file-I/O auf der lokalen Platte ermittelt und sind somit praktische Anhaltspunkte, die auch Implementierungsdetails berücksichtigen. Die Implementierung fand in C/C++ statt.

Man erkennt, daß beide Verfahren (auf obiger Plattform) wesentlich schneller als Echtzeit arbeiten. Sie sind somit z.B. geeignet, auf Webservern zu arbeiten, um bei der Internetauslieferung von Musik Rechte einzubetten oder auch auf DSP Plattformen implementiert zu werden.

6.4 Übertragungsleistung

Zur Messung der Übertragungsqualität der Wasserzeichen wurden Bitfehlerraten der extrahierten Wasserzeichendaten gemessen. Es zeigte sich, daß das PCM

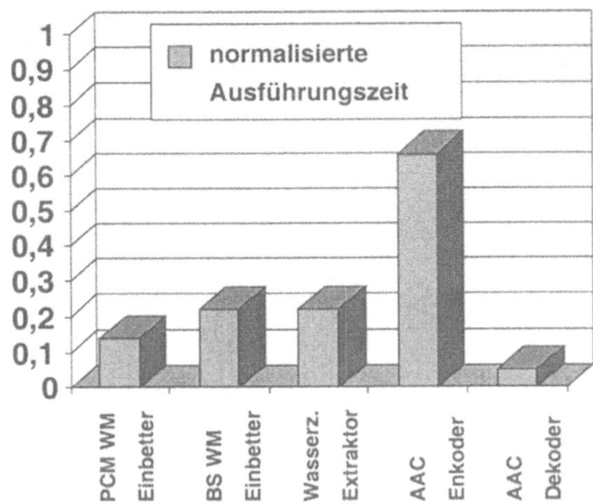

Abbildung 6. Komplexität der Wasserzeichen Verfahren im Vergleich zur Komplexität des MPEG-2 AAC Audio Codecs.

Wasserzeichen System eine Bitfehlerrate zwischen 10^{-3} und 10^{-4} und das Bitstrom Wasserzeichen System eine Bitfehlerrate von 10^{-2} und 10^{-3} aufweisen. Diese Fehlerraten wurden ohne jede Kanalkodierung ermittelt und stellen eine gute Ausgangsbasis für die Anwendung von Kanalkodierung dar. Das Musikmaterial enthielt Stücke aus allen Genres und stellt eine repräsentative Auswahl an Musik da.

7 Zusammenfassung

Nach kurzer Einführung wurde ein Überblick über allgemeine Anforderungen an Audio Wasserzeichen sowie verschiedene Prinzipien zur Einbettung nicht-wahrnehmbarer Daten in Audiosignale gegeben.

Die auch von anderen Autoren verwendete Spreizbandtechnik diente als Grundlage der vorgestellten Wasserzeichen Einbettungsverfahren, die es erlauben, in unkomprimierte und komprimierte Audiosignale Wasserzeichen einzubetten. Beiden Verfahren gemeinsam ist die Verwendung eines Maskierungsmodells, das durch Modellierung menschlicher Gehöreigenschaften die Unhörbarkeit der Wasserzeichen sicherstellt. Der vorgestellte Bitstrom Wasserzeichen Einbetter verarbeitet MPEG-2 AAC Bitströme direkt und stellt damit eine effiziente Möglichkeit dar, in bereits vorkomprimiertes Audiomaterial Wasserzeichen einzubetten.

Die Audioqualität beider Systeme wurde mit Hörtests und einem Vergleich zum Stand der Audiocodierung bewertet. Es zeigte sich, daß das PCM Wasserzeichen System nahezu transparent ist. Auch das Bitstrom Wasserzeichen System beeinflußt die Qualität der Bitströme nicht nennenswert. Weiterhin zeigten die niedrige Komplexität, hohe Robustheit und Übertragungsleistung, daß nichtwahrnehmbare Wasserzeichen sowohl in PCM Signale als auch Bitströme eingebettet werden können.

8 Danksagung

Der Autor bedankt sich bei allen, die durch fachliche Unterstützung, Programmierung und Hörtests dazu beigetragen haben, diese Entwicklung zu ermöglichen, inbesondere bei Dr.-Ing. Jürgen Herre, Dipl.-Ing. Eric Allamanche, Dipl.-Ing. Frank Siebenhaar, Dipl.-Ing. Ralph Kulessa und allen Testhörern.

Literatur

[1] Ingemar J. Cox, Joe Killian, Tom Leighton, and Talal Shamoon. A secure, robust watermark for multimedia. In *Information Hiding*. Newton Institute, University of Cambridge, May 1996.

[2] Jonathan K. Su, Frank Hartung, and Bernd Girod. Digital watermarking of text, image and video documents. *Computers & Graphics*, 22(6):678–695, Dec. 1998.

[3] Frank Hartung and Bernd Girod. Watermarking of uncompressed amd compressed video. *Signal Processing*, 66(3):283–301, May 1998.

[4] Laurence Boney, Ahmed H. Tewfik, and Khaled N. Hamdy. Digital watermarks for audio signals. In *1996 IEEE Int. Conf. on Multimedia Computing and Systems*, pages 473–480, Hiroshima, Japan, 1996.

[5] W. Bender, D. Gruhl, N. Morimoto, and A. Lu. Techniques for data hiding. *IBM Systems Journal*, 35(3&4):313–336, 1996.

[6] Daniel Gruhl, Anthony Lu, and Walter Bender. Echo hiding. In *Proceedings of the Workshop on Information Hiding*, number 1174 in Lecture Notes in Computer Science, Cambridge, England, May 1996. Springer Verlag.

[7] Xu Chansheng, Wu Jiankang, Sun Quibin, and Xin Kai. Applications of digital watermarking technology in audio signals. *Journal of Audio Engineering Sociecty*, 47(10):805–812, Oct. 1999.

[8] Jack Wolosewicz. Apparatus and method for encoding supplementary data in analog signals. WO 97/37448, International Application Published under the Patent Cooperation Treaty, Oct. 1997.

[9] R.A. Willard. ICE identification coding, embedded. In *105th AES Convention*, Berlin, Mar. 1993. Audio Engineering Society.

[10] Chong Lee. Method and apparatus for transporting auxiliary data in audio signals. WO 97/09797, International Application Published under the Patent Cooperation Treaty, Mar. 1997.

[11] Christian Neubauer and Jürgen Herre. Digital watermarking and its influence on audio quality. In *105th AES Convention*, San Francisco, Sep. 1998. preprint 4823.

[12] M. Bosi, K. Brandenburg, S. Quackenbush, K. Akagiri, H. Fuchs, J. Herre, L. Fielder, M. Dietz, Y. Oikawa, and G. Davidson. ISO/IEC MPEG-2 Advanced Audio Coding. *Journal of the AES*, 45(10):789–814, October 1997.

[13] ISO/IEC JTC1/SC29/WG11 Moving Pictures Expert Group. Generic Coding of Moving Pictures and Associated Audio: Advanced Audio Coding. International Standard 13818-7, ISO/IEC, 1997.

[14] Christian Neubauer and Jürgen Herre. Audio watermarking of MPEG-2 AAC bitstreams. In *108th AES Convention*, Paris, Feb. 2000. preprint 5101.

[15] Robert Dixon. *Spread Spectrum Systems*. Wiley & Sons Inc., 3rd edition edition, 1994.

Digitale Wasserzeichen für MIDI
Grundlagen und Konzepte

Martin Steinebach

GMD-IPSI Mobile Interactive Media
Dolivostr.15, 64293 Darmstadt, Germany
steineba@darmstadt.gmd.de

Abstract. Dem Schutz von MIDI Daten wird – im Gegensatz zu anderen Multimedia Daten wie Video und Audio – bisher kaum Beachtung geschenkt. In dieser Veröffentlichung wird die Notwendigkeit des Schutzes von MIDI Daten gezeigt. Es werden Konzepte zum Schützen von MIDI Daten anhand eines schematischen Onlinestores für MIDI-Files vorgestellt. Verschiedene Schutzmöglichkeiten, basierend auf unterschiedlichen Ansätzen, werden ebenso diskutiert wie eventuelle Angriffe auf diese.

1 Motivation und Grundlagen

MIDI (Musical Instrument Digital Interface) ist bisher nicht von den Bemühungen zum Schutz von Multimediadaten betroffen. In der Forschung wird sich hauptsächlich auf Einzelbild, Video und Audio konzentriert. Kommerzielle Lösungen sind ebenfalls kaum zu finden, Yamaha, Hersteller von Keyboards und Synthesizern, hat zwar Wasserzeichen für MIDI angekündigt, bisher aber keine Resultate veröffentlicht. Das einzige derzeit verfügbare Programm zum Schützen von MIDI-Dateien ist derzeit MIDICrypt der Firma Byzantine (http://www.byzantine.nl/midicrypt/). Zur Arbeitsweise dieses Programmes sind keine Informationen verfügbar.

Das Ziel der vorliegenden Veröffentlichung ist es, zum einen zu Begründen, warum ein Schutz von MIDI Dateien sinnvoll und notwendig ist, und zum anderen mögliche Ansätze dazu vorstellen. Neben der Motivation sollen im ersten Kapitel zuerst die Grundlagen dazu vorgestellt werden.

1.1 Motivation

Digitale Wasserzeichen werden heute als grundlegende Technologie zum Schutz von Multimedia Daten angesehen [1]. Besonders die Möglichkeit, mit ihnen das Copyright von im Internet vertriebenen Medien zu sichern, steht im Mittelpunkt des kommerziellen Interesses. Dabei werden vor allem Einzelbilder, Videos und Musikstücke betrachtet.

MIDI Daten hingegen finden bisher kaum Beachtung, obwohl sich diese besonders zum Verkauf durch Onlinestores eignen, da sie aus verhältnismäßig kleinen Dateien bestehen, meist unter hundert KB. Diese können entweder direkt heruntergeladen oder per Email versendet werden. Der geringen Größe steht ein oft recht hoher Preis entgegen. Während Musikstücke als MP3 Datei oft für ungefähr 1 DM verlangt wird, beträgt der Preis für MIDI Dateien oft 10 DM und mehr. Dieser Umstand macht MIDI Dateien zu einem Idealen Ziel von Piraten. Über Seiten im Internet oder CDs können

Daten mit einem hohen Geldwert vertrieben werden, ohne daß bisher geeignete Schutzmaßnahmen vorhanden sind.

1.2 Schutzmöglichkeiten

Einen starken Schutz bei der Übertragung der Daten über das Netz bieten kryptographische Maßnahmen. Durch kundenspezifische Kennworte kann sichergestellt werden, daß bei der Übertragung keine dritte Partei in Besitz der Daten gelangen kann. Das sonst übliche Problem bei Multimedia Daten, die nötige Fehlertoleranz bei der Übertragung großer Datenmengen, das kryptograhische Ansätze oft nicht durchführbar macht, ergibt sich bei MIDI nicht. Hier handelt es sich eher um eine Beschreibung von Notenfolgen, die ebenfalls keine Fehlertoleranz besitzt und daher auch mit nicht fehlertoleranten Mechanismen geschützt werden kann.
Dieser Schutz endet aber beim Kunden. Wenn dieser die Daten erhalten hat, muß er sie entschlüsseln und an seine Musikinstrumente versenden können. Dabei kann er die Daten beliebig aufzeichnen und gegebenenfalls weiter verbreiten. Proprietäre Formate für spezielle Wiedergabesoftware eines Anbieters sind zwar denkbar, verlieren ihre Wirkung aber ebenfalls spätestens nach der Übertragung durch die MIDI-Schnittstelle. Danach können Sequenzer die Daten erneut ungeschützt aufzeichnen.
Folglich muß ein Schutz durch Wasserzeichen erfolgen. Diese verbleiben auch nach dem Übertragen durch MIDI Geräte oder dem Wechsel von MIDI Formaten in den Daten enthalten.

1.3 Digitale Wasserzeichen

Digitale Wasserzeichen können in verschiedenen Anwendungsszenarien zur Gewährleistung von Sicherheitskriterien eingesetzt werden. Unterschieden wird hierbei zwischen Verfahren zur Urheberidentifizierung, zur Kundenidentifizierung, zur Annotation von Material, zum Nachweis der Unversehrtheit oder zur Durchsetzung des Kopierschutzes bzw. als Übertragungskontrolle [1].
Sie zeichnen sich durch eine Reihe von Eigenschaften aus. Die wichtigsten sind Transparenz und Robustheit. Transparenz ist gegeben, wenn das Einbetten des Wasserzeichen nicht mit einer Veränderung der wahrgenommenen Qualität verbunden ist. Robust sind solche Wasserzeichen, die zum einen Veränderungen des Materials wie z.B. Konvertierung zwischen verschiedenen Formaten oder das Zusammenlegen mehrerer Spuren, zum anderen aber auch gezielte Angriffe überstehen.
Weitere Eigenschaften, nach denen Wasserzeichen unterschieden werden, sind die Sicherheit gegen gezielte Angriffe, die Detektierbarkeit, die Komplexität, die Kapazität und ob die Verifikation geheim oder öffentlich durchgeführt wird.

1.4 MIDI

MIDI ist eine Spezifikation für Hard- und Software zum Datenaustausch von Musikinstrumenten, Sequenzern und Zubehör. Hier soll nur der ein Teil der Softwarespezifikation betrachtet werden: Das eigentliche MIDI Protokoll zur

Kommunikation zwischen Geräten und SMF (Simple MIDI File), das Format, in dem Daten gespeichert werden. Unter MIDI werden musikalische Vorgänge mehr beschrieben als reproduziert, diesen Teil übernehmen die angesteuerten Instrumente. Vereinfacht liefert MIDI eine Abfolge von Noten, zusammen mit eine Reihe von Angaben, wie diese Noten zu spielen sind. Wichtig sind dabei vor allem die Notenlänge und die Anschlagstärke. Weiterhin oft eingesetzt werden Aftertouch und einige Kontrollerinformationen, mit denen beispielsweise ein Vibrato oder eine Tonhöhenänderung erzeugt werden können. Weiterführende Informationen finden sich in [2], [3] und [4].

2 Konzepte

An dieser Stelle soll ein Modell entwickelt werden, wie MIDI Files über das Internet sicher verkauft werden können. Abbilung 1 zeigt ein Schema dieses Modells. Dazu sollen verschiedene Techniken zum Schutz herangezogen werden. Sowohl Wasserzeichen als auch Kryptographie sind hier sinnvoll und auch notwendig.
Zwei grundlegende Formen des Mißbrauches von MIDI Daten sind denkbar: Die unerlaubte Nutzung und die unerlaubte Weitergabe.

2. 1 Wasserzeichen zum Schutz vor unerlaubter Weitergabe

Dem Problem der unerlaubte Weitergabe kann mit kundenspezifischen Wasserzeichen begegnet werden [5]. Die vom Kunden erworbenen Daten werden mit seiner Kundennummer bzw. einem aus der Kundennummer gewonnenen Wasserzeichen gekennzeichnet. Sollten nun Dateien unrechtmäßig über dritte Parteien weiterverbreitet werden, kann anhand der Kennzeichnung der Verursacher festgestellt und zur Verantwortung gezogen werden.
Der identifizierte Kunde kann aber immer auf die unsichere Übertragung durch das Internet hinweisen. Daher muß sichergestellt werden, daß eine dritte Person ohne das Zutun des Kunden keinen Zugriff auf die von ihm erworbenen Daten erhält. Dazu sind krytographische Maßnahmen notwendig.

2.2 Kryptographie zum Schutz vor unerlaubter Aneignung

Die mit dem Wasserzeichen versehene Datei wird bei der Übertragung verschlüsselt, so daß nur der Kunde die Datei öffnen kann. Somit kann die Datei ohne Zutun des Kunden nicht Dritten zugänglich werden. Hier muß auch beachtet werden, daß Angriffe gegen Verschlüsselungen zwar möglich sind, in diesem Fall aber der notwendige Aufwand für einen solchen Angriff in keinem Verhältnis zum Nutzen steht.
Zur Verschlüsselung bietet sich hier eine Kombination aus symmetrischer und asymmetrischer Verschlüsselung an. Die MIDI Datei wird mit einem symmetrischen Verfahren verschlüsselt, der Schlüssel hierzu wiederum beispielweise über ein Public Key Verfahren gesichert dem Kunden zugesendet.

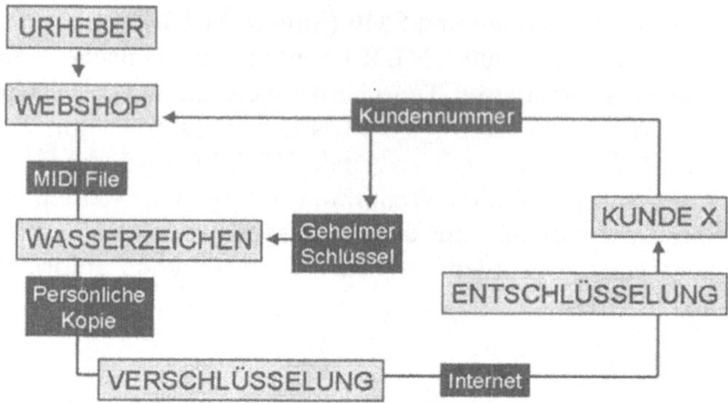

Abbildung 1: Schema eines Sicherheitskonzeptes zum Online-Vertrieb von MIDI Daten

3 Angriffe und Manipulationen

Zwei verschiedene Typen von Programmen können zu Angriffen von MIDI Wasserzeichen herangezogen werden. Zum einen die Sequenzer, mit denen Komponisten MIDI Musik erstellen und die heute eine große Auswahl an Möglichkeiten zur Manipulation bieten und zum anderen spezielle Utilities zum Manipulieren von MIDI Dateien.

Die erste Gruppe bietet die folgenden Möglichkeiten:

- Zusammenfügen und Trennen einzelner Kanäle
- Vertauschen von Kanälen
- Zufälliges oder gezieltes Verändern von Anschlaggeschwindigkeiten und Notenlängen (Abbildung 2)
- Löschen von doppelt angeschlagenen Noten
- Filtern von Sysex[1]-Informationen
- Veränderungen im Timing („Grooves") (Abbildung 3)
- Verändern von Kontrollerdaten
- Formatkonvertierungen

Mit der zweiten Gruppe sind obige Angriffe ebenfalls möglich, zusätzlich sind hier aber noch gezielte Angriffe durch statistische Algorithmen möglich. Häufig eingebettete Muster können erkannt und minimale Änderungen an Kontrollerdaten können breitbandig vorgenommen werden.

Bei diesen Angriffen kann zwischen transparenten und hörbaren unterschieden werden. Änderungen am Timing, den Anschlaggeschwindigkeiten, den Kontrollerdaten und eventuell auch das Löschen von doppelt angeschlagenen Noten

---

[1] Sysex: System Exclusive. Daten, die an einen speziellen Typ von Sythesizer adressiert sind und unter anderem Steuerbefehle oder Klangdaten enthalten können.

sind unter Umständen wahrnehmbar. Bei den Kontrollerdaten ist hierbei zu beachten, daß es verschiedene Auflösungen gibt, da entweder ein oder zwei MIDI-Bytes (7 Bit) zur Kodierung der Data verwendet werden. Daher handelt es sich entweder um 128 oder 16384 mögliche Werte, wobei im zweiten Fall Änderungen natürlich transparenter sind. Das Löschen von Sysex-Informationen kann zu einem Verlust von Funktionalität führen, bei speziell für bestimmte Instrumente erstellten MIDI-Dateien kann es auch zur Änderung des wahrgenommenen Klanges kommen.

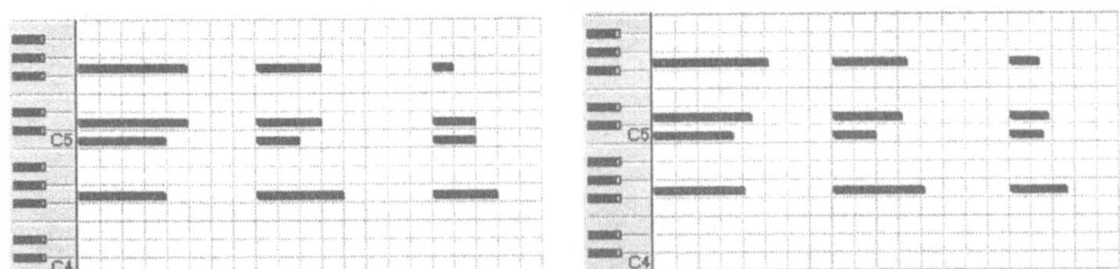

Abbildung 2. Das Quantisieren der Notenlängen gleicht Ungenauigkeiten beim manuellen Einspielen von MIDI-Informationen aus. Es läßt sich auf verschiedene Rastergrößen und Genauigkeiten einstellen.

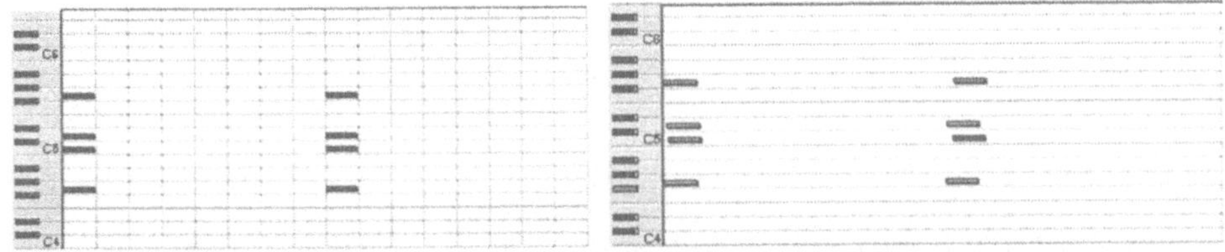

Abbildung 3. Das Quantisieren der Anschlagszeitpunkte der Noten gleicht Ungenauigkeiten beim Einspielen von Sequenzen wie beispielsweise nicht zeitgleich gegriffene Akkorde aus. Die Notenanfänge werden an einem wählbaren Raster ausgerichtet.

4 Ansätze zum Einbetten von digitalen Wasserzeichen in MIDI

Wasserzeichen können entweder im Speicherformat SMF oder dem MIDI Protokoll selbst eingebettet werden. Das Kennzeichnen von SMF wird hier nicht weiter verfolgt. Konvertierung in ein anderes Format, beispielsweise ein proprietäres Sequenzerformat, oder die Übertragung und Aufzeichnung der Daten als MIDI Protokoll, sind nur zwei mögliche Wege, Wasserzeichen, die ausschließlich in das Speicherformat eingebettet sind, zu umgehen.

Daher soll hier auf Methoden eingegangen werden, das MIDI Protokoll selbst mit einem digitalen Wasserzeichen zu versehen. Wir stellen eine Reihe von Ansätzen vor, diskutieren die Transparenz und zeigen mögliche Angriffe auf. Abbildung 4 zeigt den schematisches Aufbau von MIDI-Informationen. Im Folgenden werden nur die einzelnen Noten betrachtet.

4.1 Einbringen von Mustern

Muster in Sequenzen von Informationen können als Träger für ein Wasserzeichen dienen [6]. Dazu werden vorhandene Daten leicht manipuliert, um wieder auffindbare, relative oder absolute Folgen bestimmter Werte einzubetten. Unter absoluten Folgen versteht man eine Reihe von Werten, die in den Informationen explizit vorkommen müssen, unter relativen solche, die sich ausgehend von einem Anfangswert aus beispielsweise Differenzen zu diesem berechnen. Relative Verfahren haben hier den Vorteil, schwerer detektierbar zu sein und häufiger vorzukommen.

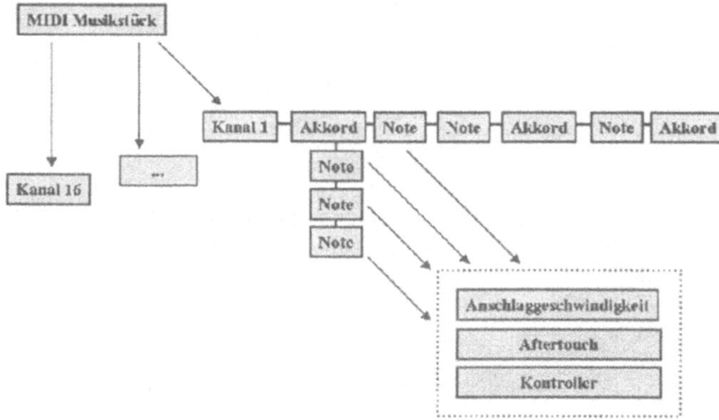

Abbildung 4. Schematischer Aufbau der Informationen eines MIDI-Musikstückes

Im Fall von MIDI eignen sich besonders Anschlaggeschwindigkeit, Aftertouch und die verschiedenen Kontrollerdaten zum Einbetten von Mustern. Die Anschlaggeschwindigkeit beispielsweise wird mit jeder Note übertragen und hat eine Auflösung von 7 Bit, diese Daten kommen also häufig vor und bieten genug Raum für leichte Veränderungen. Um die Robustheit eines Wasserzeichens zu erhöhen, sollte hier mit mehreren Datentypen gearbeitet werden. Bei starker Quantisierung oder Filtern eines Datentyps bleiben die Informationen in den restlichen Daten erhalten.
Eine Aussage über die Transparenz der Veränderungen läßt sich schwer treffen. Die Musikinstrumente interpretieren die eingehenden MIDI Daten unterschiedlich. Beispielsweise erzeugt eine Anschlaggeschwindigkeit von 0 bei manchen Geräten keinen Ton, bei anderen ist dieser bereits schwach hörbar. Synthesizer sind meist variabel in der Stärke, mit der sie auf empfangene Modulationen reagieren. Folglich sind schwache Änderungen an den Daten vertretbar, wenn auf einige Faktoren geachtet wird. Werte unter 0 und über 127 führen zu Abstürzen oder Fehlverhalten, wenn nur 7 Bit zu Kodierung zur Verfügung stehen. Zu beachten ist auch, daß manche Werte oft als Grenzen für ein bestimmtes Verhalten des Synthesizers verwendet werden. Beispielsweise treten bei Anschlagwerten über 120 bei einigen Geräten beabsichtigte Verzerrungen auf. Andere Synthesizer wählen abhängig von der Anschlaggeschwindigkeit verschiedene Instrumentensamples aus. Oft sind Vielfache von Zehn oder Potenzen von 2 die Grenzen für ein solches Verhalten. Diese Werte sollten beim Einbetten eines Wasserzeichens vermieden werden.
Bei mit einem MIDI Keyboard von Hand gespielten Stücken treten viele unterschiedliche Werte bei der Anschlaggeschwindigkeit auf. Hier fallen leichte

Änderungen durch das Einbetten von Mustern nicht auf. Wenn allerdings direkt am Computer erzeugte Musik vorliegt, kann die Anschlaggeschwindigkeit über viele Noten hinweg gleich sein. Hier ist eine Änderungen einzelner Wert auffällig, Angriffe durch statistische Mittel sind deshalb einfach. Deshalb sollte in diesem Fall zuerst eine Art „Rauschen" in die Anschlagwerte eingebracht werden, z.B. durch zufällige Addieren und Subtrahieren eines geringen Wertes. In Abbildung 5 ist hierzu ein Beispiel aufgeführt. Die v-Werte auf der linken Seite sind Vielfache von 32, auf der rechten Seite wurden leichte Veränderungen eingebracht. Durch ein Quantisieren der Anschlagwerte würde das Wasserzeichen allerdings zerstört werden, und in diesem Fall sogar der Originalzustand wiederhergestellt.

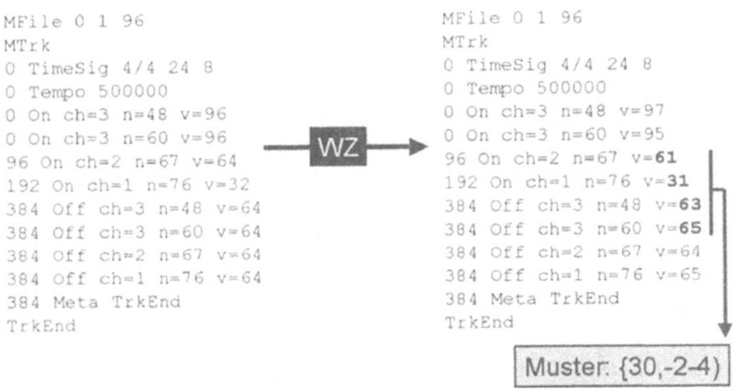

Abbildung 5. Einbetten eines Musters in MIDI Daten

4.2 Zeitbasierende Wasserzeichen

Neben den Noten selbst ist deren zeitliche Abfolge die wichtigste musikalische Information. Sequencer erlauben eine sehr genaue Festlegung dieser Abfolge, was Freiräume für geringe beabsichtigte Veränderungen mit sich bringt. Durch Verschieben von MIDI Ereignissen um minimale Zeiten können Informationen in den MIDI Daten versteckt werden (Abbildung 6). Auch hierbei liefern die Ungenauigkeiten bei den zum Erzeugen der Musik verwendeten Geräten das erforderliche Rauschen zum Verdecken der Manipulationen. Sowohl MIDI selbst als auch die Instrumente bringen Verzögerungen in die Wiedergabe eines Musikstückes ein [4].

Wie bei den Anschlagwerten kommt es auch hier zu Unregelmäßigkeiten, wenn ein Stück per Hand eingepielt wird. Der Musiker wird nicht genau die zeitlichen Raster treffen, auf denen beispielsweise die 32stel Noten liegen. Dies ist allerdings meist erwünscht, da das wiedergegebene Stück somit "wärmer" und "menschlicher" klingt, Man spricht hierbei auch von einem "Groove". Bei am Computer erstellten Stücken entfallen diese Unregelmäßigkeiten, da hier die Noten in den Rastern eingetragen werden. Die meisten Sequenzer bieten allerdings Funktionen an, mit denen nachträglich Ungenauigkeiten erzeugt werden können.

Liegt ein Stück vor, das solche Ungenauigkeiten enthält, dann kann darin auch ein Wasserzeichen eingebettet werden. Ein Ansatz wäre, jeweils ausgehend vom Taktanfang das n-te Ereignis zu betrachten. N sei dabei von einem geheimen Schlüssel abhängig. Als Information könnte dienen, ob das Ereignis auf einen geraden oder ungeraden Zeitpunkt fällt. Somit können einfach binäre Daten eingebettet werden.

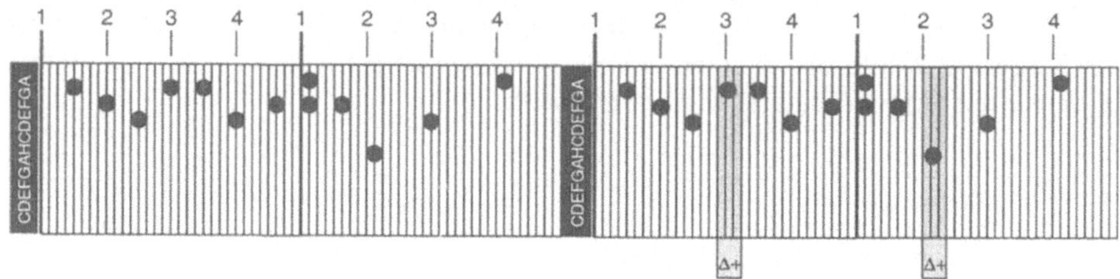

Abbildung 6. Notenfolge (links) und Notenfolge mit leichten Änderungen jeweils bei dem 4. Ereignis eines Taktes (rechts)

Eine andere Möglichkeit besteht darin, gleichzeitige oder sehr kurz aufeinanderfolgende Ereignisse zu betrachten. In die zeitliche Abfolge von Akkorden (Abbildung 7) könnten Muster eingebracht werden, indem ausgehend vom höchsten Notenwert die Zeitpunkte des Anschlags verglichen werden.

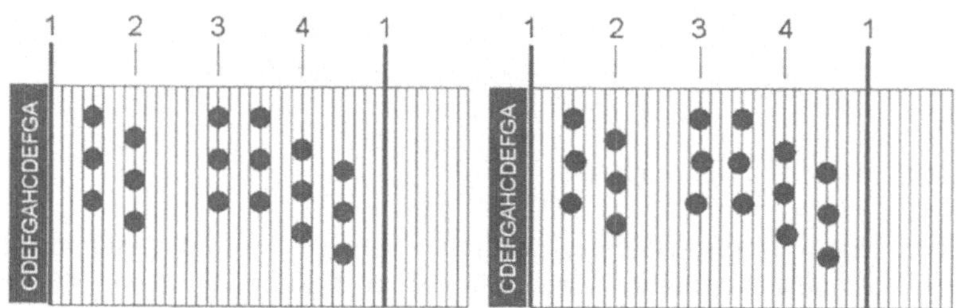

Abbildung 7. Quantisierte (links) und markierte (rechts) Akkorde

Angriffe auf dieses Verfahren sind mit jedem MIDI Sequenzer möglich. Die Option "Quantisieren" bietet eine Funktion zum automatischen zeitlichen Diskretisieren der Noten. Dabei ist meist Genauigkeit und Auflösung der Funktion frei wählbar. Ein "Groove" geht hierdurch allerdings verloren, weshalb der Angriff nicht als transparent gelten kann.

Eine andere Möglichkeit besteht darin, mit einem Utility zufällig Ereignisse um geringe Werte zu verschieben. Um sicher zu sein, daß das Wasserzeichen gelöscht wurde, müssen allerdings sehr viele Ereignisse verschoben werden, was unter Umständen ebenfalls nicht mehr transparent ist.

4.3 Einbetten von Inhaltsbeschreibungen

Dieser Ansatz wendet sich nicht an das Problem, die Urheberrechte zu sichern. Hier soll sichergestellt werden, daß die MIDI Daten tatsächlich von einem Komponisten oder Vertrieb stammen. Denn nicht nur die illegale Weitergabe von Eigentum kann Schäden verursachen, sondern auch die fälschliche Angabe von Urhebern bei minderwertiger Ware. Vertreibt eine Website im Internet illegale MIDI-Files und erzielt durch Werbung Gewinn, kann diese minderwertige, also beispielsweise schlecht eingespielte, Files unter einem bekannten Namen anbieten. Viele Interessenten vertrauen diesem Namen, ungeachtet der Herkunft der Dateien, und sind beim Hören der Daten enttäuscht. Der Ruf das Herstellers nimmt Schaden.
Durch die geringe Datenmenge in einem MIDI File ist es allerdings möglich, die wichtigsten Informationen zu einem Musikstück, also beispielsweise die Notenfolge der Hauptstimme und der Begleitung, verschlüsselt als Sysex-Information in das File einzubetten. Ähnliche Ansätze für Video- und Audiodaten finden sich in [7].
Durch ein Public Key Schlüsselpaar kann hiermit sehr einfach die Sicherung von Qualität erfolgen. Der Urheber verschlüsselt mit seinem geheimen Schlüssel. Der Kunde überprüft mit dem öffentlichen Schlüssel und einem kleinen Utility, das die MIDI-Daten und die verschlüsselte Inhaltsbeschreibung vergleicht, ob ein authentisches File vorliegt. Die Sysex-Daten sind zwar leicht zu entfernen, dadurch verliert die Datei aber auch ihr "Gütesigel". Somit bietet diese Vorgehensweise einen einfachen Weg zur Sicherung von Authentizität und Integrität.

5 Zusammenfassung und Ausblick

MIDI ist ein Thema, das bei dem zu erwartenden Wachstum von eCommerce sicher noch größere Beachtung finden wird, da MIDI-Files ideale Produkte zum Verkauf über das Internet sind. Dementsprechend wird auch der Wunsch der Anbieter nach Sicherheit ansteigen

5.1 Ausblick

Die beschriebenen Konzepte müssen prototypisch implementiert werden, um ihre Verwendbarkeit als Wasserzeichen bezüglich der Robustheit gegen Angriffe, der Datenmenge, die eingebettet werden kann, und der Gewährleistung der Transparenz zu prüfen. Danach kann eine Klassifikation hinsichtlich der Paramter [1] Robustheit, Security, Invertierbarkeit, Detektierbarkeit, Wahrnehmbarkeit, Komplexität, Kapazität und geheime oder öffentliche Verifikation erfolgen.

5.2 Mögliche Anwendungen und Zusammenfassung

In dieser Veröffentlichung werden drei Ansätze vorgestellt, die sich an verschiedene Sicherheitsaspekte wenden. Die ersten beiden sind Wasserzeichen, mit denen das Urheberrecht durchgesetzt werden kann. Der dritte Ansatz stellt Authentizität und Integrität sicher.
Die ersten beiden Verfahren basieren auf einer Veränderung wichtiger MIDI Daten. Ohne die genaue Kenntnis der Position der Veränderungen kann die eingebettete

Information nicht gelöscht werden, ohne dabei einen merklichen Qualitätsverlust zu verursachen. Die Wasserzeicheninformationen werden als relative Muster in den MIDI-Daten eingebracht, dabei können den einzelnen Mustertypen Informationen zugeordnet werden, wodurch n-Bit Wasserzeichen möglich sind. Die Verfahren ist blind, sie benötigt die ursprünglichen MIDI-Daten nicht, um die Informationen aus den gekennzeichneten Dateien zu lesen.

Diese Verfahren finden Anwendung in der Durchsetzung von Urheberrechten. Mit ihnen können MIDI Daten markiert werden, um zu verfolgen, welche Kunden die Dateien unerlaubt weitergeben. Alternativ können Markierungen eingebettet werden, die die Urheberschaft nachweisen.

Das Verfahren zur Gewährleistung der Integrität von MIDI-Daten basiert auf einer Abstraktion der beschriebenen Notenfolgen in Kombination mit kryptographischen Maßnahmen zur Sicherstellung der Unveränderbarkeit der eingebetteten Daten.

Dieses Verfahren eignet sich zum Nachweis der Integrität von MIDI Daten. Hier kann festgestellt werden, ob die Daten wesentlich verändert worden sind. Dadurch kann eine Gewährleistung der Qualität durchgesetzt werden.

Literaturangaben

1. Dittmann,J.: Digitale Wasserzeichen, Springer Verlag, ISBN 3 - 540 - 66661 - 3, 2000
2. Kientzle, Tim, A programmers guide to sound, Addison-Wesley Developers Press, 1997
3. Rumsey, Francis, MIDI Systems & Control, Focal Press, 1994 Buick, Peter; Lennard, Vic, Music Technology Referenece Book, PC Publishing, 1995
4. Steinebach,Martin, MIDI – Eine Bestandsaufnahme, Studienarbeit TU Darmstadt, 1997
5. Dittmann, J., Behr, A., Stabenau, M., Schmitt, P., Schwenk, J., Ueberberg, J.: Combining digital Watermarks and collision secure Fingerprints for digital Images, In Proc. of the SPIE Conference on Electronic Imaging '99, Security and Watermarking of Multimedia Contents, 24-29 January 1999, San Jose USA, Proceedings of SPIE Vol. 3657, [3657-51], pp. 171-182, 1999
6. Dittmann, J, Steinebach, M., Steinmetz, R., Digital Watermarking for MPEG Audio Layer 2, to appear in Proceedings of ACM Multimedia'99
7. Dittmann, J., Steinebach, M., Rimac, I., Fischer, S., Steinmetz, R.: Combined video and audio watermarking: Embedding content information in multimedia data, in Proc. of the SPIE Conference on Electronic Imaging 2000, Security and Watermarking of Multimedia Contents II, 24-26 January 2000, San Jose USA, Proceedings of SPIE Vol. 3971, pp. 176-185, 2000

Optimierung eines Wasserzeichenverfahrens zum Einbringen von kundenspezifischen Informationen in digitales Datenmaterial

Enrico Hauer

GMD-IPSI
Dolivostrasse 15
64921 Darmstadt, Germany

Abstract. Es wurde ein Wasserzeichenverfahren entwickelt, das in digitale Imagedateien einen digitalen Fingerabdruck einbettet, der robust gegenüber dem Koalitionsangriff ist. Das Wasserzeichenverfahren besitzt gegenüber der visuellen Qualität und der Robustheit gegenüber Veränderungen des Trägerobjektes, wie die Ausschnittbildung, die Skalierung und Rotation, Mängel. In diesem Paper wird zuerst ein visuelles Modell und danach eine Methode zur Dedektion der Angriffsparameter vorgestellt. Das visuelle Modell, Smooth-Block/ Edge-Detection Verfahren genannt, ermittelt die visuelle Kapazität der Markierungspunkte des Wasserzeichens und bewertet so die Wasserzeichenstärke für jeden Markierungspunkt einzeln. Die Methode der Dedektion der Angriffsparameter besteht darin, dass ein Vergleichsbild zwischen dem Original und dem Trägerobjekt gebildet wird.

1. Motivation

Generell können digitalen Wasserzeichen die folgenden Sicherheitsaspekte zugeordnet werden:
- Gewährleistung der Authentizität von Daten, dadurch garantierte Identität des Besitzers oder Senders und Durchsetzung der Urheberrechte des Besitzers
- erfolgreicher Nachweis der Integrität des markierten Datenmaterials, um Manipulationen zu unterbinden.

Um auch nachzuweisen, wer das Urheberrecht verletzt hat, kann man digitale Fingerabdrücke nutzen. Das Prinzip von digitalen Fingerabdrücken besteht darin, spezifische Kundendaten in das ausgegebene Datenmaterial einzufügen. Somit kann der Urheber zurückverfolgen, welcher der Kunden das Urheberrecht gebrochen hat. Der Urheber liest den Fingerabdruck aus dem gefundenen Datenmaterial aus und kann dann überprüfen, ob der ausgelesene Fingerabdruck mit einem der vergebenen Fingerabdruck übereinstimmt.

Der Koalitionsangriff bildet eine Angriffsmöglichkeit auf digitale Fingerabdrücke. Dabei wird ein Differenzbild aus den Fingerprint-Kopien der Kunden erstellt. In dem Differenzbild werden somit die Unterschiede zwischen den einzelnen Fingerprint-Kopien sichtbar. Die zusammenarbeitenden Kunden sehen die dedektierten Unterschiede als die Unterschiede zwischen ihren digitalen Fingerabdrücken an. Nachdem die Unterschiede verfälscht oder beseitigt wurden, entsprechen die ausgelesenen Fingerprintdaten nicht mehr den eingelesenen Fingerprintdaten.

Ziel ist deshalb die Erstellung eines koalitionsangriffssicheren Fingerabdruckes. Der Fingerabdruck muß die Eigenschaft besitzen, daß nach der Durchführung eines Koalitionsangriffes der ausgelesene Fingerabdruck die Kunden enthalten muß, welche zusammen den Koalitionsangriff angewandt haben. Falls aber kein Koalitionsangriff durchgeführt wird, muß der Fingerabdruck ausgelesen werden, der die vom Urheber eingebetteten Kundendaten enthält.

In diesem Beitrag betrachten wir in Kapitel 2 und 3 zuerst die verwendeten Fingerprint- und Wasserzeichenalgorithmen. In Kapitel 4 diskutieren wir Probleme der Erstimplemtierung in Bezug zur visuellen Qualität sowie Robustheit des Wasserzeichenalgorithmus und beschreiben mögliche Optimierungen. In Kapitel 5 betrachten wir die Testergebnisse und ziehen eine Schlußfolgerung daraus.

2.   Der Fingerprint-Algorithmus

Die Deutsche Telekom hat zusammen mit der Universität Gießen und der GMD Darmstadt einen FingerprintEditor für Einzelbilder entwickelt. Mit dem FingerprintEditor wird das Fingerprint Watermark [Ditt1999] mit der Erstellung von Kundenkopien in das Datenmaterial eingebettet und ausgelesen.

Der angewandte digitale Fingerabdruck von Schwenk/Ueberberg [ScUe1998] ist resistent gegenüber dem Koalitionsangriff. Der Fingerprint-Algorithmus ermittelt die Markierungspositionen für das zu markierende Datenmaterial auf der Basis von endlichen Geometrien. Der Vorteil der angewandten Technik liegt darin, daß durch einen bitweisen Vergleich der markierten Dokumente nicht alle Markierungspositionen erkannt werden. Es bleiben Restinformationen in der Schnittmenge erhalten, die auf die Angreifer schließen lassen.

In [Hauer1999], Seite 23-27, wird die Erstellung des digitalen Fingerprint-Schema erläutert. Die Implementierung des Fingerprint-Schemas wurde von der Universität Gießen vorgenommen.

3.   Der Wasserzeichen-Algorithmus

Die Aufgabe des Wasserzeichen-Algorithmus ist es, die durch den Fingerprint-Algorithmus gelieferten kundenspezifischen Daten in das Bildmaterial einzufügen [DiSta1998].

Der Wasserzeichenalgorithmus generiert unter Zuhilfenahme eines geheimen Schlüssels und des Originals eine fixe Anzahl von pseudo-zufälligen Markierungspunkten. Die Markierungspunkte sind in allen zu erstellenden Kopien des

Originals identisch. Der erstellte binäre Fingerprintvektor wird in die Markierungspunkte eingebettet. Da die Markierungspunkte in allen Kopien gleich sind, bleibt nach einer möglichen Anwendung des Vergleichsangriffs eine Schnittmenge der Fingerprintinformationen erhalten, womit auf die Piraten geschlossen werden kann.

Der Fingerprintvektor hat eine Länge von $l= q^d+q^{d-1}+...+q+1$. Mit Hilfe dieses Fingerprintvektors können maximal $q+1$ Kopien erstellt werden und es können d zusammenarbeitende Piraten dedektiert werden. Da für jeden Kunden ein eigener Fingerprint erstellt wird, entstehen dementsprechend unterschiedliche Kopien. Der Vergleichsangriff kann nur die Markierungspunkte mit unterschiedlichen Informationen ermitteln, die Markierungspunkte mit den gleichen eingebetteten Informationen werden nicht aufgespürt und bilden dadurch die Schnittmenge, womit die Piraten ermittelt werden.

Zudem wird der Fingerprintvektor r_1 mal eingebracht. Dadurch entsteht eine Redundanz, wodurch die Robustheit des Wasserzeichen erhöht wird. Mit Anwendung der Redundanz werden nun $r_1* (q^d+q^{d+1}+...+q+1)$ Markierungspunkte benötigt. Die Markierungspunkte werden im Original unter Zuhilfenahme des geheimen Schlüssels ermittelt und gelten für alle Kopien.

Das Original selbst wird in $n_{breite}*n_{höhe}$ Blöcke aufgeteilt, wobei die Größe eines Blockes 8x8 Pixel beträgt. Jeder Block bildet eine potentielle Markierungsposition. Zum Einbringen der Fingerprintinformationen wird der Frequenzraum des Bildes benutzt, d.h. mit Hilfe der DCT-Transformation (Direct Cosinus Transformation) werden die Daten des Blockes in den Frequenzraum transformiert. Entspricht ein Block einem Markierungspunkt, werden seine DCT-Koeffizienten in Bezug zu dem Fingerprintvektorelement verändert. Nach der Modifizierung werden die DCT-Koeffizienten zurück in den Bildraum transformiert und die neu entstandenen Bilddaten bilden die Fingerprint-Kopie.

3.1 Einbringen des Fingerprints

In Fig. 1 wird der Fingerprint-Vektor in drei Schritten eingebracht[Hauer1999], Seite 30-33.

Im ersten Schritt wird der Fingerprint-Vektor generiert. Die Anzahl der möglichen Fingerprints, die in das Bild eingesetzt werden können, richtet sich danach, in wieviele Blöcke das Bild unterteilt werden kann. Im zweiten Schritt werden mit Hilfe des geheimen Schlüssels die Markierungspositionen ermittelt, in welche die Elemente des Fingerprint-Vektors eingebettet werden. Im dritten Schritt werden die Bilddaten der Markierungsblöcke DCT transformiert, quantisiert, das Vektorelement eingebracht und die veränderten DCT-Koeffizienten rücktransformiert.

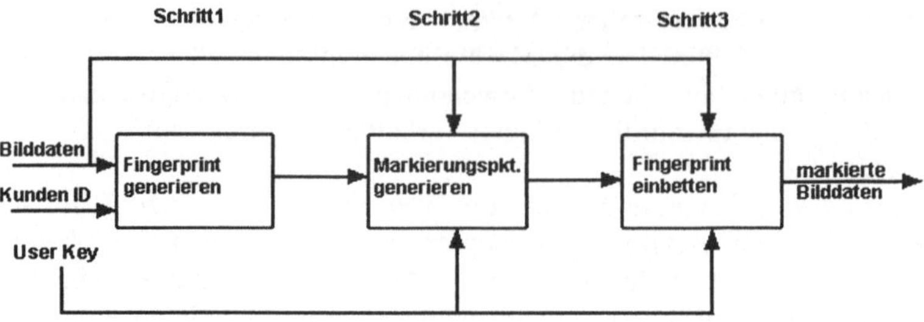

Fig. 1. Einbringen des Fingerprints

3.2 Auslesen des Fingerprints

Bei der Abfrage des Fingerprints wird das Original mit berücksichtigt, so daß es sich um ein nicht-blindes Wasserzeichenverfahren handelt. Durch den Vergleich des Originals mit dem markierten Bild sollen die Markierungspunkte und die Wertigkeit in den Markierungsblöcken wiedergefunden werden.

Im Abfragealgorithmus wird unter Zuhilfenahme von Original und Prüfbild ein Differenzbild generiert. In dem Differenzbild werden mit Hilfe des geheimen Schlüssels UK die Positionen generiert. An den ermittelten Markierungspositionen werden die Luminanzwerte ausgelesen, in die DCT-Koeffizienten transformiert und quantisiert. Zudem werden mit dem geheimen Schlüssel die Zahlenfolgen R_i berechnet. Die berechneten Zahlenfolgen werden mit den ausgelesenen Zahlenfolgen in den Markierungsblöcken verglichen. Wird eine Übereinstimmung gefunden, wird es als eine „1" interpretiert, bei keiner Übereinstimmung wird es als „0" angesehen.

Die Ermittlung des Fingerprints läßt sich in drei Schritten grob unterteilen [Hauer1999], Seite 33-35:

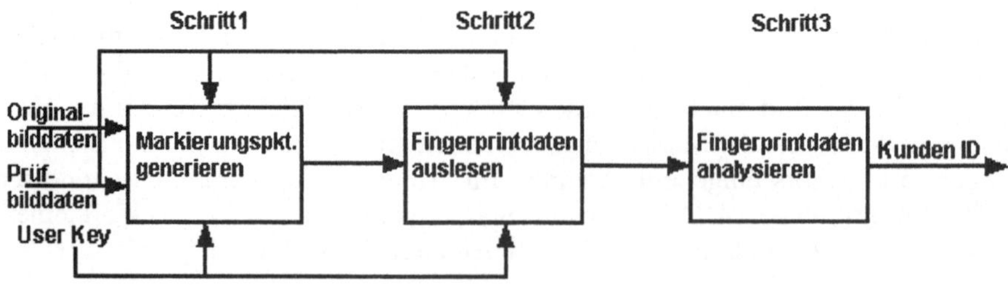

Fig. 2. Schema zum Auslesen des Fingerprints

4. Optimierung des Wasserzeichenalgorithmus'

Die Optimierung des Wasserzeichenalgorithmus wird für die folgenden Probleme durchgeführt:

1. zu schnelle visuelle Wahrnehmung des Wasserzeichens in bestimmten Bildbereichen
2. nicht vorhandene Robustheit des Wasserzeichen gegenüber geometrischen Medienoperationen, wie z.B. Rotation, Skalierung und Ausschnittbildung

Zu (1): Für alle Markierungsblöcke wird die gleiche Wasserzeichenstärke angewandt. Die Wasserzeichenstärke selbst richtet sich nicht nach den Bildeigenschaften innerhalb des Markierungsblockes. Vor allem im Bereich von Kanten und glatten Flächen werden die visuellen Veränderungen durch das Wasserzeichen sichtbar. Um die Nicht-Wahrnehmbarkeit besser zu garantieren, muß das Wasserzeichen an die Bildeigenschaften des Markierungsblockes angepaßt werden. Eine Lösung dieses Problems ist die Anwendung eines visuellen Modells. In dieser Arbeit wird für den Wasserzeichenalgorithmus ein Smooth-Block/ Edge-Detection Verfahren eingebaut, welche die Wasserzeichenstärke anhand der visuellen Eigenschaften in dem Markierungsblock bewertet. In Kapitel 4.1 wird das Verfahren beschrieben.

Zu (2): Der Wasserzeichenalgorithmus besitzt keine Robustheit gegenüber geometrischen Veränderungen. Wenn am Prüfmaterial bspw. Rotation oder Skalierung angewandt wurden, kann der Fingerprint nicht mehr korrekt ausgelesen werden. Das Problem hierbei ist, daß sich durch den Angriff die Markierungspositionen entweder verschoben haben oder nicht mehr existieren. Eine Lösung, die hier behandelt werden soll, besteht darin, daß mit Hilfe des Originals die Attacken erkannt werden, und daß das Prüfmaterial in den Zustand vor der Anwendung der erkannten Attacken zurückgeführt wird. Eine genauere Beschreibung folgt in Kapitel 4.2.

3.3 Smooth-Block/ Edge-Detection

Fig. 3 zeigt die Erweiterung des Schema von Fig. 1 unter Berücksichtigung des Smooth-Block/ Edge-Detection Verfahren.

Das für diese Arbeit aus [StDi1998] entnommene Smooth-Block/Edge-Detection Verfahren liefert einen Indikator über die visuelle Kapazität des Markierungsblockes. Der Indikator zeigt an, wie groß die Störungen in dem Markierungsblock sein dürfen, ohne sichtbar zu werden. Mit Hilfe des Indikators kann die Wasserzeichenstärke bewertet werden.

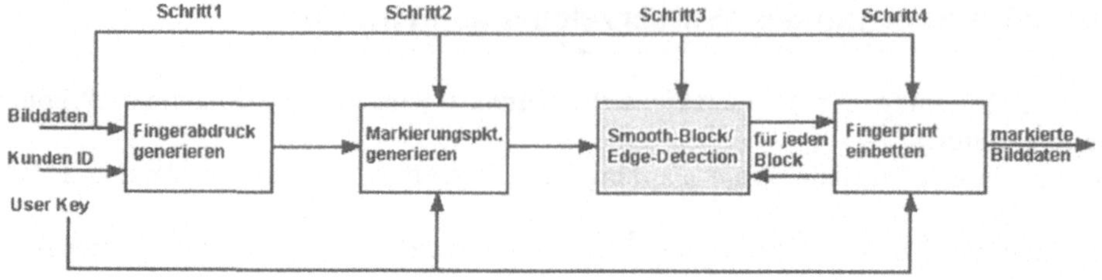

Fig. 3. Einbringen des Fingerprints unter Verwendung des visuellen Modells Smooth-Block/ Edge-Detection

Speziell für dieses Projekt wird die Wasserzeichenstärke wie folgt bewertet:

Level= 1 → Wasserzeichenstärke= 0.3

Level= 2 → Wasserzeichenstärke= 0.4

...

Level= 11 → Wasserzeichenstärke= 1.3

Bei Anwendung des Verfahrens werden die Werte von *smoothscale*, *edgescale* und *offset* vom Urheber frei eingegeben. Dabei muß aber beachtet werden, daß sich die Parameter *smoothscale* und *edgescale* gegenseitig beeinflussen. Wird *smoothscale* auf eine starke Markierung von hochfrequenten Bereichen gestellt, werden auch Kanten stärker markiert und wird *edgescale* auf eine schwache Markierung von Kanten eingestellt, werden auch hochfrequente Bereiche entsprechend schwächer markiert. Der Wert des Parameters *offset* hat eine indirekte Wirkung zu der errechneten Wasserzeichenstärke.

3.4 Erkennen von geometrischen Attacken

Fig. 4 stellt den neuen schematischen Aufbau des Retrieve Modus vom Wasserzeichenverfahren mit der Hinzunahme der Robustheit gegenüber geometrischen Veränderungen.

Bisher wird der Abfrage-Modus wie folgt unterteilt:

1. Auslesen der Bilddaten von Original und Prüfmaterial
2. Auslesen und Analysieren der Fingerprintdaten aus den ausgelesenen Bilddaten

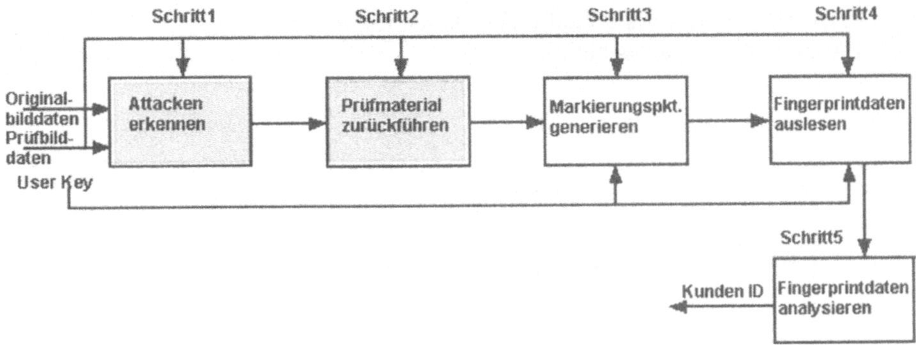

Fig. 4. Auslesen des Fingerprints nach Erkennen der Attacken und Rückführen des Prüfmaterials

Wir schlagen eine zusätzliche Analyse und Rückführung der folgenden geometrischen Angriffe vor:
- Ausschnitt
- Skalierung
- Rotation und
- die Kombinationen der Angriffe.

Die Bearbeitung der Angriffe setzt sich generell aus den folgenden Schritten zusammen:
1. Zuerst gibt der Benutzer des Editors ein, welcher oder welche Angriffe an der Fingerprint-Kopie durchgeführt wurden.
2. Der Editor erkennt die notwendigen Angriffsparameter und führt das Prüfmaterial zurück.
3. Nachdem der Angriff mit den Parametern auch am Original angewandt wurde, werden die Fingerprint-Daten ausgelesen und analysiert.

Der Angriff wird in seine Grundangriffe aufgeteilt und nach der folgenden Priorität untersucht:
1. Rotation
2. Skalierung
3. Ausschnitt

- (a)Rotation

Um den Rotationswinkel zu ermitteln, besteht generell die Möglichkeit, das Original von 0° bis 359° zu drehen, um es dann mit dem Prüfmaterial zu vergleichen. Nach anfänglichen Testen hat sich dies als fehleranfällig erwiesen, weil sich durch die Rotation die Farbwerte der Pixel innerhalb des Bildes so stark verändern, daß eine genaue Bestimmung des korrekten Rotationswinkels als problematisch erwies. Deshalb wird von vornherein schon versucht, den Wertebereich des Rotationswinkels einzuengen, um die Fehlerquote zu senken. Die Größe des Bildes nach einer Drehung wird vorher berechnet und so der angewandte Rotationswinkel bestimmt. Die Vorgehensweise zur Ermittlung des korrekten Winkels ist wie folgt:

1. Dieser Algorithmus basiert auf rechteckigen Bildern
1.1 Zustand des Rechtecks bei 0°

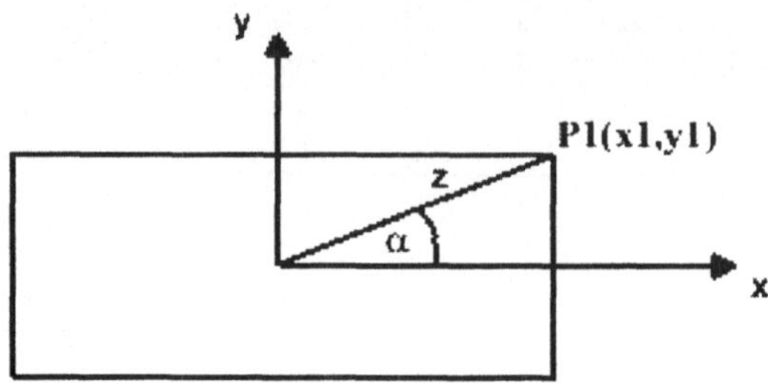

Fig. 5. Zustand des Bildes bei 0° Drehung

Wie Fig. 5 zeigt, wird um das Bild ein Koordinatensystem aufgebaut. Der Nullpunkt liegt genau in der Mitte des Bildes. Mit Hilfe des Koordinatensystems lassen sich die vier Eckpunkte des Bildes berechnen. Mit den vier Eckpunkten werden die Seitenverhältnisse des Bildes bestimmt, auch wenn das Bild gedreht wurde. Der Winkel α ist Bestandteil der Drehung und muß bei dem augenblicklich angewandten Drehwinkel zuaddiert werden. Hinzu kommen noch folgende Berechnungen:

$$x = \text{Spalten}_{\text{Original}}/2 \qquad y = \text{Zeilen}_{\text{Original}}/2 \quad z = (x^2+y^2)^{1/2} \qquad \alpha = \cos^{-1}(x/z)$$

1.2 Berechnung der vier Eckpunkte des Bildes nach der Drehung von 0° bis 359°

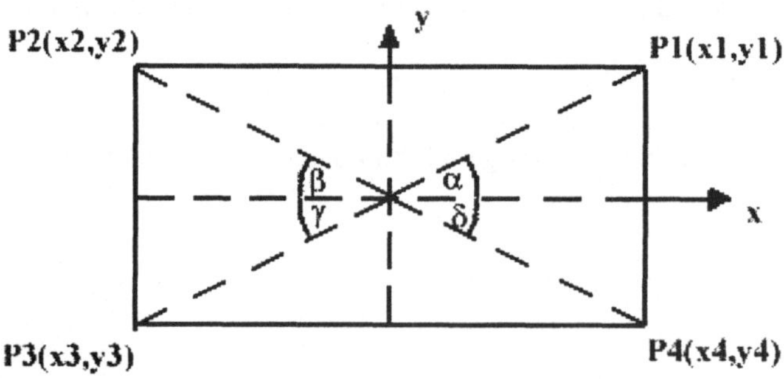

Fig. 6. Verhältnis des Bildes in Bezug zum Koordinatensystem

Die Eckpunkte P_1, P_2, P_3 und P_4, in Fig. 6 bildlich dargestellt, werden nach der Drehung durch den Winkel i wie folgt berechnet:

$$x_1 = \cos(\alpha + i) * z \qquad y_1 = \sin(\alpha + i) * z$$
$$x_2 = \cos(\beta + i) * z \qquad y_2 = \sin(\beta + i) * z \qquad \beta = 180 - \alpha$$
$$x_3 = \cos(\gamma + i) * z \qquad y_3 = \sin(\gamma + i) * z \qquad \gamma = 180 + \alpha$$
$$x_4 = \cos(\delta + i) * z \qquad y_4 = \sin(\delta + i) * z \qquad \delta = 360 - \alpha$$

Die Eckpunkte werden für die Winkel von 0° bis 360° berechnet. Anhand der Eckpunkte läßt sich die Größe des Bildes nach einer Drehung ermitteln. Fig. 7 zeigt den Zustand des neu entstandenen Bildes nach einer Drehung:

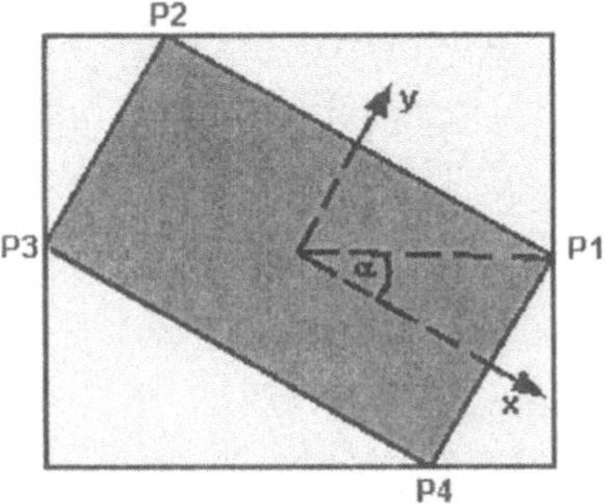

Fig. 7. Verhältnis von Original (dunkel) und Rest des Bildes (hell) nach einer Drehung

1.3 Größe des gedrehten Bildes berechnen

$$x_{min} = \min\{x|x_1,x_2,x_3,x_4\}$$
$$x_{max} = \max\{x|x_1,x_2,x_3,x_4\}$$

$$y_{min} = \min\{y|y_1,y_2,y_3,y_4\}$$
$$y_{max} = \max\{y|y_1,y_2,y_3,y_4\}$$

Länge des gedrehten Bildes $l = x_{max} - x_{min}$
Höhe des gedrehten Bildes $h = y_{max} - y_{min}$

1.4 Vergleich der berechneten Seiten mit den gemessenen Seiten

Es wird der Winkel gesucht, wo die berechnete Höhe h und Länge l mit den Seitenverhältnisse des markierten Bildes übereinstimmen. Der so ermittelten Winkel gilt als der Angriffsparameter, mit dem die Fingerprint-Kopie zurückgedreht wird.

– (b) Skalierung

Normalerweise muß bei der Skalierung der Skalierungsfaktor ermittelt werden. Da aber in diesem Fall auch die Seitenverhältnisse von Original und Prüfmaterial vorliegen, ist es ausreichend, das Prüfmaterial auf die Größe des Originals zu skalieren.

– (c)Ausschnitt

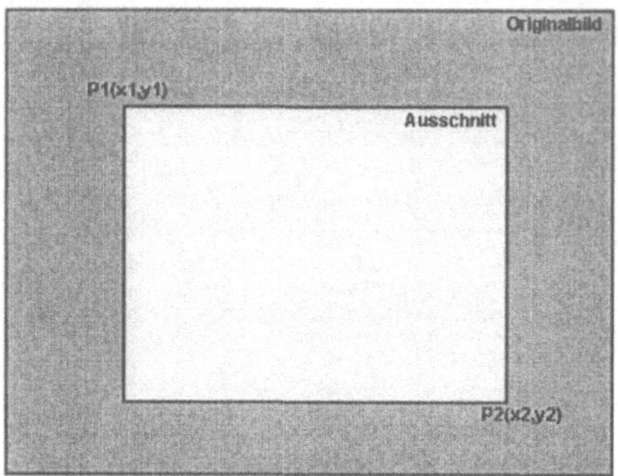

Fig. 8. Verhältnis von Original (dunkel) und signiertem Bild (hell)

Fig. 8 zeigt das Verhältnis zwischen Original (dunkel) und signiertem Bild (hell), welches bei der Bearbeitung des Ausschnittes in dieser Arbeit betrachtet wird. Die zu ermittelnden Angriffsparameter sind die Punkte $P_1(x_1,y_1)$ und $P_2(x_2,y_2)$. Punkt P_1 ist der Anfangs- und Punkt P_2 der Endpunkt des Ausschnittes im Original.

Zur Ermittlung der Punkte P_1 und P_2 wird wie folgt vorgegangen:

1. Anzahl der Möglichkeiten, den Ausschnitt in das Original zu legen:
– m= $\text{Zeilen}_{\text{Original}}$ – $\text{Zeilen}_{\text{Prüfmaterial}}$ +1
– n= $\text{Spalten}_{\text{Original}}$ – $\text{Spalten}_{\text{Prüfmaterial}}$ + 1
– → So sind n*m Verschiebungen zwischen Original und Prüfmaterial möglich.

2. Suche nach der richtigen Verschiebung aus den n*m möglichen Verschiebungen:

2.1 Bildung eines Differenzbildes bestehend aus den RGB-Farbwerten

2.2 Vergleichsobjekt: sum = Summe(dedektierten Farbunterschiede) pro Verschiebung

2.3 Zur Laufzeitoptimierung wird nur die Summe über dem mittelgrau gekennzeichneten Bereich berechnet (Fig. 9)

2.4 Mit Hilfe der Wahl der Parameter ze und sp kann die Laufzeit zusätzlich beeinflußt werden

2.5 Suche nach der kleinsten Summe *endsum* aus der Menge {sum}

2.6 Kommt *endsum* mehr als einmal vor, wird eine weitere Berechnung durchgeführt, wobei der zu vergleichende Bereich vergrößert wird

2.7 Die mit *endsum* zusammenhängenden Punkte P_1 und P_2 gelten als Angriffsparameter

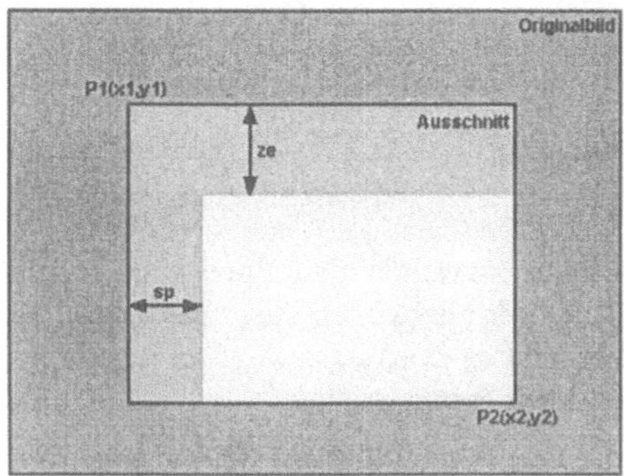

Fig. 9. Überprüfungsbereich (mittelgrau) bei der Ausschnittsberechnung

Im Analyseprozeß werden nur die Markierungsblöcke betrachtet, die zwischen den Punkten P_1 und P_2 liegen. Dabei wird jeder der r_1 Markierungsblöcke pro Vektorbit einzeln betrachtet. Liegt er innerhalb von P_1 und P_2 wird die Wertigkeit ermittelt und zur späteren Auswertung vorgemerkt. Nachdem alle r_1 Markierungsblöcke pro Vektorbit getestet worden, wird untersucht, welche Wertigkeit am häufigsten vorkommt und dem entsprechenden Vektorbit zugeordnet.

Um die Fehlerquote zu senken, ist es ratsam, daß die Angriffe mit den ermittelten Parametern (Skalierungsfaktor und Rotationswinkel) auch am Original angewandt werden. Dabei sollte das Original mit dem Skalierungsfaktor skaliert und rückskaliert werden, sowie mit dem Rotationswinkel ein erstes Mal rotiert und mit dem Restwinkel zu 360° ein zweites Mal rotiert werden.

5. Testergebnisse und Ausblick

In der Beurteilung des Smooth-Block/ Edge-Detection Verfahren ist zu erkennen, daß bei einer niedrigen Wasserzeichenstärke auch mit Anwendung des Verfahrens keine oder kaum Veränderungen in der visuellen Qualität vernehmbar sind. Erst mit Erhöhung der Wasserzeichenstärke kann mit Hilfe der Parameter *smoothscale*, *edgescale* und *offset* des visuellen Modells die visuelle Qualität beeinflußt werden.

Zusätzlich wurde die Robustheit des Wasserzeichenverfahrens gegenüber der verlustbehafteten Kompression getestet. Hier zeigt sich eine direkte Beziehung zwischen der Wasserzeichenstärke und dem Grad der Kompression. So kann das Wasserzeichen je nach Höhe der Wasserzeichenstärke auch bei einem Kompressionsgrad von 75% dedektiert werden. Dies zieht aber Nachteile in der visuellen Qualität der Fingerprint-Kopie mit sich.

Zur Dedektion der Angriffsparameter wurden nur die Rotwerte des RGB-Farbmodells von den entsprechenden Testobjekten herangezogen. Dabei haben sich die folgenden Grenzen der jeweiligen Angriffsparameter ergeben:

- Ausschnitt: der Ausschnitt kann bis zu 50% der Größe des Originals haben bei einem maximalen Kompressionsgrad von 50%
- Skalierung: die minimale Grenze des Skalierungsfaktors liegt bei 50%
- Rotation: es können nur die Rotationswinkel von $i*90°$, für $i=0$ bis 3 dedektiert werden

Speziell bei der Rotation ist die Interpolation zwischen den Pixel und seinen Nachbarpixeln das größte Problem. Um die Möglichkeiten der erfolgreichen Dedektion der Angriffsparameter zu verbessern, ist es ratsam, zusätzlich die Grün- und Blauwerte des RGB-Farbmodells zum Vergleich heranzuziehen.

Es hat sich gezeigt, daß mit Hilfe der Bildung eines Vergleichsbildes zwischen dem Original und der Fingerprint-Kopie die Angriffsparameter nur teilweise erfolgreich ermittelt werden können. Deshalb ist es ratsam, zusätzlich zu dieser Methode noch andere Methoden zur erfolgreichen Dedektion der entsprechenden Angriffsparameter heranzuziehen. Dies kann z.B. das Einbetten von zusätzlichen Informationen in die Fingerprint-Kopie im Einbettungsprozeß sein, welche zur Erkennung der Angriffsparameter herangezogen werden.

Referenzen

[ScUe1998]   **Dr. Jörg Schwenk, Dr. Johannes Ueberberg**: Verfahren zum sicheren Einbringen Digitaler Fingerabdrücke in elektronische Dokumente, Patentantrag, 1998, Seite 1-2

[DiSta1998]   **Jana Dittmann, Mark Stabenau**: Digitale Fingerabdrücke als digitales Wasserzeichen zur Kennzeichnung von Bildmaterial mit kundenspezifischen Informationen, DuD Fachbeträge, 1999, Seite 242-263, ISBN 3-528-05728-9

[Hauer1999]   **Enrico Hauer**: Optimierung eines Wasserzeichen-verfahrens zur kundenspezifischen Markierung von Bildmaterial mit digitalen Fingerabdrücken, Diplomarbeit, FH Anhalt Köthen FB Informatik, November 1999

[StDi1998]   **Mark Stabenau, Jana Dittmann**: Digitale Wasserzeichen für MPEG Video Seite 49-52, GMD Report 34, September 1998, Seite 49-52

[Ditt1999]   **Jana Dittmann**: Digitale Wasserzeichen, Springer Verlag Berlin, August 1999, Seite 30, ISBN 3-540-66661-3

Robustheit und Sicherheit Wavelet-basierter Watermarking-Algorithmen

Peter Meerwald und Andreas Uhl

Department of Scientific Computing, Universität Salzburg, Jakob-Haringer-Str. 2,
A-5020 Salzburg, Österreich
{pmeerw, uhl}@cosy.sbg.ac.at

Zusammenfassung In diesem Artikel betrachten wir den Stand der
Entwicklung Wavelet-basierter Watermarking-Algorithmen. Dabei konzentrieren wir uns auf Verfahren zum Schutz des Urheberrechts bzw. zur Prüfung der Integrität und Authentizität von digitalen Bilddaten.
Nachdem wir die Vorteile von Wasserzeichen im Wavelet-Transformationsbereich identifiziert haben, untersuchen wir, ob sich tatsächlich eine höhere Robustheit, insbesondere gegenüber JPEG2000, erzielen läßt.

1 Einführung

Mit der fortschreitenden Standardisierung von JPEG2000[1] als Ersatz für das
auf die diskrete Cosinus-Transformation beruhende JPEG-Verfahren wird in den
kommenden Jahren ein Wavelet-basiertes Kompressionsverfahren weite Verbreitung finden. Den gesteigerten Anforderungen von heute wie progressive Übertragung und Skalierbarkeit kann das in den achtziger Jahren entwickelte JPEG
nicht – oder nur mehr bedingt – gerecht werden. Mittlerweile läßt die verfügbare Rechenleistung auf den meisten Arbeitsplätzen auch wesentlich aufwendigere
Kodierschemen und damit höhere Kompressionsraten zu.

Durch die rasante Entwicklung der Übertragungs- und Speicherkapazität und
nicht zuletzt durch das Wachstum des Internets, wurde es aber auch notwendig,
Verfahren zu entwickeln, die den Schutz des Urheberrechtes digitaler Medien ermöglichen bzw. die Integrität und Authentizität der Inhalte sicherstellen. Digitale Wasserzeichen (Watermarks) sind Signale, die für das menschliche Auge nicht
wahrnehmbar in Bilddaten eingebettet werden. Mittels geeigneter Programme
ist es möglich, die versteckte Information auszulesen und zur Feststellung des
Urhebers (watermarking for copy protection) oder des rechtmäßigen Käufers
eines digitalen Bildes zu verwenden (watermarking for circulation tracking) –
dazu ist eine darüberliegende Sicherheitsinfrastruktur erforderlich. Für einige
Anwendungen wie dem Schutz der Bilder einer digitalen Bibliothek können auch
sichtbare Wasserzeichen verwendet werden, geeignete Verfahren beschreibt etwa
Braudaway [2]. Die Anforderungen an sichtbare Wasserzeichen unterscheiden
sich wesentlich von den hier behandelten nicht wahrnehmbaren Watermarks,
weshalb wir nicht weiter auf sie eingehen wollen.

---

[1] ISO/IEC JTC1/SC29/WG1 (JPEG working group)

Grundsätzlich ist ein Wasserzeichen unabhängig vom Dateiformat oder dem Kompressionsschema, da das Wasserzeichen direkt in das Bildsignal eingebunden ist (spread-spectrum communication). Trotzdem kann es von Vorteil sein, das Kompressionsverfahren zu kennen. Die zu erwartenden Störungen, die bei einer verlustbehaftete Kompression auftreten, können bei der Einbettung des Watermarks vorweg genommen werden bzw. bei der Erkennung berücksichtigt werden. Diese zusätzliche Information führt im allgemeinen zu robusteren Wasserzeichen. Aus diesem Grund ist es wichtig, Wavelet-basierte Kompressionsverfahren zu untersuchen und geeignete Watermarking-Algorithmen zu entwickeln.

1.1 Einteilung der Verfahren

Die bisher in der Literatur beschriebenen Wavelet-basierenden Verfahren (siehe auch Tabelle 1) lassen sich im wesentlichen nach dem Anwendungsgebiet (Urheberschutz oder Integritätsprüfung), der optionalen Verwendung des Originalbild zur Rekonstruktion des Watermarks und der Art des Wasserzeichens einteilen. Watermarks für den Urheberrechtsschutz müssen sowohl robust gegenüber typischen Bildbearbeitungsoperationen wie Skalieren der Größe, Verändern des Kontrasts und Kompression sein, als auch genügend Kapazität zur Identifizierung des Urhebers bieten – zum Beispiel durch Einbettung einer 64-Bit-Zahl, wie es der ISO Standard 10918 ('Multimedia License Plate') vorsieht. Die Verfahren zum Nachweis der Unverfälschtheit hingegen müssen sicher sein und sollten die Art der durchgeführten Manipulation aufdecken können.

Die Verwendung des Originalbildes zur Rekonstruktion des Wasserzeichens erhöht die Robustheit eines Verfahrens wesentlich, bringt aber auch das Problem der Umkehrbarkeit mit sich, wie Craver [9] gezeigt hat. Für viele Anwendungen ist es praktikabel, auf das Originalbild verzichtet zu können (blind detection/reconstruction).

Die Information eines Wasserzeichens besteht entweder aus einer beliebigen Folge von Bits oder aus einer pseudo-zufälligen Folge von Zahlen, die um 0 normal verteilt sind[2]. Auf die Verfahren zur Einbettung eines kleinen Bildes (etwa das Logo des Urhebers), vorgestellt etwa in [16] und [4], wird hier nicht weiter eingegangen, da in diesem Fall die Erkennung des Wasserzeichens nicht auf einem statistischen Test beruht, sondern die Fähigkeit des menschlichen Auges für die Rekonstruktion ausschlaggebend ist. Ebenso betrachten wir hier keine Verfahren, die nur das Vorhandensein eines Watermarks feststellen können – dazu zählen etwa Algorithmen, wie sie in [11] und [1] beschrieben werden.

In Abschnitt 2 werden wir auf einige für das sichere und robuste Einbetten von Wasserzeichen wichtige Vorteile der diskreten Wavelet-Transformation (DWT) gegenüber der DCT eingehen und einen Überblick über einige Watermarking-Verfahren geben. Resultate zur Robustheit insbesondere gegenüber JPEG und einigen DWT-basierten Kompressionsalgorithmen finden sich in Abschnitt 3. Abschließend geben wir einen Ausblick auf die künftige Entwicklung Wavelet-basierter Watermarking-Verfahren.

---

[2] Herrigel beschreibt in [13] ein Verfahren, wie beliebige Symbole als Folge von Zahlen mit den gewünschten Eigenschaften kodiert werden können.

Tabelle 1. Einteilung Wavelet-basierter Watermarking-Algorithmen

Algorithmus	Anwendungsgebiet	Originalbild erforderlich	Binäres Watermark	Einbettung in ...
Chu [6]	Urheberschutz	Nein	Ja	Bildbereich
Corvi [7]	Urheberschutz	Ja	Nein	LL_n
Inoue [14]	Urheberschutz	Ja/Nein	Ja	HL_3, LH_3 zerotree
Kundur [17]	Urheberschutz	Nein	Ja	HL_i, LH_i, HH_i
Kundur [18]	Integritätsprüfung	Nein	Ja	HL_i, LH_i, HH_i
Ohnishi [23]	Urheberschutz	Nein	Ja	HL_i, LH_i, HH_i
Pereira [24]	Urheberschutz	Nein	Ja	LL_1
Wang [29]	Urheberschutz	Ja/Nein	Nein	nicht LL_n
Wolfgang [31]	Urheberschutz	Ja	Nein	HL_i, LH_i, HH_i
Xia [32]	Urheberschutz	Ja	Nein	HL_i, LH_i, HH_i
Xie [33]	Integritätsprüfung	Nein	Ja	LL_n
Zeng [34]	Urheberschutz	Ja	Nein	HL_i, LH_i, HH_i
Zhu [35]	Urheberschutz	Ja	Nein	HL_i, LH_i, HH_i

2 Wasserzeichen im Wavelet-Bereich

Aufbauend auf die Arbeit von Cox [8] hat man in den letzten Jahren festgestellt, daß Wasserzeichen, die in den Transformationsbereich (DCT, DFT, ...) eines Bildes eingebettet werden, oft robuster sind als solche, die direkt im Bildbereich kodiert werden. Das zeigen auch klar unsere Ergebnisse im Abschnitt 3.

Eines der ersten Watermarking-Verfahren im Wavelet-Transformationsbereich beschreibt Corvi [7]. Anstatt der DCT-Koeffizienten wie in Cox's Algorithmus werden dabei einfach die Koeffizienten im Näherungsbild (LL) der zweidimensionalen diskreten Wavelet-Transformation mit der Watermark-Information versehen. Die Vorteile und Möglichkeiten, die die pyramidale Wavelet-Zerlegung (siehe Abbildung 1) eines Bildes bietet, werden dadurch allerdings nicht genutzt.

Angelehnt an die von Cox beschriebene Methode zum Einbetten von Wasserzeichen in Form einer Folge normalverteilter Zahlen wurde eine ganze Reihe von Verfahren entwickelt, zu denen auch die Algorithmen von Xia [32], Zhu [35] und Wang [29] zu zählen sind. Anders als für das Wasserzeichen von Corvi, werden hier ausschließlich die Detail-Subbänder (HL_n, LH_n, HH_n) benutzt. Während Xia und Zhu alle Stufen der Wavelet-Zerlegung zum Kodieren des Watermarks verwendet, wählt Wang nur signifikante Subbänder und verwendet dazu ein Modell, das auch dem MTWC-Kompressionsschema [28] des selben Autors zu Grunde liegt.

Eine andere Gruppe von Wavelet-basierten Watermarking-Algorithmen nutzt die Quantisierung einzelner Koeffizienten zur Einbettung eines Bits ähnlich des von Koch [15] beschriebenen Schemas für den DCT-Bereich. Hierzu gehören die von Ohnishi [23] und Kundur [17] präsentierten Verfahren, die beide ausschließlich Koeffizienten der Detail-Subbänder in Beziehung setzen. Ähnlich funktionieren die Methoden von Xie [33] bzw. Pereira [24], die allerdings Koeffizienten des Näherungsbildes (LL) verwenden. Um geeignete Koeffizienten für das Verfahren von Xie auszuwählen und damit die Robustheit erhöhen zu können, wird hierbei auf den von Said [25] entwickelten SPIHT Algorithmus zurückgegriffen. Das von Inoue [14] beschriebene Verfahren nutzt die von Shapiro [26] eingeführten 'zerotrees' um zwischen signifikanten und nicht signifikanten Koeffizienten unterscheiden zu können. Die zwei vorgestellten Varianten des Algorithmus verwenden einmal die signifikanten, einmal die nicht signifikanten Koeffizienten, um die Watermark-Information zu kodieren. Der Ansatz von Kutter [21] zur Einbettung eines Wasserzeichens im Bildbereich wird von Chu [6] durch eine Quantisierung im Wavelet-Bereich erweitert, um die Auswirkungen Wavelet-basierter Kompressionsschemen vorwegzunehmen. Wolfgang [31] zeigt, daß ein für den DCT-Bereich entwickelter Algorithmus auch im Wavelet-Bereich gute Ergebnisse liefert und Zeng [34] schlägt das Verfahren für den JPEG2000 Standard vor[3].

Eine gute Einführung in die Problematik der Bild-Authentifizierung und Integritätsprüfung mit zahlreichen Literaturhinweisen gibt Lin[4]. Interessanterweise stellen wir fest, daß die zwei von uns betrachteten Wavelet-basierten Verfahren, Xie [33] und Kundur [18], sich in bezug auf die Einbettung des Wasserzeichens nicht wesentlich von den Methoden des Urheberrechtsschutzs unterscheiden.

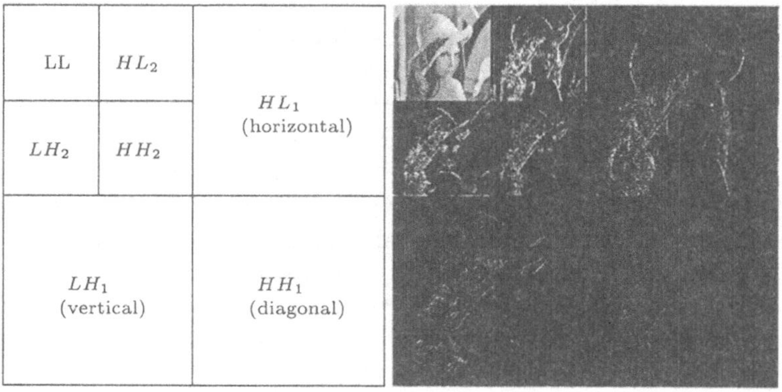

Abbildung 1. Pyramidale 2-Stufen-Zerlegung des Graustufenbildes 'Lena'

2.1 Vorteile des Wavelet-Transformationsbereiches

Der nächste Standard zur Kompression digitaler Bilder, JPEG2000, wird auf die diskrete Wavelet-Transformation aufbauen. Durch den Wechsel des Transformationsbereiches können neu hinzugekommene Anforderungen wie die progressive Übertragung (in zweifacher Hinsicht: entweder bis zur gewünschten Auflösung oder bis zur geforderten Bildqualität), die Anpassung an wechselnde Bandbreitenverhältnisse (etwa bei Übertragung in GSM-Netzen oder über das Internet) leichter erfüllt werden [5]. Aber auch der Schutz des Urheberrechts durch Wasserzeichen soll bei der Entwicklung des Standards berücksichtigt werden[5]. Geeig-

---

[3] ISO/IEC JTC1/SC29/WG1 N759

[4] siehe http://www.ctr.columbia.edu/~cylin/auth/mmauth.html

[5] 'Seminar on imaging security and JPEG2000', Juli 1999; die Arbeiten sind unter http://eurostill.epfl.ch/~ebrahimi/JPEG2000.htm verfügbar.

nete Watermarking-Verfahren können in gleichem Maße von den Eigenschaften der Wavelet-Transformation profitieren. Zu den Vorteilen gehören nach Xia [32]:

- Der hierarchische Aufbau der Zerlegung und Multiresolution-Eigenschaft. Durch den geschachtelten Aufbau der Wavelet-Zerlegung kann ein Wasserzeichen eventuell schon nach Berechnung weniger Stufen erkannt werden, was Rechenzeit – speziell bei Videoanwendungen – sparen kann. Im Gegensatz zur DCT ermöglicht die DWT auf natürliche Weise progressive Übertragung, was auch im vorliegenden JPEG2000-Entwurf in den vielfältigen Skalierungsmöglichkeiten Niederschlag findet.
- Die Lokalität der DWT-Koeffizienten. Die Änderung eines DWT-Koeffizienten wirkt sich nicht wie bei der DCT global auf das gesamte Bild aus, sondern beeinflußt nur die Bilddaten in einem kleinen Bereich, abhängig von der Länge des verwendeten Zerlegungsfilters. Dadurch werden lokale Wasserzeichen möglich, die verwendet werden können, um nur ausgewählte Bildbereiche (region-of-interest, ROI) zu kennzeichnen; eine Anwendung dieser Eigenschaft beschreibt Su [27].
- Die Ähnlichkeit der Arbeitsweise des menschlichen Auges und der dyadischen Frequenz-Zerlegung durch die Wavelet-Analyse [10]. Die Struktur der Zerlegung erlaubt es, Schwächen des Sehapparates auszunutzen, um Wasserzeichen unsichtbar einzubetten. So ist das Auge weniger empfindlich gegenüber kleinen Änderungen im Bereich von Kanten oder Texturen als in glatten Flächen eines Bildes. Kanten- und Texturinformation wird größtenteils durch die Detail-Subbänder (HL, LH, HH) repräsentiert.
  An dieser Stelle sei auf die 'duale Beziehung' zwischen Kompressions- und Watermarking-Verfahren verwiesen [19], da beide auf die Wahrnehmbarkeit von Quantisierungsfehler bzw. Fehler durch das zusätzliche Watermark-Signal Bezug nehmen müssen. Nicht geklärt ist bisher, ob die Übereinstimmung der Transformationsbereiche für Watermarking und Kompression eine höhere Robustheit des Wasserzeichens nach sich zieht. Wolfgang [30] bzw. Zeng [34] erwarten höhere Robustheit durch Übereinstimmung der Transformationsbereiche – im Gegensatz zu Kundur [19], die bessere Ergebnisse durch Verwendung verschiedener Transformationen und eines Referenzwasserzeichens [20] erzielt.
- Die Möglichkeit der effizienten DWT-Implementierung. Einige DCT-gestützte Watermarking-Verfahren verlangen die Transformation großer Bildblöcke (bzw des gesamten Bildes), was durch die Komplexität der DCT zu langen Rechenzeiten führt. Die DWT begnügt sich hingegen mit linearen Aufwand und kann somit problemlos auch auf große Bilder angewandt werden.

3 Ergebnisse und Ausblick

Um Aussagen über die Robustheit von Watermarking-Algorithmen gegenüber verlustbehafteter Kompression machen zu können, betrachten wir die Auswirkung der Bildveränderung auf die Korrelation zwischen dem originalen und dem extrahierten Wasserzeichen. Dazu wurden mit verschiedenen Watermarking-Algorithmen Wasserzeichen in das bekannte Graustufenbild 'Lena' (512 × 512 Pixel) eingebettet. Die Wahl der Parameter erfolgte so, daß das Wasserzeichen mit freiem Auge nicht wahrgenommen werden kann.

Untersucht wurde die Auswirkung der Kompression auf das eingebettete Wasserzeichen mittels JPEG, SPIHT [25] und JPEG2000[6] bei verschiedenen Kompressionsraten. Durch geeignete Wahl der Kompressions-Parameter liegt die erzielte Kompressionsrate zwischen 1:4 und 1:32 bei JPEG, zwischen 1:4 und 1:80 bei SPIHT und zwischen 1:4 und 1:100 bei JPEG2000. Tabelle 2 gibt darüber hinaus Auskunft über die PSNR des Originalbildes gegenüber dem komprimierten Bild.

Tabelle 2. PSNR der getesteten Kompressionsalgorithmen bei verschiedenen Kompressionsraten

Kompression	Rate	PSNR	Rate	PSNR
JPEG	1:4	40.78	1:32	30.40
SPIHT	1:4	45.07	1:80	30.22
JPEG2000	1:4	43.91	1:100	29.20

Über die Korrelation von Wasserzeichen, die im Wavelet-Transformationsbereich eingebettet wurden und ohne Zuhilfenahme des Originalbildes nach der Kompression rekonstruiert werden müssen, gibt die linke Spalte von Abbildung 2 Auskunft. Es zeigt sich, daß das Verfahren von Xie zur Einbettung eines Watermarks überaus robust ist gegenüber allen Kompressions-Angriffen. Dies wird durch Einbetten des Wasserzeichens in alle Koeffizienten des Näherungsbildes erreicht. Allerdings leidet darunter die Sicherheit, da keine Stellen schlüsselabhängig "übersprungen" werden wie etwa im Verfahren von Kundur. Das Verfahren von Inoue zeigt Synchronisationsprobleme beim Auslesen des Wasserzeichens ohne Referenzbild und fällt deshalb plötzlich stark ab.

Generell sind die Wavelet-basierten Watermarking-Verfahren, die auf das Originalbild zurückgreifen können, robuster, wie die rechte Spalte von Abbildung 2 deutlich veranschaulicht. Hier zeichnen sich alle Algorithmen mit Ausnahme von Inoues durch sehr gute Robustheit gegenüber Kompression aus. Durch Ausnutzen der Multiresolution-Eigenschaft der Wavelet-Zerlegung und den überlappenden, redundanten Aufbau des Wasserzeichens schneidet Zhus Methode am besten ab. Unter Verwendung des Originalbildes erzielt auch Wangs Algorithmus sehr gute Resultate und stellt eine echte Verbesserung gegenüber dem DCT-basierten Verfahren von Cox dar. Da die Algorithmen gleich vorgehen und beide im Prinzip versuchen, die für die Wahrnehmung signifikantesten Koeffizieten zu verändern, kann dieser Gewinn klar dem Modell der Wavelet-Transformation zugerechnet werden. Keiner der getesteten Algorithmen im DCT-Bereich kommt an die Robustheit der Wavelet-basierten Verfahren heran, insbesondere bei hohen Kompressionsraten. Zusätzlich zu den bekannten Algorithmen von Cox und Koch

---

[6] ISO/IEC CD15444-1; für unsere Experimente wurde JasPer 0.010 verwendet, verfügbar auf `http://spmg.ece.ubc.ca/people/mdadams/jasper/index.html`

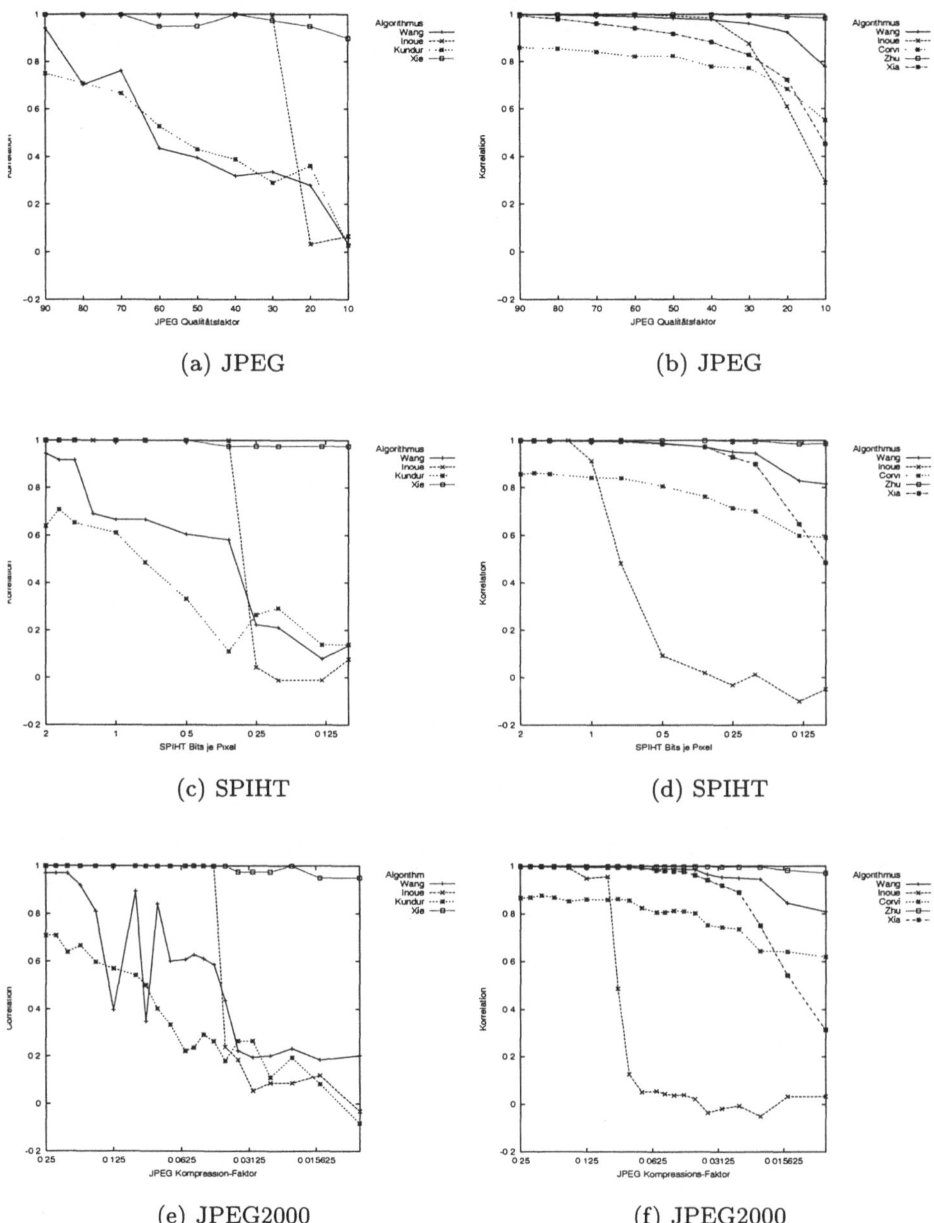

Abbildung 2. Korrelation der Wasserzeichen im Wavelet-Bereich nach Kompression des Bildes; in der linken Spalte die Watermarking-Verfahren ohne Zuhilfenahme des Originalbildes, in der rechten Spalte die Algorithmen, die das Originalbild verwenden

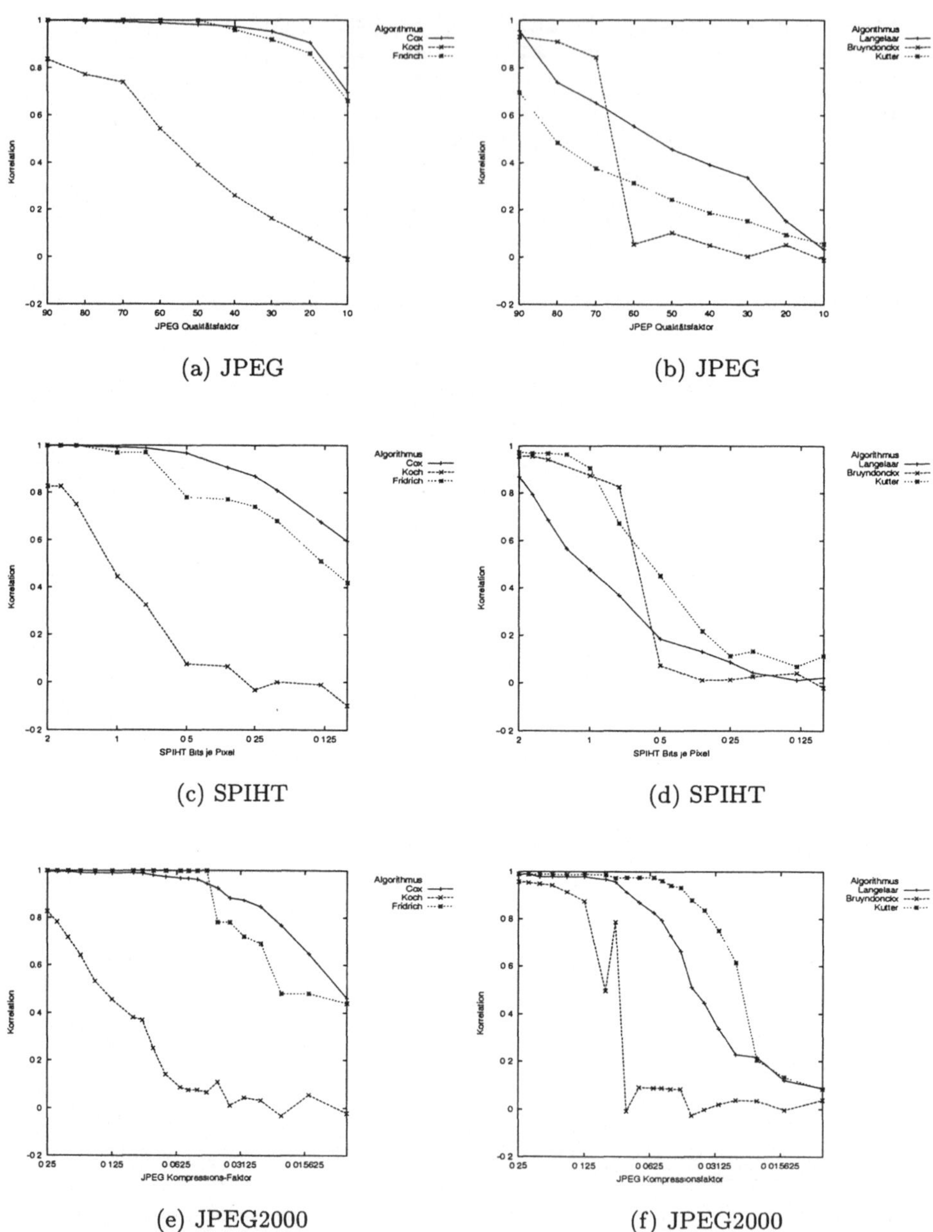

(a) JPEG

(b) JPEG

(c) SPIHT

(d) SPIHT

(e) JPEG2000

(f) JPEG2000

Abbildung 3. Korrelation der Wasserzeichen im DCT-Bereich (linke Spalte) bzw. Bild-Bereich (rechte Spalte); jeweils nach Kompression des Bildes mit JPEG, SPIHT und JPEG2000

haben wir auch eine Variante von Fridrich [12] getestet, die DCT-Koeffizieten des mittleren Frequenzbereichs verwendet.

Mit dem robusten Einbetten eines Wasserzeichens im Transformationsbereich können die Ansätze, die im Bildbereich arbeiten, nicht mithalten, wie die rechte Spalte von Abbildung 3 zeigt. Wir haben die Verfahren von Bruyndonckx [3], Langelaar [22] und Kutter [21] zum Vergleich herangezogen, die allesamt ohne Originalbild auskommen. Die Methode von Langelaar nimmt die JPEG-Kompression vorweg und ist deshalb bei diesem Test besonders robust.

Zusammenfassend kann gesagt werden, daß der Wavelet-Transformationsbereich gute Voraussetzungen mitbringt, um robuste Wasserzeichen, vor allem im Hinblick auf JPEG2000, einzubetten.

Literatur

1. M. Barni, F. Bartolini, V. Cappellini, A. Lippi, A. Piva. A DWT-based technique for spatio-frequency masking of digital signatures. In *Proc. of SPIE, EI '99*, vol. 3657, San Jose, USA, January 1999.
2. G. W. Braudaway, K. A. Magerlein, F. C. Mintzer. Protecting publicly-available images with a visible image watermark. In *Proc. of SPIE*, vol. 2659, p. 126–133, San Jose, USA, February 1996.
3. O. Bruyndonckx, J.-J. Quisquater, B. M. Macq. Spatial method for copyright labeling of digital images. In *IEEE Workshop on Nonlinear Signal and Image Processing '95, Thessaloniki, Greece*, p. 456–459, 1995.
4. J. J. Chae, D. Mukherjee, B. S. Manjunath. A robust embedded data from wavelet coefficients. In *Proc. of SPIE, EI '98*, vol. 3312, p. 308–317, San Jose, USA, 1998.
5. M. Charrier, D. S. Cruz, M. Larsson. JPEG2000, the next millennium compression standard for still images. In *Proc. of ICMCS '99*, p. 131–132, Florence, Italy, 1999.
6. C.-J. H. Chu, A. W. Wiltz. Luminance channel modulated watermarking of digital images. In *Proc. of SPIE*, p. 437–445, Orlando, USA, April 1999.
7. M. Corvi, G. Nicchiotti. Wavelet-based image watermarking for copyright protection. In *Scand. Conf. on Image Analysis '97*, Lappeenranta, Finland, June 1997.
8. I. J. Cox, J. Kilian, T. Leighton, T. G. Shamoon. Secure spread spectrum watermarking for multimedia. In *Proc. of ICIP '97*, vol. 6, p. 1673–1687, Santa Barbara, USA, October 1997.
9. S. Craver, N. Memon, B.-L. Yeo, M. M. Yeung. On the invertability of invisible watermarking techniques. In *Proc. of ICIP '97*, vol. 1, p. 540, Santa Barbara, USA, October 1997.
10. S. Daly, W. Zeng, J. Li, S. Lei. Visual masking in wavelet compression for JPEG2000. In *Proc. of SPIE, EI '00*, vol. 3971, San Jose, USA, January 2000.
11. R. Dugad, K. Ratakonda, N. Ahuja. A new wavelet-based scheme for watermarking images. In *Proc. of ICIP '98*, Chicago, USA, October 1998.
12. J. Fridrich. Combining low-frequency and spread spectrum watermarking. In *Proc. of SPIE*, San Diego, USA, July 1998.
13. A. Herrigel, J. J. K. O'Ruanaidh, H. Petersen, S. Pereira, T. Pun. Secure copyright protection techniques for digital images. In *Information hiding: second international workshop*, p. 169–190, Portland, USA, April 1998.
14. H. Inoue, A. Miyazaki, A. Yamamoto, T. Katsura. A digital watermark based on the wavelet transform and its robustness on image compression. In *Proc. of ICIP '98*, Chicago, USA, 1998.

15. E. Koch, J. Zhao. Towards robust and hidden image copyright labeling. In *Proc. of IEEE Int. Workshop on Nonlinear Signal and Image Proc.*, p. 452–455, Marmaras, Greece, June 1995.

16. D. Kundur, D. Hatzinakos. A robust digital image watermarking method using wavelet-based fusion. In *Proc. of ICIP '97*, p. 544–547, Santa Barbara, USA, October 1997.

17. D. Kundur, D. Hatzinakos. Digital watermarking using multiresolution wavelet decomposition. In *Proc. of ICASSP '98*, vol. 5, p. 2969–2972, Seattle, USA, May 1998.

18. D. Kundur, D. Hatzinakos. Digital watermarking for telltale tamper-proofing and authentication. In *Proc. of IEEE: Special Issue on Identification and Protection of Multimedia Information*, vol. 87, p. 1167–1180, July 1999.

19. D. Kundur, D. Hatzinakos. Mismatching perceptual models for effective watermarking in the presence of compression. In *Proc. of SPIE*, vol. 3845, Boston, USA, September 1999.

20. D. Kundur, D. Hatzinakos. Attack characterization for effective watermarking. In *Proc. of ICIP '99*, Kobe, Japan, October 1999.

21. M. Kutter, F. Jordan, F. Bossen. Digital signature of color images using amplitude modulation. In *Proc. of SPIE*, vol. 2952, p. 518–526, San Jose, USA, 1997.

22. G. C. Langelaar, R. L. Lagendijk, J. Biemond. Robust labeling methods for copy protection of images. In *Proc. of SPIE*, vol. 3022, San Jose, USA, 1997.

23. J. Ohnishi, K. Matsui. Embedding a seal into a picture under orthogonal wavelet transform. In *Proc. of ICMCS '96*, p. 514–521, Hiroshima, Japan, June 1996.

24. S. Pereira, S. Voloshynovskiy, T. Pun. Optimized wavelet domain watermark embedding strategy using linear programming. In *Proc. of SPIE*, Orlando, USA, January 2000.

25. A. Said, W. A. Pearlman. A new, fast, and efficient image codec based on set partitioning in hierarchical trees. In *IEEE Trans. on Circuits and Systems for Video Technology*, vol. 6, p. 243–250, June 1996.

26. J. M. Shapiro. Embedded image coding using zerotrees of wavelet coefficients. In *IEEE Trans. on Signal Processing*, vol. 41, p. 3445–3462, December 1993.

27. P.-C. Su, H.-J. Wang, C.-C. J. Kuo. Digital image watermarking in regions of interest. In *Proc. of IS&T PICS Conf.*, Savannah, USA, April 1999.

28. H.-J. Wang, C.-C. J. Kuo. High fidelity image compression with multithreshold wavelet coding (MTWC). In *Proc. of SPIE*, San Diego, USA, August 1997.

29. H.-J. Wang, P.-C. Su, C.-C. Kuo. Wavelet-based digital image watermarking. *Optics Express*, 3:497, December 1998.

30. R. B. Wolfgang, C. I. Podilchuk, E. J. Delp. The effect of matching watermark and compression transforms in compressed color images. In *Proc. of ICIP '98*, Chicago, USA, October 1998.

31. R. B. Wolfgang, C. I. Podilchuk, E. J. Delp. Perceptual watermarks for digital images and video. In *Proc. of SPIE, EI '99*, vol. 3657, San Jose, USA, 1999.

32. X.-G. Xia, C. G. Boncelet, G. R. Arce. Wavelet transform based watermark for digital images. *Optics Express*, 3:497, December 1998.

33. L. Xie, G. R. Arce. Joint wavelet compression and authentication watermarking. In *Proc. of ICIP '98*, Chicago, USA, 1998.

34. W. Zeng, S. Lei. Transform domain perceptual watermarking with scalable visual detection – proposal for JPEG2000. Technical report, Sharp Lab., USA, 1998.

35. W. Zhu, Z. Xiong, Y.-Q. Zhang. Multiresolution watermarking for images and video: a unified approach. In *Proc. of ICIP '98*, Chicago, USA, October 1998.

Wasserzeichen für Polygon basierte 3D Modelle

Oliver Benedens

Fraunhofer Institut für Graphische Datenverarbeitung
Darmstadt, Germany
`benedensigd.fhg.de`

Zusammenfassung Wir beschreiben ein System, mit Geomark bezeichnet, zur Einbettung von digitalen Wasserzeichen in Polygon basierte 3D Modelle. Das System besteht aus drei Verfahren: Ein Algorithmus, bezeichnet als *Vertex Flood Algorithm* (VFA), realisiert fragile öffentliche Wasserzeichen und ermöglicht optional Authentizitäts- und Integritätsprüfung eines Modells. Ein weiterer Algorithmus, mit *Affine Invariant Embedding* (AIE) bezeichnet, realisiert Wasserzeichen, die robust gegenüber Affinen Transformationen sind. Ein mit *Normal Bin Encoding* (NBE) bezeichneter Algorithmus realisiert Wasserzeichen mit Robustheit gegen Re-Meshing Operationen, u.a. Polygon-Reduktion. Wasserzeichen aller drei Verfahren können überlagert werden, um deren Vorteile zu kombinieren. Das System ist als Plugin für 3D Studio MAX realisiert.

1 Einleitung

Die Forschung im Bereich digitaler Wasserzeichen hat sich in den vergangenen Jahren auf die Medien Bild, Video und Audio konzentriert. In einer Vielzahl von Anwendungsgebieten wie CAD/CAM, Modellierung, Animation, Visualisierung und im Print-Bereich liegen schutzwürdige Daten nicht in Form von Rasterdaten sondern vektor-basiert vor. Solche Daten umfassen bspw. 3D Modelle in virtuellen Realitäten und 2D vektor-basierte Grafiken in Postscript und PDF Dokumenten. In dieser Arbeit beschreiben wir die Realisierung von Wasserzeichen für 3D Modelle im Modellierungs-, Animations- und Visualisierungsbereich. Eine Übertragung von zwei der geschilderten Verfahren, VFA und AIE, auf den 2D Fall ist möglich.

2 Verwandte Arbeiten

Praun et al. [11] entwickelten ein Verfahren zur Einbettung geheimer 1-Bit Wasserzeichen in 3D polygonale Modelle. Das Verfahren nutzt einen Multi-Resolution-Ansatz zur Generierung glatter markierter Meshes. Letzteres wird dadurch erreicht, daß die zur Modifikation eingesetzten, im Ortsraum operierenden Filter, den Gesamtverlauf von Flächen modifizieren. Das Verfahren benötigt das Original-Modell zur Extrahierung eines Wasserzeichens, eventuell anhaftende Affine Transformationen müssen durch Interaktion mit einem Nutzer entfernt werden. Aus diesem Grund ist das Verfahren als *forensisch* zu klassifizieren. Oh-buchi et al.[9, 10] publizierten das erste Verfahren zur Realisierung affin inva-rianter Wasserzeichen. Das mit *Tetrahedral Volume Ration* (TVR) bezeichnete Verfahren nutzt als affine invariantes Merkmal den Ratio des Volumens zweier Tetraeder. Es zeichnet sich durch große Kapazität aus. Als Nachteile sind die Beschränkung der Anwendbarkeit auf 2-Manifolds und Anforderungen an die Darstellungsgenauigkeit von Koordinaten zu nennen. Boon-Lock und Minerva [4] publizierten das erste Verfahren zur Realisierung eines Integritäts- und Au-thentizitätsschutzes für polygonale 3D Modelle. In diesem Verfahren kann unter Kenntnis eines *geheimen* Verifizierungs-Schlüssels geprüft werden, ob das Modell nach Einbettung eines fragilen Wasserzeichens modifiziert wurde (Geometrie und Topologie). Wir werden im folgenden ein Verfahren vorstellen, das ebenfalls ein fragiles Wasserzeichen für Authenzitäts- und Integritätsprüfungen realisiert aber eine andere Anwendung adressiert: Ein Anwender hat ein 3D Modell aus dem Internet heruntergeladen und möchte folgende Informationen aus dem Modell extrahieren: Allgemeine Label-Informationen (bspw. Lizenzbestimmungen, Hy-perlinks), Nachweis der Identität des Erzeugers/Copyright-Inhabers des Modells und Nachweis, daß das Modell nicht modifiziert wurde, bzw. Modifikationen sich in bestimmten Toleranzen bewegen.

3   Die Wasserzeichen-Verfahren des Geomark Systems

Dem Geomark-System liegt folgende Philosophie zugrunde: Wasserzeichen wer-den nach Fertigstellung eines Modells oder einer virtuellen Szene eingebettet. To-pologie und Konnektivität eines Modells sind Ergebnis der gezielter Modellierung des Erstellers oder teilweise Ergebnis eines automatisierten Prozesses, bspw. Er-gebnis einer Photogrammatischen Auswertung oder einer Freiform-Flächen- nach Dreiecks-Flächen-Konvertierung. Abhängig von der Anwendung unterliegt das zu markierende Modell eventuell Nebenbedingungen bzgl. tolerierten Punkte-bewegungen und Normalen-Änderungen. Bestimmte Eigenschaften, die mit den Eckpunkten eines Meshes verknüpft sind, bspw. Farben und Texturen, sind nur schwer zu reproduzieren, wenn ein Re-Meshing im Verlaufe des Einbettungsvor-gangs vorgenommen wird. Aus diesem Grund verändern alle Verfahren des Geo-mark Systems lediglich die Koordinaten von Eckpunkten (Geometrie). Konnek-tivität und Topologie werden nicht modifiziert. Alle mit Objekten verbundenen skalaren Attribute, wie bspw. Farben, Texturen, Sichtbarkeits-Eigenschaften, bleiben unverändert, ebenso die Gruppen-Struktur bzw. Hierarchien einzelner Objekte und ganzer Szenen.
Wir skizzieren im folgenden drei Wasserzeichen Verfahren: *Vertex Flood Al-gorithm* (VFA), *Affine Invariant Embedding* (AIE) und *Normal Bin Encoding* (NBE). Diese Verfahren sind unter bestimmten Bedingungen kombinierbar, d.h. ein Objekt kann simultan Wasserzeichen aller drei Verfahren tragen, wobei die Mengen der jeweiligen Informationsträger (Eckpunkte) **nicht** disjunkt sein müssen Jedes dieser Verfahren kann insbesondere Objekte mit folgenden Eigenschaften verarbeiten:

– Objekte bestehend aus mehreren (kleinen) unverbundenden Meshes.
– Meshes die nicht 2-manifold sind.
– Meshes die Doppelflächen enthalten.
– „Entartete" Meshes die kleine Flächen oder Winkel enthalten.

Alle drei Verfahren werden im folgenden skizziert. Eine ausführliche Beschreibung der Verfahren und Testergebnisse ist in [3] publiziert.

3.1 Der Vertex Flood Algorithmus

Dieses Verfahren realisiert fragile öffentlich lesbare Wasserzeichen mit der Option von Authentizitäts- und Integritätsprüfung. Der Algorithmus modifiziert Eckpunkte, so daß deren Euklidsche Distanz zum Massenzentrum eines designierten Start-Dreicks-Fläche Wasserzeichen Bits codiert. Mit Ausname der Start-Fläche operiert der Algorithmus ausschließlich auf Eckpunkten ohne Berücksichtigung von Konnektivität oder topologischer Beziehungen. Die Punkte müssen nicht zusammenhängend sein, d.h., das Verfahren kann im Extremfall auf eine 3D Punktwolke angewandt werden. Wie in diesem Fall verfahren wird, wird am Ende dieses Abschnitts erläutert. *com* bezeichne das Massezentrum des Start-Dreiecks mit den Eckpunkten $S = \{s_1, s_2, s_3\}$, V bezeichne die Menge aller Eckpunkte des Modells. Als nächstes belegen wir die Mengen

$$M_k = \{v \in V \setminus S \mid k \leq \left\lfloor \frac{|v - com|}{W} \right\rfloor < k + 1\}$$

für $0 \leq k \leq N = \lfloor \frac{r}{W} \rfloor$. r ist die maximale erlaubte Distanz eines Eckpunktes v von *com* um für das Einbetten von Wasserzeichen-Bits berücksichtigt zu werden. Die Länge eines jeden mit einer Menge assoziierten Intervalls ist W. Nun werden die Mengen M_0 bis M_N durchlaufen, wobei leere Mengen übersprungen werden. Die Punkte einer jeden Menge werden modifiziert, sodaß diese $m = 2^n$ Bits codieren. Jede Menge ist mit einem Intervall der Länge W assoziiert, das folgendermaßen unterteilt ist:

buf	I_0	$\cdots$	I_{m-1}	buf

Um den Wert *val* ($0 \leq val \leq m - 1$) in einer Menge zu codieren, wird jeder Eckpunktes der Menge modifiziert, so daß seine Distanz zu *com* in der Mitte des mit I_{val} bezeichneten Teilintervalls zu liegen kommet. Der Zweck der beiden mit *buf* bezeichneten Intervalle besteht darin, die Auswirkung von Änderungen eines Intervalls, nach Einbettung des Wasserzeichens, auf Nachbarintervalle zu reduzieren. Beim Auslesen des Wasserzeichens wird entweder das Teilintervall gewählt, in dem der Mittelwert aller Distanzen liegt oder in dem die meisten Distanzen liegen. Die Werte r und W werden vom Start-Dreieck abgeleitet. Um einen effektiven Zugriff auf das Wasserzeichen zu ermöglichen, fordern wir vom Start-Dreieck ein bestimmtes Verhältnis seiner Kantenlängen: $1 \leq R_1 \leq R_2$. Wir wählen das Dreieck, das diesem Verhältnis am nächsten kommt als Start-Dreieck und modifizieren die dessen Kantenlängen, so daß das Seitenverhältnis exakt übereinstimmt. Das Wasserzeichen ist fragil, da es sehr empfindlich auf

Lageveränderungen der Eckpunkte des Startdreiecks reagiert. Die Intervallänge W wird durch $1/3 \cdot (e_1 + e_2 + e_3) \cdot scalef$ berechnet, wobei e_i die Kantenlägen des Start-Dreiecks bezeichnen. $scalef$ bezeichnet einen weiteren konstanten Skalierungsfaktor ($scalef < 1$). Die auf diese Weise realisierten Wasserzeichen sind robust gegen Orthogonale Transformationen.

Authentizitäts- und Integritätsprüfung Das geschilderte Verfahren wird auf folgende Weise um Authentizitäts- und Integritätsprüfung ergänzt:

1. Zunächst wählen wir die maximale Distanz, um die Eckpunkte bewegt werden dürfen, ohne das fragile Wasserzeichen zu verfälschen. Von dieser Distanz und einem Kantenlängen-Verhältnis leiten wir Kantenlängen ab und modifizieren die nächstgelegene Dreiecks-Fläche so daß sie diese Längen exakt erfüllt.
2. Als nächstes bilden wir einen String über den ein Hashwert gebildet werden soll. Hierzu konkatenieren wir folgende Informationen: Labelinhalte, Zertifikat des Modell-Erstellers (im X509v3 Format), oder im Falle geringer Kapazität Issuer-, Subject-Distinguish Name und Seriennummer oder ein Link unter dem das Zertifikat heruntergeladen werden kann. Als nächstes iterieren wir über die Intervalle (es sei bemerkt, daß für die Anwendung kein *buf* bezeichneten Intervall existieren) und fügen folgende Information hinzu: Ist das Intervall nicht leer, fügen wir die Anzahl der Punkte im Intervall plus die Anzahl der Flächen und Kanten adjazent zu jedem Punkt hinzu, ansonsten die Anzahl aufeinanderfolgender leerer Intervalle. Der resultierende String wird unter Verwendung einer kryptographisch sicheren Hashfunktion „gehasht" und mit dem geheimen Schlüssel des Absenders signiert (wir verwenden als asymmetrisches Kryptosystem RSA).
3. Schließlich betten wir Label-Information, Ersteller-Zertifikats-Information und den signierten Hashwert als öffentliches Wasserzeichen ein. Die einzubettende Information wird so oft dupliziert, d.h. redundant eingebettet, bis sie in der Länge gleich oder größer der Anzahl nicht leerer Intervalle ist.

Der Empfänger des Modells extrahiert die Label- und Zertifikats-Information, berechnet den Hashwert und verifiziert die Signatur. Beim Decodieren des Wertes eines Intervalls verlangen wir, daß alle Distanzen der Eckpunkte des Intervalls in demselben Teilintervall liegen. Das beschriebene Verfahren detektiert das Entfernen eines einzelnen Eckpunktes, Lageveränderung des Eckpunktes über das festgelegte Maximum und allgemein Änderungen von Konnektivität. Die Generierung eines Meshes, das mit der Signatur eines anderen Meshes authentifizert werden kann, stellt wegen der Festlegungen bzgl. Punkt-Dichte und Konnektivität eine schwierige Aufgabe dar. Die Sicherheit kann in diesem Zusammenhang folgendermaßen erhöht werden: Existiert eine fixe Ordnung von Eckpunkten und Flächen, kann die Liste der Flächen im Eckpunkt-Indizes einfach in den zu hashenden String aufgenommen und somit Konnektivität und Topologie fixiert werden. Auf nachfolgend beschriebene Weise können Punktekoordinaten

neben Distanzen in die Checksumme miteinbezogen werden, was jegliche signifikante Lageveränderung von Eckpunkten des Modells bei gleichzeitiger Erhaltung
des Authentizitäts- und Integritätsnachweises ausschließt:

- Aus dem Startdreieck wird eine Orthonormalbasis des $\mathbb{R}^3$ berechnet. Die
  Punktekoordinaten (relativ zu dieser Basis) werden unter Verwendung eines
  von W abhängigen Wertes skaliert. Anschließend werden die Fließkomma-
  Koordinaten durch eine weitere Teilintervallbildung in Integer-Koordinaten
  überführt, d.h. die Indizes der drei Teilintervalle für (x,y,z)-Komponente
  stellen die Integer-Koordinaten dar. Die Fließkomma-Koordinaten werden
  derart modifiziert, daß sie in der Mitte der jeweiligen Intervalle zu liegen
  kommen.
- Für jedes nicht leere Intervall werden die Integer-Koordinaten der jeweiligen
  Eckpunkte (sortiert) dem String zur Bildung der Checksumme hinzugefügt.
- Nun werden die Distanzen derart modifiziert, daß in jedem nicht leeren Intervall die Eckpunkte in dem Teilintervall zu liegen kommen, das den gewünsch-
  te Wert codiert (die Länge der Teilintervalle wird so gewählt, daß die „ein-
  gestellten" Integer-Koordinaten hierdurch nicht verändert werden).

Das Verfahren kann für die Markierung von n-dimensionalen Punktewolken ge-
neralisiert werden. In diesem Anwendungsfall kann die Intervalllänge W bspw.
von der maximalen Distanz zweier Punkte abgeleitet werden. Einer der Punkte
kann dann als Startpunkt des Verfahrens dienen.

3.2 Der Affine Invariant Embedding Algorithmus

Bei der Kombinierung von 3D Modellen zu virtuellen Szenen, können diese in
vielfältiger Weise modifiziert werden. Die am häufigsten vorgenommenen Operationen, wenn ein Objekt in einer Szene plaziert wird, sind Translation, Rotation,
gleich- und ungleichmäßige Skalierung und Spiegelung. Der AIE Algorithmus
realisiert daher affin invariante Wasserzeichen durch Anwendung einer affin inva-
rianten Norm $\|\cdot\|_V$: der Nielson Foley-Norm, wie sie in [7] eingeführt wurde. Ihre
Definition für $\mathbf{E}^3$ sei an dieser Stelle kurz rekapituliert: Die Norm ist abhängig
von Daten, nämlich den Eckpunkten $V = \{V_1, .., V_n\}$ mit $V_i = (x_i, y_i, z_i)$:

$$\|P\|_V^2 = P \cdot n \cdot [\bar{V} * \bar{V}]^{-1} \cdot P^T \tag{1}$$

$$\bar{V} = \begin{pmatrix} x_1 - \bar{x}, \ y_1 - \bar{y} \\ x_2 - \bar{x}, \ y_2 - \bar{y} \\ \vdots \qquad \vdots \\ x_n - \bar{x}, \ y_n - \bar{y} \end{pmatrix}$$

$$\bar{x} = \frac{\sum_{i=1}^n x_i}{n}, \bar{y} = \frac{\sum_{i=1}^n y_i}{n}$$

(mit $P \in \mathbf{E}^3$).
Wir wenden die Norm auf eine Menge von $n = 4$ benachbarten Eckpunkten

$V = \{V_1, .., V_4\}, V_i \in \mathbb{R}^3$. Als nächstes definieren wir

$$M_V = \tfrac{1}{4} \sum_{i=1}^{4} V_i$$
$$Norm(P)^2 = \|P - M_V\|_V^2 \quad (P \in \mathbb{R}^3) \tag{2}$$

Wir benutzen folgende Beziehung, um Informationen durch Änderung eines Norm-Wertes einzubetten: Gegeben sei ein Eckpunkt $P \in \mathbb{R}^3$, der nicht in einer Ebene mit jeweils drei Eckpunkten aus der Menge V liegt:

$$P' = M_V + (1 + k)(P - M_V) \Rightarrow \frac{Norm(P')^2}{Norm(P)^2} = (1 + k)^2 \tag{3}$$

Wenn die Distanz des Punktes P zum Massenzentrum M um den Faktor $1 + k$ geändert wird, ändert sich der Norm-Wert um Faktor $(1 + k)^2$.

Wir unterteilen das kontinuierliche, nach oben hin offene Intervall möglicher Norm-Werte in Teilintervalle der Länge w, wobei jedem Intervall ein Wert zugeordnet wird: Sei n die Anzahl der Bits, die in einem Norm-Wert codiert werden soll. Wir nummerieren das i-te Interval mit $i \bmod 2^n$. Wenn der Wert $val \in \{0, .., m - 1\}$ $(m = 2^n)$ codiert werden soll, ändern wir den Norm-Wert, so daß er in die Mitte des nächstgelegenen Intervalls bewegt wird, der mit val nummeriert ist.

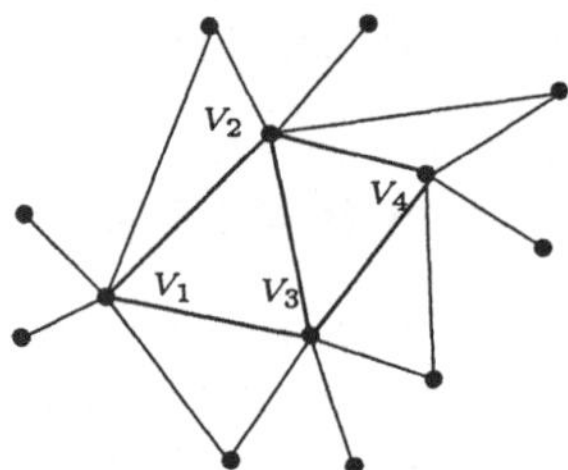

Abbildung 1. Ein Einbettungs-Primitiv bestehend aus zwei Startflächen und Eckpunkten.

Der Einbettungs-Vorgang Im Einbettungsvorgang werden Fragmente eines globalen Bit-Strings lokal in sogenannten Einbettungs-Primitiven codiert. Jedes Einbettungs-Primitiv codiert ein $(Index, Wert)$ Paar. *Index* verweist auf die Startposition des Fragments *Wert* im globalen Bit-String. Ein Primitiv besteht jeweils aus zwei kanten-adjazenten Dreiecks-Flächen, Start-Flächen genannt, und adjazenten Eckpunkten. Die Startflächen dürfen nicht in oder nahe einer Ebene liegen. Die Eckpunkte der beiden Startflächen seien mit $V_1, .., V_4$ bezeichnet. Diese vier Punkte stellen nun die Menge V von Eckpunkten zur lokalen Auswertung des Norm-Wertes $Norm()$ dar. Als nächstes werden zwei Mengen G_1 und G_2 gebildet: G_1 besteht aus allen Eckpunkten, die zu *genau einem Punkt* in V adjazent sind. G_2 besteht aus allen Eckpunkten, die Teil einer Dreiecksfläche sind, die kanten-adjazent zu einer der beiden Startflächen ist. Ist $|G_1| < 4$ und

$|G_2| < 4$ setzen wir $G := G_1 \cup G_2$, ansonsten $G := min_{1 \leq i \leq 2}\{G_i \mid |G_i| \geq 4\}$. Wenn $|G| < 4$ ist, verwerfen wir die Start-Flächen-Kombination. Abbildung 1 zeigt ein Primitiv für das $G := G_2$ gewählt wird. Als nächstes wird G in vier Teilmengen $g_1, .., g_4$ mit gleicher Anzahl von Elementen aufgeteilt (sofern möglich). Die Information $(Index, Wert)$ wird folgendermaßen eingebettet:

Teilmenge	Eingebettete Bits
g_1	00 I_5 I_4 I_3 I_2
g_2	01 I_1 I_0 D_9 D_8
g_3	10 D_7 D_6 D_5 D_4
g_4	11 D_3 D_2 D_1 D_0

In diesem Beispiel wurde der globale Bit-String in Fragmente der Länge 10 bits unterteilt. Ein Index der Länge 6 Bit wird verwendet, um diese Fragmente zu adressieren, was eine Limitierung der Länge des globalen Bit-Strings auf 640 bits bedeutet. Die ersten beiden eingebetteten Bits jeder Teilmenge dienen der Sortierung der vier Teile in $Index$ und $Wert$. $I_5, .., I_0$ ist der 6 Bit Index, $D_9, .., D_0$ sind die 10 Daten-Bits (Fragment).
Jedes Fragment wird mehrfach eingebettet (in der aktuellen Implementierung drei Mal als Voreinstellung). Modifizierte Eckpunkte und Eckpunkte der Startflächen werden als „besucht" markiert und nur einmal verwendet.

Der Lese-Vorgang Im Lese-Vorgang wird durch die Menge von Flächen iteriert. Für jede Fläche werden kanten-adjazente Flächen als mögliche zweite Startfläche getestet. Es werden jeweils, wie zuvor beschrieben, die Teilmengen $g_1, .., g_4$ gebildet und eingebettete Information gelesen. Sofern jedes der Sortierungs-Bits (00,01,10,11) mindestens einmal auftritt und gleiche Sortierungs-Bits jeweils vom gleichen Bit-Muster gefolgt werden, speichern wir die Kombination $(Index, Wert)$ in einer globalen Hashtabelle. Nachdem alle *relevanten* Kombinationen getestet wurden, kombinieren wir die Fragmente, die am häufigsten an ihrer jeweiligen Position auftraten, zu dem Resultats-Bit-String. *Relevante* Kombinationen bedeutet, daß wir auf einfache Weise den Suchraum einschränken können, bspw. durch Sortierung aller Flächen, basierend auf der Anzahl von Adjazenzen zu Kanten und Flächen und Limitierung der Anzahl zu testender Kombinationen. Durch redundante Einbettung unter Einbeziehung der Lokalität von Primitiven, kann der Lese-Vorgang nach erstmaligem Lesen des Wasserzeichens abgebrochen werden.

3.3 Der Normal Bin Encoding Algorithmus

Der in [1, 2] publizierte Algorithmus erlaubte das Einbetten eines geheimen Wasserzeichens mit Robustheit gegen komplexe Geometrie- und Topologie verändernde Operationen, insbesondere Polygon-Reduktion. Der Algorithmus war *forensischer* Natur, da er Nutzer-Interaktionen beim Lese-Vorgang erforderte. Der Nutzer mußte das Originalmodell erkennen, um den zugehörigen Merkmalsvektor zu selektieren. In diesem Abschnitt beschreiben wir eine Variante des Normal

Bin Encoding (NBE) Algorithmus, die ein 1-Bit Wasserzeichen einbettet und keinerlei a priori Information, außer einem geheimen Schlüssel, zum Lesen benötigt. Wir beschreiben im folgenden die Realisierung des Wasserzeichen-Detektors.

Die 1-Bit Wasserzeichen Variante Das Verfahren baut auf den in [1, 2] skizzierten Verfahren auf. 1-Bit Wasserzeichen werden erfolgreich in verschiedenen Anwendungen [8, 11] eingesetzt. In dem Verfahren werden Flächennormalen eines Modells auf die Einheitssphäre projeziert und dort zu disjunkten Gruppen, als Bins bezeichnet, zusammengefaßt. Eine Normale wird einem Bin zugeordnet, wenn ihre Abstand (Winkel) zu einer vorgegebenen Zentrums-Normale des Bins kleiner als ein vorgegebener Winkel ist (Bin-Radius). Im folgenden seien die Zentrumsnormale des Bins mit Index i mit n_i ($1 \leq i \leq N_B$), die dem Bin zugeordneten Flächennormalen mit N_{ij} ($1 \leq j \leq n_i$) bezeichnet. N_B sei o.B.d.A. gerade und gibt die Gesamtanzahl der Bins an. Die Bins sind nicht überlappend. Basierend auf einem geheimen Schlüssel werden die Bins in zwei disjunkte Teilmengen aufgeteilt: $M_1 = \{m_{11}, .., m_{1n}\}$ und $M_2 = \{m_{21}, .., m_{2n}\}$, jede enthält $n = N_B/2$ Elemente (Bin-Indices). Im Einbettungsvorgang werden nun Flächennormalen aus Bins der Menge M_1 möglichst nahe zum Bin-Zentrum hinbewegt. Normalen in Bins der Menge M_2 werden nicht intentional verändert. Gleichwohl können ihre Normalen modifiziert werden, um Änderungen für Bins der Menge M_1 zu erzielen. Flächennormalen werden im Einbettungsverfahren durch Lageveränderung von Eckpunkten modifiziert.

Im Lese-Vorgang wird ein Treshold-Detektor eingesetzt, der für einen gegebenen geheimen Schlüssel K_s, einen Wert liefert, der die Wahrscheinlichkeit für den Fall angibt, daß das Modell **nicht** unter Verwendung dieses Schlüssel markiert wurde (*false negative propability*). Für N Schlüssel $K_{s_1}, .., K_{s_N}$ „vermuteter" Wasserzeichen, liefert der Detektor die Information, welches Wasserzeichen am wahrscheinlichsten eingebettet wurde.

Sei die mittlere Winkeldifferenz von Normalen im Bin mit Index i zur Zentrumsnormalen mit $\bar{Y}_i$, die Differenzen mit X_{ij} ($1 \leq j \leq n_i$) bezeichnet.

$$\bar{Y}_i = \frac{X_{i1} + \ldots + X_{in_i}}{n_i} \tag{4}$$

Um ein statistisches Modell anwenden zu können, treffen wir die „approximative" Annahme, das die Flächennormalen gleichverteilt in ihrer Repräsentaton auf der Einheitssphäre seien. Unter dieser Annahme betrachte wir die Winkeldifferenz X_{ij} als statistische Meßgröße: Die X_{ij} seien für alle Bins identisch verteilt mit unbekanntem Mittelwert und Varianz und unabhängig. Sei nun angenommen, wir beobachteten den Mittelwert m und die Varianz s^2 für $\bar{Y}_i$ Werte zu Bins in M_2. Wenden wir den Zentralen Grenzwertsatz an, ist die Variable $\bar{Z}$ mit

$$\bar{Z} = \frac{\bar{Y}_1 + \ldots + \bar{Y}_n}{n} \tag{5}$$

$N(m, \frac{s^2}{n})$ verteilt (for $m >> 30$).
Seien m_2 und s^2 die beobachteten Werte der $\bar{Y}_i$ zu Bins der Menge M_2: Die

Wahrscheinlichkeit

$$P = \Phi\left(\frac{m_1 - m_2}{\sqrt{s^2 \cdot n_2/n_1}}\right) \tag{6}$$

kann nun folgendermaßen interpretiert werden: Sie sagt aus, wie wahrscheinlich es ist, eine Abweichung der Werte m_1 und m_2 für die Mengen M_1 and M_2 zu beobachten. Je kleiner P, desto größer ist die Wahrscheinlichkeit, daß intentionale Modifikationen an den Normalen in Bins der Menge M_1 vorgenommen wurden.

4 Testergebnisse

Test-Modelle wurden mit Wasserzeichen aller drei Verfahren markiert. Hierbei wurden, mit abnehmender Einbettungsstärke, zunächst ein NBE-Wasserzeichen, dann ein AIE-Wasserzeichen und schließlich ein VFA-Wasserzeichen eingebettet. Im Bezug auf NBE, wurde die Robustheit gegenüber Polygon-Reduktion getestet. Angewandt wurden hierbei zwei Verfahren: *qslim* [6] and *plycrunch*. Letzteres ist Teil der *Simplification Envelopes* Distribution [5]. Beide Verfahren können Modelle verarbeiten, die keine 2-Manifolds sind.

No	Model	vertices	faces	orig. probability
1	cow	6083	12075	3.241080E-45
2	skateboard	23584	46785	1.486888E-10
3	bunny	22610	44622	1.709180E-22
4	viper	20759	38732	9.982807E-23
5	bridge	16177	24714	3.536744E-22

Tabelle 1. Modell-Größe und Detektor-Wahrscheinlichkeiten der mit NBE-Wasserzeichen markierten Modelle.

5 Zusammenfassung und aktuelle Entwicklungen

Die drei vorgestellten Verfahren realisieren fragile öffentliche Wasserzeichen mit optionaler Authentizitäts- und Integritätsprüfung, geheime und öffentliche affin invariante Wasserzeichen und ein 1-Bit Verfahren für geheimer Wasserzeichen mit Robustheit gegen Remeshing-Operationen, insbesondere Polygon-Reduktion. Eigene aktuelle Arbeiten umfassen die Realisierung affin invarianter Wasserzeichen für polygonale und NURBS-Flächen basierte 3D Modelle unter speziellen Nebenbedingungen, u.a. maximal tolerierte Punktebewegungen und Genauigkeit mit der Koordinaten repräsentiert werden. Weitere Entwicklungen haben zum Ziel, die Skalierbarkeit des NBE-Verfahrens zu verbessern, indem dieses zunächst auf reduzierte Polygonnetze angewandt wird, um anschließend vorgenommene Änderungen in die Original-Polygonnetze zurück zu propagieren.

No	red.	vertices	faces	probability	No	red.	vertices	faces	probability
1	25%	1550	3000	8.778222E-09	1	29%	1540	3504	2.292422E-11
1	8%	545	1000	2.775433E-05	1	23%	1257	2819	1.599228E-07
2	11%	2694	5000	4.116683E-13	2	60%	13522	27995	7.196427E-11
2	4%	1183	2000	1.427411E-06	2	44%	9683	20599	2.588654E-07
3	45%	10235	20000	1.750314E-10	3	77%	17237	34311	2.608362E-10
3	34%	7720	15000	8.759356E-07	3	58%	12944	25816	1.937350E-05
4	26%	6222	10001	4.230604E-22	4	37%	7486	14435	2.379935E-12
4	15%	4084	6001	5.942947E-05	4	31%	5895	11822	1.139079E-05
5	61%	10162	15000	4.529004E-06	5	78%	10837	19299	1.057597E-08
5	40%	7042	10000	7.861884E-01	5	67%	9164	16471	5.908176E-04

Tabelle 2. Die Tabelle zeigen Modell-Größe und Detektor-Wahrscheinlichkeit nach Polygon-Reduktion. Linke Tabelle zeiht Ergebnisse nach Anwendung von *qslim*, die rechte Tabelle nach Anwendung von *plycrunch*.

In diesem Kontext werden allgemein Verfahren zur Reduzierung der Problemgröße und Erhöhung der Robustheit untersucht: Durch Polygonreduktion unabhängig von geometrischen Größen, Markierung der reduzierten Polygonnetze und Zurückpropagierung von Modifikationen, läßt sich zum einen die Verarbeitungszeit senken, zum anderen können Wasserzeichen-Inhalte statt von einzelnen Lagekoordinaten vom Massezentrum mehrerer Punkte abhängig gemacht werden, was u.a. die Robustheit gegenüber der Randomisierung von Punkten erhöht. Eine zentrale Herausforderung im Bereich digitaler Wasserzeichen für 3D Modelle besteht in der Realisierung von Wasserzeichen, die *gleichzeitig* robust gegen Affine Transformationen und Re-Meshing Operationen, insbesondere Polygon-Reduktion, sind und eine Detektion/Extrahierung des Wasserzeichens erlauben, ohne das Originalmodell zu benötigen. Erst solche Verfahren ermöglichen die vollständig automatisierte Suche nach Wasserzeichen in großen Datenbeständen. Das NBE-Verfahren ist in der Lage, Modelle basierend auf zentralen Momenten zu reorientieren, d.h. orthogonale Transformationen rückgängig zu machen. Ungleichmäßige Skalierung und Scherung können hingegen nur in sehr geringem Maße kompensiert werden (vom Algorithmus selbst). Daher besteht weiterer Forschungsbedarf zur Realisierung genannter Verfahren.

Literatur

1. O. Benedens. Geometry-Based Watermarking of 3D Models. *IEEE Computer Graphics, Special Issue on Image Security*, pp. 46–55, January/February, 1999.
2. O. Benedens. Watermarking of 3D polygon based models with robustness against mesh simplification. *Proceedings of SPIE: Security and Watermarking of Multimedia Contents*, pp. 329–340, 1999.
3. O. Benedens and C. Busch. Towards Blind Detection of Robust Watermarks in Polygonal Models. *To be published in: Eurographics 2000 Conference Proceedings*, 2000.

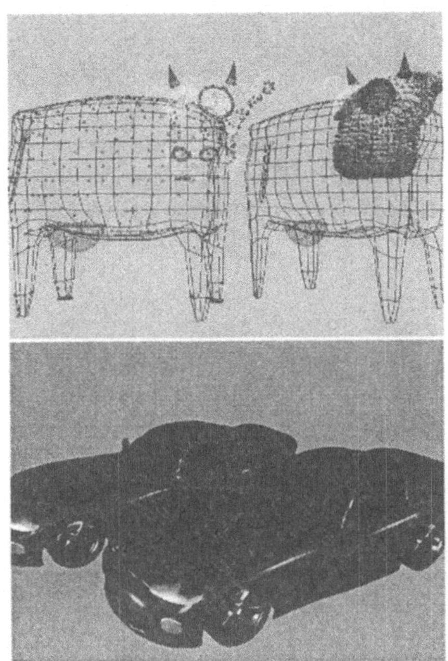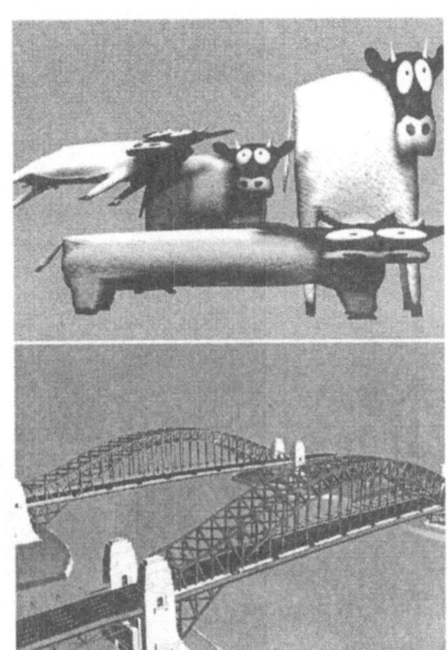

Abbildung 2. Erste Zeile: Im linken Bild sind Eckpunkte, die ein AIE- (linke Kuh) und VFA-Wasserzeichen (rechte Kuh) codieren, hervorgehoben. Das rechte Bild zeigt die Auswirkungen verschiedener affiner Transformationen, z.B. ist die Kuh ganz links Ergebnis einer nicht-gleichmäßigen Skalrierung, gefolgt von einer Scherung. In allen Fällen war das AIE-Wasserzeichen (ein 15x11 bitmap) stabil. Zweite Zeile: Das linke Modell zeigt jeweils das Original, das rechte Modell eine mit Wasserzeichen **aller** drei Verfahren versehene Kopie.

4. Y. Boon-Lock and M. Minerva. Watermarking 3D Objects for Verification. *IEEE Computer Graphics, Special Issue on Image Security*, pp. 36–45, January/February 1999.
5. J. Cohen et al. Simplification Envelopes. *SIGGRAPH 96 Proceedings*, pp. 119–128, 1996.
6. M. Garland and P. Heckbert. Surface Simplification Using Quadric Error Metrics. *SIGGRAPH 97 Proceedings*, pp. 202–216, 1997.
7. G. Nielson and T.Foley. A Survey of Applications of an Affine Invariant Norm. *Mathematical Methods in Computer Aided Design*, Academic Press, pp. 445–467, 1989.
8. N. Nikolaidis and I. Pitas. Robust image watermarking in the spatial domain. *Signal Processing*, **66**(3), pp. 385–403, May 1998.
9. R. Ohbuchi, H. Masuda, and M. Aono. Watermarking Three-Dimensional Polygonal Models. *ACM Multimedia 97*, pp. 261–272, 1997.
10. R. Ohbuchi, H. Masuda, and M.Aono. Watermarking Three-Dimensional Polygonal Models Through Geometric and Topological Modifications. *IEEE Journal on selected areas in communications*, **16**(4), pp. 551–559, May 1998.
11. E. Praun, H. Hoppe, and A. Finkelstein. Robust Mesh Watermarking. *SIGGRAPH 99 Proceedings*, pp. 69–76, 1999.